UZBEK EMBROIDERY
IN THE NOMADIC TRADITION

UZBEK EMBROIDERY
IN THE NOMADIC TRADITION

*The Jack A. and Aviva Robinson Collection
at the Minneapolis Institute of Arts*

KATE FITZ GIBBON AND ANDREW HALE

With contributions by Irina V. Bogoslovskaya, Frieda Sorber, and Lotus Stack

Distributed by Art Media Resources, Chicago

© 2007 Minneapolis Institute of Arts
2400 Third Avenue South
Minneapolis, Minnesota 55404
www.artsmia.org

All rights reserved under international and Pan-American Copyright Conventions. Except for legitimate excerpts customary in reviews or scholarly publications, no part of this publication may be reproduced or transmitted in any form or by any means, electronic or mechanical, without permission in writing by the publisher.

Introduction and Chapters 1–4 text
© 2007 by Kate Fitz Gibbon and Andrew Hale

Distributed by Art Media Resources, Chicago

Front cover:
At torba ilgich
Lakai, 19th century
2004.259.88

Back cover:
Detail of front cover

Facing title page:
Ilgich
Lakai, 19th century
2004.259.82

Editors: Phil Freshman, St. Louis Park, Minnesota, and Susan C. Jones, Minneapolis

Designer: Brent Marmo, Design:Marmo, Excelsior, Minnesota

Objects photographer: Dan Dennehy, Minneapolis Institute of Arts

Digital-photography production: Charles Walbridge, Minneapolis Institute of Arts

Publishing and production management: Jim Bindas, Books and Projects LLC, Minnetonka, Minnesota

Printer: Tien Wah Press, Singapore

This book was set in Perpetua and Gill Sans typefaces.

Printed in Singapore

ISBN: 1-58886-094-9
ISBN: 978-1-58886-094-1

A bazaar street in Samarkand, 1900.

Library of Congress Cataloging-in-Publication Data

Minneapolis Institute of Arts.
Uzbek embroidery in the nomadic tradition : the Jack A. and Aviva Robinson collection at the Minneapolis Institute of Arts / Kate Fitz Gibbon and Andrew Hale.
    p. cm.
  Includes bibliographical references and index.
  ISBN 978-1-58886-094-1 (hardcover)
 1. Embroidery–Uzbekistan–Exhibitions. 2. Robinson, Aviva–Art collections–Exhibitions. 3. Robinson, Jack A. (Jack Albert), 1930– Art collections–Exhibitions. 4. Embroidery–Private collections–Minnesota–Minneapolis–Exhibitions. 5. Embroidery–Minnesota–Minneapolis–Exhibitions. 6. Minneapolis Institute of Arts–Exhibitions. I. Fitz Gibbon, Kate. II. Hale, Andrew. III. Title.
  NK9275.67.U9F58 2007
  746.4409587'074776579–dc22
                                        2006038926

CONTENTS

Director's Foreword   7
William M. Griswold

Acknowledgments   10
Kate Fitz Gibbon and Andrew Hale

Preface   13
Lotus Stack

Introduction   15

1. EPICS AND HEROES: THE STEPPE UZBEK   19
     Three Origin Tales   44

2. TEXTILES AND RITES OF PASSAGE: THE RHYTHMS OF LIFE   49

3. RENEWING ANCIENT FORMS: *ILGICH* AND THE ART OF EMBROIDERY   89

4. URBAN EMBROIDERY: SHAHRISABS AND *SUZANI*   129

Chapter Notes   163

THE JACK A. AND AVIVA ROBINSON COLLECTION OF CENTRAL ASIAN EMBROIDERIES   172

Appendix I: Materials and Techniques Used in Uzbek Embroideries   181
    Irina V. Bogoslovskaya

Appendix II: Edge Treatments on Uzbek Embroideries in the Robinson Collection   192
    Frieda Sorber in collaboration with Lotus Stack

Glossary   199

Selected Bibliography   202

Index   205

Reproduction Credits   208

Uuk kap ilgich
Lakai, early 20th century
Silk, cotton, metal; cross-stitch,
chain stitch
2004.259.81

DIRECTOR'S FOREWORD

The generous gift to the Minneapolis Institute of Arts (MIA) of ninety-seven Central Asian embroideries from the collection of Jack A. and Aviva Robinson augments an area of our collection that was established in the late 1920s with a gift of ten textiles. In the years that followed, little Central Asian material appeared on the international market. Consequently, few pieces were added to that core group.

During the 1970s and 1980s, however, when ikat and embroidered textiles from Central Asia became more widely available outside that part of the world, the MIA judiciously took advantage of the opportunity to enhance this area of the collection. During the past twenty-five years, our holdings have continued to grow. But it is only now, with the addition of the Robinsons' superb acquisitions, that the MIA's group of Central Asian textiles can be considered a major resource.

In addition to the connoisseurship and aesthetic sensibility manifested in their collecting choices, the Robinsons were keenly aware of the need for greater scholarship in the field, as well as of the importance of gaining a broader understanding of the objects themselves and the roles they played in the culture that produced them. With their characteristic attention to quality and detail, they persuaded Kate Fitz Gibbon and Andrew Hale, recognized experts in the field, to become involved. The Robinsons' funding support for scholarly research and collaboration with institutions and colleagues in Russia, Uzbekistan, and Tajikistan exemplifies their grasp of the needs of museums today.

MIA curator Lotus Stack guided this immense undertaking from inception to completion. Sharing the Robinsons' passion for Central Asian textiles, she gladly contributed her own expertise and wealth of experience to the project that is vividly documented in this catalogue and in the beautiful exhibition it accompanies.

None of this would have been possible without the Robinsons' foresight, and it is with gratitude that we acknowledge their continuing generosity to the Minneapolis Institute of Arts.

William M. Griswold
Director and President,
Minneapolis Institute of Arts

This 1880 photograph shows the ruins of Aq Saray palace in Shahrisabs, built by Timur Leng (Tamerlane) between 1379 and 1396.

ACKNOWLEDGMENTS

We owe thanks to the many colleagues and friends who made our research both fruitful and enjoyable. Our dear friend Dr. Igor Klochkoff was a tireless guide to the streets of St. Petersburg and Moscow. In St. Petersburg, Alexander Nikitin led us through hidden depths of the Hermitage, Elena Tsareva and Rahimov Rahmat Rahimnovich gave us every assistance at the Museum of Anthropology and Ethnography (Kunstkammer), and Larissa Popova and Karina Solovyeva opened the Central Asian collections and photographic archives of the Russian Ethnographic Museum to us. Ekaterine Stanislavovna Ermakova reviewed Lakai and Kungrat materials with us at the Oriental Museum in Moscow. Also in Moscow, the staff of the Russian State Library helped us locate and photocopy many rare books in their entirety.

The Internet message board of the Central Eurasian Studies Society (CESS) at Harvard University was an incredible research resource. Our request for contacts in Uzbekistan and Tajikistan let loose a flood of helpful replies. We regret that we lack sufficient space to list all those who responded — and to whom we are most grateful. We wish especially to acknowledge Gabriele Rasuly-Paleczek, who provided us with numerous publications and an extensive bibliography. Through CESS contacts such as Oleg Grabar, Scott Levi, Elena Neva, and Douglas Northrop we were able to arrange meetings in Dushanbe with the historians Guzel Maitdinova and Rahim Masovich Masov and with museum professionals Said Murad Babamulloev, Zukhra Mahmedjanova, Abdulwali Sharipov, and Mumina Shovaleva. Heartfelt thanks go to Saodat Marafova, chief of the Museum of Ethnography in Dushanbe, and her colleague, Nadezhda Vasitova, who spent many hours going through materials with us. Tojiniso Rahmanova, a young scholar, and Mumina Sadullaeva, a gold embroiderer, provided important insights into that ancient craft. Muratali Umarov, the organizer of a craft-development project in Dushanbe, introduced us to his Lakai family in Hissar. There, Aimkhal Ernazarova — matriarch, storyteller, and accomplished needleworker — welcomed us into her home and helped us understand contemporary Lakai culture. Our extensive travels were made easy through the help of the marvelous Gafarov Abduahad Abdusamadovich, Mamadnazarov Vafonazar Abdusalomovich, Valisher and Jahongir Ashurov, Firdavs Ishaky, Abdulaev Ravshan, and Vakhidova Sharkia.

In Uzbekistan, Kamil Khojaev was a generous friend and advisor. Colleague Irina V. Bogoslovskaya helped us in a thousand ways; this book, which is enhanced by her appendix essay in these pages, would not have been possible without her. The Central Asian scholar Adam Albion of the East West Institute in Tashkent gave generously of his time and made many thoughtful suggestions. At the State Fine Arts Museum in Tashkent, deputy director Svetlana Manasyan and chief textile curator Azoda Alimdjanova gave us hours of their valuable time. Also in Tashkent, we were warmly received by the distinguished director of the State Historical Museum, Inoyatov Hamdamovich Kutlugjon, and by the museum's curator of ethnology, Rahima Mokhtarey. At the Samarkand National Museum, we received courteous and collegial assistance from Mirsaddievna Lutfiya Ergasheva and Lushnikova Elizaveta Valentinovna. Marifat Mirzaeva of Shahrisabs provided many details on contemporary *suzani* production. Special thanks also go to Shahnoza Karimbaeva, director of the Tashkent House of Photography, for her help. Vladimir and Denis Karasev gave us numerous insights into the ancient cultures in Uzbekistan. Boris Golender advised us on vintage photography. The distinguished photographer Dina Khojaeva lent us her granddaughter Marina as a most charming guide and intelligent companion. Alexandra Drobova was a superb tour guide and text translator.

In addition, we wish to recognize the numerous contributions of Binafsha Nodir, a young Uzbekistan scholar who has already done fine work on the costume and way of life of the Kungrat. Fully conversant with the work of past researchers, passionately dedicated to her work (and to her growing family), fluent in Uzbek as well as in the language of social science, and respectful of traditional culture, Nodir represents the bright future of Uzbekistan scholarship.

We cannot possibly acknowledge all those who aided us during our time in Afghanistan; our hearts will always be with them. Our friends Mir Ayaz Elyasi, Abdul Hai, Abdur Rauf, Ghullam Siddiq, and their delightful families must be recognized for their many kindnesses over the years.

The outstanding British textiles collector Doris (Pip) Rau shared her collection, her friendship, and her excellent advice. Sarah Posey, formerly of the British Museum, gave generously of her time. Sharon Schenck of Santa Fe lent us many useful books on textiles from her extensive library. As she has in the past, translator Liv Bliss brought humor as well as depth of linguistic and historical understanding to texts antique and modern alike. Gail Martin made an outstanding contribution in building the Robinsons' collection and then deepened it with her generous assistance and hospitality. Lotus Stack, curator of textiles at the Minneapolis Institute of Arts, encouraged, shepherded, and sustained this project through months of work and thousands of miles of good-humored companionship on our travels.

Particular appreciation is due to the staff at the Minneapolis Institute of Arts. Evan Maurer, Director Emeritus, helped initiate the publication, and William Griswold, the museum's current director, maintained the museum's support for it. Chief Photographer Dan Dennehy and Digital Imaging Specialist Charles Walbridge worked beyond the call of duty. Without the initiative, intelligence, and dedication of the Textile Department staff — Curatorial Assistant Patty Martinson, Conservation Technician Christine Pradel-Lien, and Senior Conservator Beth McLaughlin — all of whom helped in countless ways, this project would not have turned out successfully. Virginia Hjelmstad worked extensively on technical analysis of the objects in the collection, in particular consolidating and standardizing the details in the image captions. This proved to be a formidable challenge, and Virginia met it admirably.

We are immensely grateful to Jack A. and Aviva Robinson for granting us the privilege of working with their collection and researching in depth a subject we had wanted to pursue for many years. The professional skills of editor Phil Freshman (ably assisted by Susan C. Jones), graphic designer Brent Marmo, and publication manager Jim Bindas helped bring this book to fruition.

Finally, we must express our deep gratitude to the late scholar Belkis Khalilovna Karmysheva, whose research forms the basis for much of the work in this book. In her last years, Karmysheva welcomed us to her Moscow apartment, gently corrected our misapprehensions, and brought us tea, photographs, texts, and textiles.

At every step of the way, the courtesy and generosity of our colleagues enabled us to overcome logistical difficulties. Closed museums opened their doors, archivists dug through piles of textiles and documents to locate rare materials, and, everywhere, people took time from their busy lives to stop and assist us. All good work is collaborative: we have tried to be worthy of our sources and our distinguished colleagues.

Kate Fitz Gibbon and
Andrew Hale
Santa Fe, New Mexico

The pattern of this late-nineteenth–early twentieth-century Kungrat ilgich *is comprised of five circular medallions at the center surrounded by jillik bashi designs (2004.259.31).*

PREFACE
Lotus Stack

The greatest pleasure of curatorial work is bringing a unique private art collection to a major public institution. The opportunity to introduce a museum audience to the largely unfamiliar Central Asian culture of the Uzbek has been much enhanced by the privilege of working with the farsighted, adventurous collectors Jack A. and Aviva Robinson. Their generous gift of textile art to the Minneapolis Institute of Arts (MIA) also provided for important scholarly research in the field by Kate Fitz Gibbon and Andrew Hale and for two technical essays. This exhibition and its accompanying catalogue are sources of considerable satisfaction to everyone at the MIA.

Central Asia's embroidered-textile heritage includes two distinct forms of artistic expression: the refined, systematically ordered urban aesthetic and the enormously vital arts of the nomadic tradition. For centuries, Bukhara and Samarkand, major cities on the Silk Road, were famous for their elegant and sophisticated woven textiles, characterized by costly silk and metal threads, bold patterns, and complex techniques. In the nineteenth century, however, exotic, opulently embroidered *suzani* wall hangings, created predominantly by women for their dowries, were brought to Europe and the United States. During the early twentieth century, a few American museums acquired examples of these works for their collections, but except for certain types of carpets, non-urban textile traditions received little attention. The addition of the Jack A. and Aviva Robinson Collection to the holdings of the MIA allows the museum to present nomadic and rural embroideries as well as urban pieces. This focused group of objects splendidly articulates the range and dynamism of the Uzbek style.

The collection is rich in textiles from the Lakai Uzbek that show the value placed on individual expression. These *ilgich* wall hangings have a singularly compelling aesthetic that resonates within the Lakai's steppe culture. The intense, kinetic energy of their embroideries is manifest in several Robinson *ilgich* that feature vibrating, double-tailed scorpions as well as in others whose designs are powerfully abstract. The Kungrat Uzbek's appreciation for floral and spider motifs inspired them to devise design elements that transform familiar representations of natural forms into enigmatic imagery. Lakai and Kungrat embroiderers alike experimented with stitch variations, thread structure, and fiber sources to create exceptional luminosity, and they played symmetry against asymmetry to balance space within their compositions.

Aviva and Jack A. Robinson, 2006.

Fitz Gibbon and Hale's catalogue text emphasizes the many interpretations of iconic imagery in the Robinson Collection and explores the ways cultural identity is expressed in Uzbek artistry. The authors demonstrate that the primary purposes of these embroideries were to showcase the individual embroiderer's artistic skills and to bring honor to her family through the preservation of a communal culture.

The creation of such a wide-ranging collection of embroidered art required exceptional dedication; fittingly, the Robinsons are an exceptional couple. Lifelong learners, they have pursued their interests in the visual arts with passion and intellectual discipline. Jack and Aviva have traveled extensively, seeking out the new, the beautiful, and the unusual in museums and marketplaces worldwide. Their collection of Uzbek embroideries reflects an aesthetic sensitivity that is informed, but not encumbered by, Western cultural perspectives. They have collected with assurance, their intuitive responses supported by extensive interaction with textile experts. The Robinsons' gift of their collection to the MIA is a manifestation of their philosophy that personal resources should be shared to benefit the society that nurtured their growth.

This tabaklau ilgich, *with its characteristic false flap, is probably from the Durmen tribe. It was collected by the 1930 SAMIIR expedition and dated to before 1914. The composition includes circular forms with toothed edges enclosing a central star or cruciform shape and smaller* jillik bashi *designs.*

INTRODUCTION

The Jack A. and Aviva Robinson Collection gathers together of some of the most animated and creative textiles from Central Asia: the embroidered *ilgich* tent hangings of the Lakai and Kungrat tribes of present-day Uzbekistan, Tajikistan, and Afghanistan and the *suzani* wall hangings from the region embracing the cities of Shahrisabs and Kitab. The Lakai and Kungrat share a history of steppe pastoralism as well as a language, rituals, and bonds of kinship. Their embroideries express a distinct ethnic identity, and their imagery reflects the natural forces of the open steppe. In contrast, the embroideries of Shahrisabs and Kitab have a regional, not an ethnic, style. They come from an urban environment, and their subjects are idealized floral forms. In the cities, people of varied ethnic backgrounds worked at embroidery both as a commercial occupation and to produce goods for their own households. They made large hangings suited for urban homes, and they crafted robes and accessories for the market. Each of these traditions produced works of extraordinary virtuosity, eccentricity, and dynamism. As collectors, the Robinsons sought out textiles with the individuality and vitality that characterize the finest Central Asian art.

Until about thirty years ago, Kungrat and Lakai embroideries were rarely included in the literature on Central Asian art, and they almost never appeared in Soviet publications. Members of a Soviet field expedition collecting various items from the Lakai and Kungrat in 1930 stressed the rarity of these embroideries, which had not been sold before 1914, when famine forced their sale for the first time. They came to the attention of Western collectors only in the 1970s, when a severe drought in northern Afghanistan forced Lakai, Kungrat, and other Dasht-i-Kipchak peoples to sell their most valued possessions on the Kabul market. Over the past three decades, recognition and enthusiasm have grown among private collectors and in museums worldwide, but scholarship surrounding their role in traditional culture has remained limited. While attention has been given to urban *suzani* in general, and while the Shahrisabs area's embroideries have been much admired for their artistic qualities, no study has addressed the relationship of the Shahrisabs style to that of neighboring rural and nomadic peoples.

This book covers the historical and cultural backgrounds of these disparate textile-producing communities and considers how they were affected by changing political and economic circumstances. Chapter One describes the history of Uzbek pastoralist peoples in Central Asia, the development of ethnic and clan identity, and the adaptation of nomadic peoples to settlement in the late nineteenth and early twentieth centuries. Chapter Two summarizes textile production by the Lakai and Kungrat and examines how textiles help perpetuate cultural identity as well as how they are integrated into ceremony and ritual, especially in relation to marriage and motherhood.

Chapter Three is primarily devoted to identifying design elements, styles, and techniques characteristic of the Lakai and Kungrat and to mapping the distribution of textiles among different tribes. We look at the abstracted forms of pre–Islamic steppe art and consider the resonance — or lack of it — of shamanic and other traditions within embroidery design. Textiles acquired during early twentieth-century expeditions that are now in Russian and Central Asian museum collections help provide a chronology for embroideries from different regions; later examples demonstrate the ways textile production faltered under Soviet rule.

Chapter Four examines *suzani* production in Shahrisabs and Kitab. We compare the function of embroidered *suzani* in an urban setting with rural usage, and we outline the effects of commercialization of embroidery. Finally, we examine the relationship of the inventive Shahrisabs embroidery design to rural and nomadic design styles from the surrounding region.

The book concludes with two appendices. The first, by Irina V. Bogoslovskaya, an independent scholar from Tashkent, provides valuable details on materials, dyestuffs, weaving, and embroidery techniques. The second appendix, written by Frieda Sorber of the Mode Museum, Antwerp, Belgium, in collaboration with Minneapolis Institute of Arts textiles curator Lotus Stack, examines the construction of the distinctive edgings and trims utilized by the Lakai and Kungrat, as seen in examples from the Robinson Collection.

The ethnological research undertaken by colonial-period and Soviet-era scholars provided a foundation for this study. Books by early travelers to Central Asia contributed exotic detail as well as useful information on the textile trade. Among many important Russian and Soviet sources, the following are especially noteworthy: the collections made by the ethnographer Samuel Martinovich Dudin at the turn of the last century; the expeditions of M. S. Andreev to Samarkand in 1921 and Tajikistan in 1925; the inventories of S. T. Rusyaikina from the Central Asian Museum of History and History of the Revolution (SAMIIR) expedition in 1930; the photographs and notes of one Jurabaev, an ethnographer who doubled as an agent for the NKVD (the internal Soviet police force that preceded the KGB) among the Lakai in 1929; and the writings of Belkis Khalilovna Karmysheva, an exceptionally diligent and clear-sighted scholar who worked in the 1940s and 1950s, as well as those of her colleagues G. L. Chepelevetskaya, Valentina Georgievna Moshkova, Antonina Konstantinovna Pisarchik, and Olga Aleksandrovna Sukhareva, among others. The work of these scholars and the field collections from museums in Tajikistan, Uzbekistan, and Russia, acquired fifty to one hundred years ago, are of inestimable value today. Issues of ethnicity have been illuminated by a remarkable number of academic works on Central Asia that have appeared since the dissolution of the Soviet Union in the early 1990s.

We were fortunate to have traveled widely in northern Afghanistan more than thirty years ago, when we first encountered the textiles of the Lakai, Kungrat, and other Dasht-i-Kipchak peoples living between Balkh and Kunduz. The time remaining for fieldwork, not only in Afghanistan but all across Central Asia, is short. The modern world is fast encroaching on even the most remote places in Central Asia; memories are fading, and the older generation is passing away. These circumstances bring particular value to the work of Binafsha Nodir, a colleague in Uzbekistan who currently is doing fieldwork in Kungrat regions and has been able to answer many pressing questions for us.

Soviet ideology encouraged distortions that some scholars in the former U.S.S.R. and in the West continue to embrace. One perspective imposes rigid divisions of culture based on the "ethnic" identities of the titular nationalities of the present republics — that is, the notion that whatever is from Uzbekistan is Uzbek and from Tajikistan, Tajik. We have tried to build a framework for understanding the material that is free of colonial-period paternalism and nationalist social analysis. It seems more useful to examine material culture on the basis of small social groups, local economies, and trade patterns and to look at ways Central Asian culture is shared broadly across ethnic lines.

Another group of Soviet scholars defined aspects of Central Asian culture as either "Islamic" or "shamanist," "animist" or "Zoroastrian." This approach was foisted upon Soviet anthropologists, in accordance with the party line, in an attempt to promote atheism and to denigrate and weaken Islam as a social force. Marxist-Leninist theory already provided the explanation of how all societies functioned, so these scholars focused on a detailed study of materials — not on why they were made. In comparison, Western scholars have tended to look at cultures as a whole and to ask, "How does this society operate?" We prefer the second approach for discussing relationships between material culture and belief. Central Asia's rich and complex history is reflected in the syncretism of Islamic practice, and the separate roles of men and women in community and family ritual have made ceremonies related to the woman's world more durable.

Our hope is that this book will serve as an accurate source and grounding for future work. There are many gaps in the available data, but rather than offer speculative solutions, we have attempted to draw attention to these questions as deserving additional fieldwork. We confess to having little patience with contemporary spiritual interpretations of the meaning of embroidery patterns or with the grafting of Central Asian materials onto a foreign analytical framework. Valid interpretations should make sense to the people who actually made the art. Although our explanations may not be what the Lakai and Kungrat consider most meaningful, we hope they would not find them misguided or absurd.

As students of Central Asian culture, we have been fascinated by the creative adaptation of designs and artistic styles from ancient models by both steppe and urban peoples. For us, this process is an essential component of the history of art in the region. Each movement of peoples into Central Asia brought new artistic as well as social, economic, and spiritual contributions to a rich cultural mixture. The materials in the Robinson Collection help us understand the art of Central Asia as evolutionary rather than static. They also help us appreciate and value the continuing interchange of artistic ideas in the region.

A Lakai at torba ilgich collected by the 1930 SAMIIR expedition and dated to before 1914.

I. EPICS AND HEROES: THE STEPPE UZBEK

Uuk kap ilgich
Lakai, early 19th century
2004.259.79 (detail)

There are few places of more austere beauty than the heart of Central Asia. The brown, silt-laden Amu Darya river tumbles out of the mountains at the center of the world's largest landmass, where the Karakorum, Pamir, and Tien Shan ranges join. The river runs for hundreds of miles, forming the boundary between Afghanistan and Tajikistan, Uzbekistan and Turkmenistan. The first region it crosses is mountainous; pastures and deep gorges are woven with clouds, and they are empty but for the occasional shepherd and his flock. Below, lush valleys are dotted with clusters of mud-brick houses, and still lower there are dusty villages. A hot sun beats down upon wide, hand-hoed fields, and the irrigation ditches are lined with tall, straight *chinar* trees.

These mountain valleys and the uplands are home to the Lakai tribe. In the eighteenth and nineteenth centuries, Lakai warriors pastured their horse herds in this strategic area, sharing it with the settlements of their Tajik neighbors, the Kulabi and Chagatai highlanders.[1] By the time the Amu Darya reaches the Surkhandarya region of Uzbekistan, which is inhabited by the Kungrat tribe, the mountains have become sloping hills, and flocks of goats and the enormous Hissar sheep are common sights. Corrals walled with stones mark the sites of winter grazing grounds. Around the town of Termez, the land on either side of the river is flat and hot — in some places, desert and, in others, moist with salt marshes. In the spring, silkworms munch on mulberry leaves in the walled gardens. Fruits and vegetables ripen here a month earlier than anywhere else in Central Asia, and in the fall, the people living on the Uzbekistan side of the river make wine. All year round, camels chew moodily on seemingly inedible thorns and *sauksal*. The camel's ill temper notwithstanding, this place has been, at times, a paradise for both man and beast.

The area seems peaceful until one comes closer and notes the marks left by the perpetual struggle to possess it. Some signs are blatant: after the decade-long war with the Soviet Union and the subsequent civil war, crippled men and scarred children are all-too-common sights in Afghanistan. Some signs are harder to interpret. Is the tumbledown wall in a Tajikistan village a relic of recent years of civil strife or just the result of poor construction? Then there are the remnants of the seven decades of Soviet conquest and rule in Central Asia; the ugly sign for a collective farm that hangs rusting from a gate, or the antique tractors that sit idle while women open sluices and weed the fields by hand.

Often, the larger towns originally served as market centers along the Silk Road or as fortresses guarding disputed highways and passes. Just beyond the thoroughfares, offices, and shops are giant walls of citadels rising two hundred feet above the roadway, their towers now crumbling.

The cheerful and determined faces in the street tell another story — of people simply getting on with life. The children are boisterous, the women mostly shy, and the men polite, but they are all remarkable in their variety. Some faces are pale, with long-lashed eyes and smooth cheeks; others have nut-brown or olive skin. There are wide cheekbones and narrow ones. There are almond eyes and round ones, and some are like tiny slits in a fabric of wrinkles. On the Afghanistan side of the river, where men are hirsute, some sport beards as luxurious as hedges, while others wear the long moustache and sparse goatee of a Chengiz or a Tamerlane. These varied faces bear the marks of long contention over Central Asia's riches and over who should rule the countryside and the roads. The faces also

EPICS AND HEROES 21

A nineteenth-century Lakai uuk kap ilgich *whose design includes a stylized double-tailed scorpion figure at the center, enclosed within a diamond, and edged with a varicolored pattern (2004.259.79).*

A Lakai family in the village of Upaii, Tajikistan, seated on a striped woolen kilim, c. 1929. The woman's scarf is embroidered with a geometric pattern.

Map of Central Asia.

A nineteenth-century Lakai at torba ilgich *with a characteristic pattern that includes a diamond–based central figure with hornlike elements in each corner. The small medallions with contrasting red-and-white or red-and-yellow sections resemble the flower forms often found in* suzani *from the Shahrisabs region (2004.259.88; detail opposite).*

An Uzbek man on the open steppe, about 1900, with a donkey bearing all the components of a small yurt. Felts are wrapped around the lattice, reed, and roof poles. The roof wheel, an iron tripod, and other household utensils are lashed on top.

speak of alliance, of union, and of having learned to share a generous land.

This book is about the embroideries of the Lakai and the Kungrat tribes and of the cities of Shahrisabs and Kitab. It is also about the people who made them and their history. Without knowing these people and how they have lived, we cannot understand what their embroideries mean or why and how they were made.

The Lakai and Kungrat first appeared in Central Asia as part of the movement of Dasht-i-Kipchak steppe peoples into the Balkh region at the time of the Shaibanid confederation in the early sixteenth century. This movement was the last great migration of Turkic tribes into the southern steppe, a process that began during the first millennium. It is also the first indication of a solid connection between the historical and present-day Uzbek peoples. Common notions of ethnic identity cannot be applied to the name Uzbek. They are not a racial group, nor have they been tied for many centuries to a single geographical region or a single dialect. In Central Asia, ethnicity is a political construction that has varied according to historical circumstance. The molding of ethnic identity allowed transitions between loyalty to dynasty, to clan, to a region, or to a specific religious or political leader. What remained constant in these temporary attachments was the readiness with which groups merged and dissociated and the relevance of previous alliances and betrayals to political choices that were made generations later.

The name Uzbek originated during the Mongol administrative and military alliance known as the Golden Horde. The section of the Mongol empire ruled by Jochi, the eldest son of Chengiz Khan, the Golden Horde had become assimilated with nomadic and semi-nomadic Turkic tribes in the Dasht-i-Kipchak steppe, a region approximating present-day Kazakhstan.[2] In Central Asia, unrelated clans often united under a powerful leader, using his name as that of the new alliance. According to the seventeenth-century Khivan historian Abul Ghazi, the followers of one successful and popular leader, Uzbek Khan (1282–1341; reigned 1312–40), took the name Uzbek.[3] Uzbek Khan was both a military strongman and a fighter for the faith, a Muslim ruler who succeeded in uniting all four groups of the Golden Horde.

The first consolidation of Uzbek peoples took place during the disintegration of the Golden Horde over the next century, but the Uzbek did not move into the agricultural regions of the southern steppe until the sixteenth century. The Timurid empire, centered in Central Asia's southern oases, was wracked by infighting, and several political groups sought to regain the upper hand by forming alliances with new peoples moving into the area. Under the leadership of the ambitious Muhammad Shaibani (1451–1510), Dasht-i-Kipchak tribes from the steppe exploited Timurid weakness.

The Timurids invited Shaibani into their territory to defend them from Mongol raiders who were plundering the northern borders of the empire. He successfully repelled the Mongols, and more followers flocked to him. As the Timurid empire imploded through dissension, the ranks of Shaibani's followers grew by integrating Turk, Tajik, Mongol, and other local tribal populations.[4] Shaibani made and broke alliances, defeating a succession of Timurid chiefs and princes and absorbing their lands until he ruled a vast stretch of Central Asian territory. Under the Shaibanids, Balkh and the heartland of Central Asia comprised one of the region's three great powers. To the south and west lay Safavid Persia; to the east, Kabul was an outpost of the great Mughal empire of India, founded by Babur, a Timurid prince whom the Shaibanids had driven from Central Asia.

The tribes of the Shaibanid confederation inherited rich lands on both sides of the Amu Darya. The names Qunghrat and

Loqai are listed in several early sources as two of the ninety-two tribes in the Uzbek orbit.[5] According to the historian and ethnographer Belkis Khalilovna Karmysheva, the Lakai, Durmen,[6] Kungrat, Qataghan, Marka, Kauchin, Kesamir, and Semiz tribes form part of the Kipchak group that was the center of the Shaibanid confederation.[7] These are among the tribes named in the genealogical stories told by the Kungrat and Lakai even today (see pp. 44–46). What the various tribes shared, aside from a common origin in the Dasht-i-Kipchak steppe and a mobile, pastoral way of life, was their willingness to adapt to new military and social organizations despite their heterogeneous character.

Soon after Shaibanid suzerainty was established, the Kungrat coalesced into distinct clan groupings that were comparatively large and powerful; three Kungrat emirs are noted among the chieftains of the Shaibanid state.[8] The large town of Kungrat, near the Aral Sea, is mentioned in many early sources; for example, in 1740 the Russian envoys Gladyshev and Muravin wrote that the town's inhabitants lived in tents.[9] The name Lakai does not appear in these early sources, but that simply may indicate that the Lakai were not important parties to political events.

During the Shaibanid period (1506–98) and then the Janid dynasty (1598–1740), the Lakai and Kungrat established nomadic communities in the crescent of fertile lands that stretched from the mountains of present-day southern Tajikistan to the Surkhandarya region of Uzbekistan. Like other steppe–based tribes drawn from the Dasht-i-Kipchak region, they were pastoralists. For the most part, they disdained agriculture, content to reap the benefits of domination over preexisting Turk and Persian-speaking peoples in the region.[10] According to local traditions, the Kungrat were sheepherders, and the Lakai primarily bred horses, which they pastured along with other stock throughout the year. Fluctuating groups ranging from a few to a few hundred families moved between summer and winter pastures, setting up their latticed tents (*kherga*, or yurts) in seasonal camps.

By the late nineteenth and early twentieth centuries, when the first demographic data on Turkic tribes were collected in the region, the Kungrat were inhabiting lands on both sides of the Amu Darya, including several centers in northern Afghanistan between Kunduz and Balkh, especially the town of Aibak in Samangan province.[11] The Lakai took up residence in Baljuan and the Hissar Valley, in what was then called Eastern Bukhara and today forms part of southeastern Uzbekistan and southern Tajikistan. Groups of Lakai also crossed the Amu Darya to live in the Kunduz region of Afghanistan during periods of internecine strife or when they were attacked by forces of the Bukharan emir. Each group adapted a traditional steppe way of life that included part-time agriculture, trade with their neighbors, and raids and warfare for plunder in the service of various rulers.

The region known to both the British and Russians as Turkestan had fluctuating internal borders: the western end was ruled by the Bukharan emir, while the eastern end was under the *beg* of Kunduz. The *begs*, or nobility, of the Qataghan Uzbek were the de facto rulers of large tracts of present-day northern Afghanistan, dominating settled Turk and Tajik peoples through a loose system of chiefdoms under the *beg* of Kunduz.

The Kunduz *begs* and the Bukharan emirs followed standard Central Asian carrot-and-stick practices with respect to the local leaders under their jurisdiction. They dispensed protection and patronage to gain allegiance, conscripted troops and recompensed them with plunder, attempted occasionally to collect taxes and impose duties, and periodically sent out punitive expeditions when local leaders became recalcitrant. Most often, they followed a policy of noninterference. Local administration and local wars were left in the hands of

EPICS AND HEROES   29

The design at the center of this late-nineteenth–early twentieth-century Lakai at torba ilgich *is based on a whirling-circle pattern usually found on red ground cloth (2004.259.83). This silk, cross-stitched ilgich references a style that is more commonly embroidered with chain stitches and slanted buttonhole stitches. The Kungrat call the whirling-circle design* burni kiyushik, *or "crooked nose."*

An early twentieth-century Kungrat or Durmen ilgich *with unusually bold and well-defined pattern elements in saturated, contrasting colors (2004.259.56).*

This late-nineteenth–early twentieth-century piece, possibly from the Durmen tribe, is one of a group of ilgich *in the Robinson Collection that appear to combine Lakai and Kungrat design styles (2004.259.68).*

Top:
This Lakai woman was head of the Liaur Village Soviet, Tajikistan, 1929.

Bottom:
Lakai farmers clear irrigation ditches for their fields, Tajikistan, 1929.

local leaders, who settled disputes, meted out justice, organized important social events, and acted as intermediaries between their populations and the *beg* or the emir.

Political borders were secured in the second half of the nineteenth century, when Russian military forces advanced into the oasis towns north of the Amu Darya, and the Afghan Amir Abdur Rahman implemented an aggrandizing nationalist strategy.[12] The region was divided into two essentially colonial regimes. Abdur Rahman annexed a large section of northern Afghanistan that had been ruled for centuries by Uzbeks, and the emirates of Bukhara, Khiva, Khojent, and Samarkand became parts of the Russian protectorate of Turkestan.[13] At this point, the histories of the Lakai and Kungrat on opposite banks of the Amu Darya diverged, as each became subject to different political pressures.

Though nominally under the rule of the Bukharan emir, the Lakai area north of the Amu Darya had remained largely independent and its inhabitants notably reluctant to pay their taxes. In 1869 the ruling emir crushed the tribe in attacks so ruthless that the Russians called them pogroms. Within a few decades, the Lakai lost all their herds and were forced into settled agriculture. However, after enduring years of abject poverty, they managed to become successful grain producers, reestablish their horse herds, and forge an opportunistic political and military alliance with Bukhara, which ended with the Bolshevik Revolution of 1917.[14]

Many in Central Asia were eager for independence — or simply were eager to be rid of colonial rule. Under the leadership of Mullah Ibrahim Beg, the Lakai achieved notoriety in the 1920s as guerrilla fighters against the Bolsheviks. The Soviets characterized this movement as a *basmachestvo*, a class struggle in which feudal chieftains and religious leaders resorted to banditry in an attempt to reinstate the rule of the Bukharan emir. Although the exiled emir did play a part in directing resistance, as did pan-Turkic activists such as Enver Pasha, the movement was multifaceted. In the rural areas, religious sentiments prevailed over political ones, but the revolt was also in reaction to the economic hardship resulting from Bolshevik policies. Photographs of Lakai settlements made in 1929 by the ethnographer and NKVD agent known as Jurabaev depict a devastated community: people wear old, ragged clothes, and only humble household goods are visible.[15] Single-crop cotton cultivation had made it impossible for the formerly rich region to feed itself; included among the photographs are woeful images of Lakai returning from trips to "bread centers" to collect basic staples. For more than a decade, local support enabled Ibrahim Beg's fighters to use hit-and-run tactics against Soviet troops as the *basmachi* movement waxed and waned. The fighters were often forced to cross into Afghanistan in order to evade pursuit. Eventually, in 1931, Ibrahim Beg was pushed back into Soviet territory, captured, and executed.[16]

The Lakai regions were finally pacified and organized into cotton-producing collective farms. The *basmachi* movement had compromised the Lakai's Soviet credentials, although in the end they were politically rehabilitated, and only the *begs* were condemned. The Lakai themselves were splintered. The Badra-Oglu Lakai clan went over to the Bolsheviks in the 1920s, while many of the Ishan Khoja Lakai moved into northeastern Afghanistan, as did numerous other Uzbek peoples fleeing political and religious oppression.

Today, the majority of Lakai live in southern Tajikistan, concentrated in the Hissar and Baljuan regions. Southern Tajikistan has a mixed Uzbek and Tajik population, but the large collective farms where most Lakai work tend to operate under brigades that replicate clan divisions, and the rural administrative hierarchy is

A late-nineteenth-century Kungrat ilgich *in which in floral pattern elements are constrained within a rigorous, formal design (2004.259.54).*

The complex pattern on this early twentieth-century Lakai uuk kap ilgich *was achieved by the use of different-colored threads integrated into a regular geometric repeat (2004.259.24).*

made up of tribal heads from important families.[17] The Lakai are loyal citizens of Tajikistan, but they maintain strong notions of kinship and Lakai identity, especially regarding their warrior past and their pre–twentieth-century political dominance of the region. Their continued self-differentiation underscores the fallacy of an already compromised "ethnic Tajik culture" in Tajikistan. Tajikistan is a titular Tajik state, but it does not include any of the great Tajik/Persian historic cities, all of which were encompassed within the Uzbek Soviet Socialist Republic and today are part of the Republic of Uzbekistan.

The officially engineered creation of a Tajik national identity under the Soviets excluded the Lakai, who, as Uzbeks within a Tajik state, seem smaller and more isolated. The Durmen, Karluk, and Kungrat, whom the Lakai claim among their clans, as the historian Olivier Roy writes, "distinguish themselves explicitly from the Lakay. . . . [W]hat now dominates is their Uzbek ethnic identity."[18] Important passages from history are disappearing from the collective memory. Because the Lakai are not Tajik, the state has no interest in honoring their past or in exploring nomadic traditions, which instead are often denigrated as primitive. As a result, the Lakai themselves must preserve their historical memory; unfortunately, only a small portion of the stories known a few generations ago remains today.

In Uzbekistan, the Kungrat comprised a significant population in a mixed region that included Turkic-language-speaking peoples of both Turk and Dasht-i-Kipchak steppe origin and Persian-speaking people with a lengthy agricultural tradition.[19] Despite the obvious difference in standing of the Lakai and the Kungrat within their respective national environments — the Lakai as Uzbeks in a titular Tajik state and the Kungrat as a majority ethnicity in a titular Uzbek state — the Soviet imposition of an ethnic identity on each population was similar. In the early Soviet years, Uzbeks were perceived as "progressive" and Tajiks as "reactionary." With state interests behind them, the Kungrat in the Surkhandarya region became a socially dominant group, so much so that Persian-speaking people often identified themselves as Uzbek for censuses or on official identity cards.[20]

Although three-quarters of all livestock in Central Asia perished in the 1920s as a result of forced-collectivization policies, the Kungrat were able to retain and even revive a semipastoral way of life under state administration. They are skilled shepherds, and their access to sheep and camel wool also enabled them to perpetuate numerous weaving and felting crafts that disappeared in other areas. Like the Lakai, the Kungrat have a strong sense of self-differentiation; their approach to modernization is more conservative than that of other Uzbek and Tajik groups in Central Asia. Traditional women's costume and adornment remain important elements in weddings and other family rituals, and older women still wear a distinctive Kungrat costume and headgear.

Kungrat who are today in their seventies and eighties display remarkably detailed memories of clan organization and descent. Older men are aware of genealogical ties to the Karakalpak region and know stories of movements between Balkh in Afghanistan and Surkhandarya, and older women remember many rituals of childbirth and protection.[21] The same elders, however, say that these things are no longer important to young people and that many of the tales their own grandparents knew have been lost.

The combination of retained Kungrat cultural traditions and limited economic opportunity has encouraged the domestic manufacture of clothing and furnishings. Surkhandarya is Uzbekistan's largest cotton-growing province, and it also produces large amounts of grain, fruits, and vegetables. Nevertheless, the average income is lower than in most of Uzbekistan, good jobs are hard to find, communications are poor, and the infrastructure is aging. Ironically, the poverty and isolation of the region have been transformed into cultural assets for the state, as the Surkhandarya and Baisun regions have become folkloric showplaces for Uzbek culture.[22] The inhabitants are subjected to scrutiny by cultural expeditions, and their elaborate regional costumes, textiles, music, dance, and even time-honored games are celebrated in festivals. This has both positive and negative aspects. Luckily for ethnographers, if not for themselves, modernization has bypassed many of the Kungrat, whose remote villages remain preserves of traditional culture.

By the end of the nineteenth century, very different political and cultural forces were at work in Afghanistan. The Afghan Amir Abdur Rahman set the pattern for central-government rule, forcibly moving large Pashtun populations into the north, allocating the best lands to them, and giving them control of administrative affairs. This placed considerable pressure on Uzbeks living in Samangan, Kunduz, and Takhar provinces, home to the Kungrat and other Qataghan tribes.[23] The role of the local Uzbek *begs* was reduced to that of brokers for tribal interests.[24] Although stripped of their official power, the *begs* continued acting as intermediaries, and those who successfully kept government interference to a minimum were regarded as heroes in their communities. Wealth and local influence tended to accrue to the *begs*; dependency increased among poorer people, and social stratification became greater. Community obligations were met through patronage and lavish entertainments, which increased the number of people in a *beg*'s loyalty network.

In Afghanistan, the Kungrat were engaged primarily in agriculture and sheep herding, and some moved seasonally with their flocks to pasture. Settlements were a combination of mud-brick homes and yurts. Although always conscious of tribal differentiation and hierarchy, the Kungrat established commercial and social alliances with their Uzbek neighbors, with whom they shared a similar way of life and traditions of household organization. Until the Soviet invasion of 1979, most Kungrat villagers led a quiet life, without much interference from the government. In fact, for Uzbeks who had acquired a higher education, life often seemed almost *too* quiet. The Afghan state did not promote Uzbek identity, and because Uzbek was not recognized as an official language, instruction in all schools was conducted in Persian and Pashtu. There were no development projects that benefited Uzbeks, and there was little hope for advancement through government service. A growing consciousness of discrimination arose among Uzbek intellectuals beginning in the 1960s, but a popular Uzbek identity did not emerge in Afghanistan until the war against the Soviets and, then, the Taliban, when the military successes of the Uzbek general Abdul Rashid Dostum became a locus of ethnic pride.[25]

For the minuscule Lakai population in Afghanistan, ethnic-group identity remained closely equivalent to the tribe. After the Soviet border with Tajikistan closed in the 1930s, the small Lakai villages located near Kunduz almost seemed to disappear into the landscape. People still traveled back and forth, crossing the border illegally to visit family, but only rarely. The borders were porous during the *basmachi* war, the Afghan conflict with the Soviet Union, and the Tajikistan civil war.[26] The continued Lakai reluctance to move into the Uzbek orbit may have been the result of their noninvolvement in such trans-ethnic activities as the bazaar trade, from their relative isolation as farmers and herders, and from a strong sense of self-differentiation — even from other immigrant Uzbek groups.

What has remained consistent in the development of identity in different countries and within both Lakai and Kungrat clan

A late-nineteenth–early twentieth-century Lakai at torba ilgich *whose field pattern is made up of five hexagonal medallions (2004.259.71; detail opposite). Although the four hornlike elements in the intervening spaces are not connected to the hexagonal medallion at the center, the resulting composition is similar to that of Lakai* ilgich *with a central diamond and horned corner elements.*

A twentieth-century Lakai uuk kap ilgich *with an unusual pattern of six medallions. Winglike or hornlike forms extend from the top of each medallion (2004.259.91). The fill pattern of the circular medallions is similar to those on a Lakai* ilgich *collected during the 1930* SAMIIR *expedition.*

The central element in this late-nineteenth–early twentieth-century Lakai at torba ilgich *is a diamond-shaped central figure that is surrounded by four fanlike shapes with spiraling, multiple hornlike elements (2004.259.72).*

Three Kungrat women, c. 1930.

groups is that multiple forms of solidarity and affinity groups operated at the same time. Villages or neighborhoods (*mahallas*), religious ties to Sufi groups, memories of historic alliances and betrayals, and patron-client relationships all formed different levels of group identity known as *qaum*.[27] While lineage and clan remained of central importance in local hierarchies, communal obligations, and marriage, relationships between the tribe and the state were essentially political.[28]

Courtesy, deference to elders, and the integration of traditional social behaviors into ceremonies are important elements of traditional and contemporary Central Asian "ethnic" identity. Part of this identity involves being Muslim: almost all the Uzbek, including the Kungrat and Lakai, are Sunnis, following the Hanafiyya school of Islamic law. (In the former Soviet Union, Muslim self-identity does not depend upon active participation in religious activities. Islamic practices, even if limited to name-giving ceremonies and funerals, are conflated with urban as well as tribal social norms.[29]) Rural dwellers such as the Lakai and Kungrat often are more observant of Islamic traditions than their urban countrymen; since independence, it has become easy to determine the number of local *quam* by counting the number of mosques in a given village or town. There are also communal activities that sustain Lakai and Kungrat identity in ceremonies surrounding childbirth, marriage, and death. The rural regions of Afghanistan and former-Soviet Central Asia are less subject to the pressures of modernization, and kinship-based, neighborhood, and occupational groupings remain distinct.[30] Modernist tendencies and conservative practices coexist — for the most part harmoniously — in Lakai and Kungrat societies.

Group identity is a meaningful concept to every individual, affecting both everyday experiences and significant rites of passage.

In Afghanistan, Uzbekistan, and Tajikistan, the most potent forms of cultural continuity exist within the woman's sphere — as domestic ritual and, especially, in the creation of handmade textiles.

A Lakai at torba ilgich *collected by the 1930* SAMIIR *expedition and dated to before 1914. Its pattern consists of a large central medallion that is surrounded by four smaller medallions and four partial-medallion designs.*

THREE ORIGIN STORIES

A Lakai Origin Story

Khan Mahmud of Balkh sent for Dugan the *cinchi,* a great expert on horses. He ordered Dugan to search through all his horses to find a *tulpar,* a racing horse with invisible wings that only a very experienced *cinchi* can see. There was not a single *tulpar* among the khan's horses, but a *diwana,* a person touched by God, brought Dugan a skinny nag. He said to the khan, "Here is a *tulpar!*" The khan was angry and offended and ordered Dugan's eyes put out. After this, Dugan was known as Sukir, or blind.

Dugan Sukir told his younger brother, Dumbugul, to buy the nag and return to the khan and say to him: "Give us forty days, and then the best racer among your horses shall race my nag. If your horses cannot keep up with her, you must go to the judges and pay compensation for my eyes." After forty days, Dugan Sukir ran his hands over the body of the horse and found a small dimple, which he filled with butter. He told Dumbugul to request an additional forty days from the khan. Once that period ended, the horse was ready and eager for the contest. But the brothers, realizing that the khan intended to kill them, fled to Hissar.

The khan's men gave chase, but the *cinchi* cunningly evaded pursuit, and the horse jumped over the Amu Darya river, saving the brothers. They lived by the riverbank for a time, and the younger one became known as Dumbugul Mergen, the hunter. One day he saw a trunk floating in the river and discovered inside it two girls — one of them a princess. The older brother, Dugan Sukir, married the princess, and Dumbugul Mergen wed the other girl.

This is how the girls had come to be inside the trunk: One of the descendants of Isaac, a son of the prophet Abraham, was called Adkham. He had a younger sister named Anar. The people in the town where they lived noticed that Anar had begun leaving her home in the evenings and spending them with strange men. They told Adkham this, expecting him to punish her. But he discovered that Anar had been passing the nights learning from the *chilitani,* or wise men, in their cave. Still, the neighbors reported the girl's absences to the king and complained that her brother would not punish her. The ruler ordered that Adkham and his sister be killed. But before he died, Adkham cried out that neither he nor his sister had done anything wrong: "Anar ham khak, min ham khak!"

After Adkham's death, his corpse continued speaking the same words. The angry king ordered the corpse burned, but even the ashes cried out. Then the king's minions threw the ashes in the river. But the foam of the ashes declared, "Anar ham khak, min ham khak!" The river carried the foam into the reservoir in the king's courtyard. The princess and the vizier's daughter were curious: They stuck their fingers into the foam, licked them, and became pregnant. Furious, the king ordered that the girls be put to death. But the executioner took pity on them, stowing them inside a trunk and throwing the trunk into the Amu Darya.

Not long after the girls wed Dugan Sukir and Dumbugul Mergen, they gave birth from these ashes to two boys. People witnessing the difficult birth of the princess's child called her "Chin Kiz," a true virgin. Her son was given the name Chengiz. When the vizier's daughter gave birth, she cried out, "Dur men!" or "I am the best pearl!" Her child, called Durmen, was the forefather of the Durmen tribe.

In time, the princess had forty sons by Dugan Sukir. When they grew up, they banished Chengiz, saying he had no father. Shortly after the khan of this kingdom died, the bird of the kingdom flew over the steppe and landed on the head of a bald man — who was Chengiz and who was elected khan.

Chengiz Khan wished to avenge himself on his brothers, and he began killing them. His mother was able to hide only one, Karmysh. At this time, there also lived four brothers, whose late father had left them but a single lame goat; each brother owned one leg of the animal. Once, when the goat was lying in hot ashes, its lame leg caught fire, and as the creature ran to a threshing floor, it set fire to the grain that was stored there. The angry owner of the threshing floor seized the owner of the lame leg and brought him to Chengiz Khan, who fined the man who owned the lame leg. The owner of the lame leg, grieving, dragged himself off home. On his way, he encountered Karmysh, who advised him to return to the khan and say that the lame leg had not run to the threshing floor and so was not responsible for the mishap; the owners of the three healthy legs should be fined instead. Karmysh then begged the man not to tell the khan who had given him this advice. After the man made his appeal, the khan asked: "Why didn't you say this before? Who told you this?" At first he refused to say, but when threatened again with the fine, he revealed that it had been Karmysh.

Chengiz Khan now felt remorse over having killed his brothers, reasoning that if only one of them could have given such good advice, perhaps all would have been great supporters of the state. Chengiz Khan then married Karmysh to sixteen women, who had sixteen sons, from whom are descended the sixteen clans of the Qataghan tribe. The youngest of these sons was named Lakai. During his life, Karmysh gave all his possessions to his sons, but he forgot Lakai, who demanded his rights from his father. Karmysh replied: "The property of your brothers is yours. When you have a need, you can ask it of them." And that is why the Lakai believed they were permitted to take the property of the Qataghan tribe; their forefather had permitted them to do so.

Lakai had four sons from two wives. Because these four brothers could not live together, Essen Khodja and Badragli (one son from each mother) ventured forth and lived as nomads in Hissar, while Turt Aul and Bairam remained in Baljuan.

Collected by Belkis Khalilovna Karmysheva, this tale is included in her book *Uzbeki-Lokaitsi Iuzhnovo Tadjikistana* [Uzbek-Lakai of Southern Tajikistan] (Stalinabad: Academy of Science of the Tadjik SSR, Institute of History, Archaeology, and Ethnography, 1954), 24–26.

The Amu Darya tumbling forth from the mountains, c. 1900.

Another Lakai Origin Story

Many men wanted to marry the khan's daughter, but she refused each of them. People asked, "Why does she turn them all down?" One of these men, whose name was Lakai, gossiped too much about the young woman and her family. The angry khan threw Lakai into a river, trying to drown him. As Lakai thrashed about, he asked over and over, "Am I right, or are you right?" The khan's daughter, watching from the roof of the palace, saw the man in the water and heard his words. She had him rescued and demanded, "What do you mean, am I right or are you right?" He answered, "If you want to see who is right, drink the water." So she cupped her hands and drank the foam on the water.

Although she was a pure virgin, she became pregnant from the foam and, nine months later, gave birth to a baby — from her mouth. Later, she married Lakai. One day, when the baby was old enough, the khan's daughter put the child in a saddlebag on the back of a gray horse, struck the horse, and told it to go. The horse traveled a great distance, and where it stopped became the home of the Kungrat tribe.

All the people — the Kungrat, the Qataghan, the Barlas, the Karluk, and the Turk — intermingled, except for the Lakai; they are the only ones who have kept their Chagatai lineage pure. The Lakai are like the trunk of a tree, while the others are branches.

The authors collected this story in 2005 from Aimkhal Ernazarova, a Lakai woman who lives in Hissar, Tajikistan.

A Kungrat Origin Story

One day, Chengiz Khan and his army moved to conquer the neighboring country, but they lost the battle. The ruler fled on foot and along the way met an old man named Kungir-bii, who was riding a dark-brown horse; *kungir* means dark brown. The old man said to Chengiz Khan: "If I were to die, nothing would happen. I am just an old man. But if you were to die, there would be no one to rule the country." He offered his horse to Chengiz Khan, who accepted it and invited the old man to visit him any time. When the old man came to his castle, the khan received him with delicious food and then asked what he wanted as a gift. The old man asked for sheep and steppe land on which to pasture them. Chengiz Khan presented him with the steppe called Guzar-Baisun. Thus the Kungrat tribe originated.

Binafsha Nodir collected this story in 2005 from O. T., a Kungrat man who was born in 1916, is a member of the Vahtamgali tribe, and lives in the Sherabad district of Uzbekistan.

The Lakai town of Karatag, on the Karatag River, 1929. The river flows into the Kafirnigan and then into the Amu Darya.

2. TEXTILES AND RITES OF PASSAGE: THE RHYTHMS OF LIFE

At torba ilgich
Lakai, late 19th–early 20th century
2004.259.70 (detail)

For centuries, the yurt represented freedom, mobility, and the heritage of the steppe to the Kungrat and Lakai. This distinctive structure was the family's social and spiritual center. Children were born close to, and new mothers were purified by, its hearth fire. Lucky young brides and grooms received an *aq oy*, a white yurt, as their marriage portion.[1] And old men had a saying: "Let this yurt serve me until my death. Let them carry out my dead body from this yurt."[2]

In the past, a yurt or two housed a single family; whole clans gathered to form yurt villages. But the Lakai in Tajikistan no longer use this structure, and for the Kungrat in Uzbekistan and Afghanistan it has become a secondary, temporary dwelling. Many of the prestige textiles that once decorated the yurt have been moved to the house. Nonetheless, patterns of family life, divisions of labor, and women's traditions revolving around the yurt remain intact. Its symbolic presence continues to be felt throughout the lives of the Lakai and Kungrat.

During the nineteenth century, the largest tribes of Dasht-i-Kipchak Uzbek origin were the Durmen, Kungrat, and Lakai; splinter groups included the Marka, the Turkman of the Yuz, the Kesamir, the Qataghan, the Naiman, and the Semiz.[3] These tribes have a common history of nomadic pastoralism and similar social structure, rituals, and beliefs. Many aspects of their material culture are so similar as to be indistinguishable. Each group developed economic specialties suited to its local environment, and each retained a distinct tribal identity that was expressed in the details of cultural life — in costume, household decoration, and artistic style. The Lakai specialized in horse breeding, but sheep herding was also economically important.[4] According to a Lakai saying, "The old woman strikes fear by saying she is dying; the sheep herder strikes fear by saying he is leaving." (Concern about the expense of a funeral is expressed in the first case and the expense of losing a herder in the second.) Sheep were the most important herd animal for the Kungrat, who also raised goats and camels.

Until the end of the nineteenth century, Dasht-i-Kipchak herders lived primarily in yurts, moving along the watersheds that were tributaries to the Amu Darya and the Panj rivers. These territories are now divided among southern Tajikistan, southeastern Uzbekistan, and Afghanistan.[5] From the sixteenth century to the present day, the Lakai and Kungrat have shared these lands with settled Turkic- and Persian-speaking peoples who were largely agrarian. Except when their chiefs were engaged in short-term warfare, these neighbors maintained peaceful relations, and economic ties encouraged cultural exchange. Before the 1920s, most goods changed hands through barter. Each of the various communities had acquired special craft skills. The Lakai traded jewelry, horse harnesses, and embroidery work for Tajik-made carved wooden chests, agricultural products, and ironwork.[6] Among the more striking examples of cultural borrowings is that the Lakai and Kungrat replaced their herds of horses and sheep with superior local breeds, and several Persian-speaking groups that raised goats and sheep began using yurts as residences at the summer pastures.[7]

The Lakai remained yurt dwellers until the 1920s, but by the early twentieth century, many Dasht-i-Kipchak Uzbeks, including the Kungrat, had settled into compact farming and herding communities. Yurts were considered more prestigious than the simple *lochik* or than mud-brick houses, but only the affluent could afford to purchase them.[8] Villages (*kishlaq*) were laid out in a line along an irrigation source or clustered together and surrounded by fields. Although land was collectivized in Soviet Uzbekistan

The pattern of this late-nineteenth–early twentieth-century Lakai at torba ilgich *consists of a central spiral-edged form and four spike-edged, diamond-shaped design elements in each corner. The bands on the sides and bottom edge are cross-stitched. The top band, part of which would have been covered when the object was hung, is unadorned (2004.259.70).*

TEXTILES AND RITES OF PASSAGE 53

Left:
The design of this late-nineteenth-century Lakai uuk kap ilgich *is embroidered on a rarely seen green-flannel ground cloth. Note the dramatically contrasting colors and elaborate edging of the pepper-shaped motifs (2004.259.74).*

Above:
A twentieth-century tasseled tent decoration, sewn from two embroidered strips with a double-spiral repeat pattern on blocks of contrasting ground (2004.259.90). Such embroideries could be hung anywhere in a tent or house.

The ground for this nineteenth-century Dasht-i-Kipchak scissor bag (kaichidon) was pieced together from fabric of contrasting colors and then embroidered with chain stitch (2004.259.60). Women of the household treated the long iron scissors that were used for working fabrics and for trimming pile in weaving with great care.

TEXTILES AND RITES OF PASSAGE 53

Left:
The design of this late-nineteenth-century Lakai uuk kap ilgich *is embroidered on a rarely seen green-flannel ground cloth. Note the dramatically contrasting colors and elaborate edging of the pepper-shaped motifs (2004.259.74).*

Above:
A twentieth-century tasseled tent decoration, sewn from two embroidered strips with a double-spiral repeat pattern on blocks of contrasting ground (2004.259.90). Such embroideries could be hung anywhere in a tent or house.

The ground for this nineteenth-century Dasht-i-Kipchak scissor bag (kaichidon) *was pieced together from fabric of contrasting colors and then embroidered with chain stitch (2004.259.60). Women of the household treated the long iron scissors that were used for working fabrics and for trimming pile in weaving with great care.*

An elderly Kungrat man in his garden, Uzbekistan, 2005.

A contemporary Kungrat yurt, used as a secondary dwelling, Sherabad district, Uzbekistan, 2005.

in the late 1920s and during the 1930s, many households continued raising and marketing their own crops.[9] The majority of Uzbeks in northern Afghanistan owned their homes and parcels of agricultural land (typically only five to ten acres). Throughout the first half of the twentieth century, most Lakai and Kungrat lived in small flat-roofed or domed mud-brick dwellings, which often included a separate room for receiving guests. A walled courtyard contained a brick bread oven and cooking area as well as space for seasonal activities such as weaving. A yurt was often set up in the courtyard or adjacent to the home for use as an auxiliary dwelling in summer. Today, those Kungrat who take their flocks to spring and summer pastures continue to live in yurts, even in the former Soviet Union.

Regardless of whether Kungrat and Lakai lived in yurts or in settled communities, there was a definite division of labor between men and women. Because status in the household was based on age rather than gender, decision-making was the province of older men and women, and young brides had less authority than mothers. Children were generally treated with great affection, and girls were often their fathers' special favorites. Bias certainly existed against those women who attempted to assert themselves outside traditional gender roles, but men recognized the rights of women to exercise power fully in the household and to make decisions in family matters.

Traditionally, women cooked, made bread, cleaned, and cared for the health of family and domestic animals. Men worked with flocks, in the fields, or in the marketplace.[10] This continues to be the pattern of household management in Afghanistan; in Uzbekistan, women often work in the fields as well as performing domestic duties. They also are expected to produce textiles for dowries and household decoration and to help furnish new homes for younger family members. Virtually all Lakai and Kungrat women are skilled at sewing and embroidery; in the past, most also wove cloth for clothing and flat-woven wool rugs or pile carpets, for domestic furnishings, and for sale to supplement family income. Whenever women were not engaged in other household tasks, they would spin floss silk, weave or braid decorative trims, and do embroidery. Aside from clothing, all the textile items women make today originally were made to decorate the yurt. Familiarity with the structure of the yurt helps clarify the textiles' original functions.

The Yurt and Its Ornamentation

The Kungrat call the yurt an *utov*. An old yurt, with felts blackened by smoke and weather, is called a *kara oy*, or black yurt. And a very old yurt was once called a *turt keraga*. Like other seminomadic Uzbeks, the Kungrat build their yurts with willow (*tol*), a springy, pliable wood.[11] Women assemble and decorate the structure, while men help only with the most arduous tasks. The yurt base consists of four latticework sections (*keraga*; each is called a *kanot*, or wing), made from narrow wooden poles that are laced together with small straps fashioned from felted camel wool or ox hide (*kuk*); these sections can be compressed, accordionlike, into small bundles for transport. Curved wooden poles (called both *uvuk* and *uuk*) are attached to the top of the lattice. The opposite ends are fitted into slots (*kuz*) surrounding the circumference of a large wheel (*changarok*) that forms the yurt dome and serves as both window and chimney. The roof wheel has two crossed arcs that curve upward, forming a sort of skeletal cap. There is also a hinged door (*bosaga*), set in a doorframe.

Ornamental textiles help stabilize the yurt. A wide woolen tent band (*bogich*) is intertwined between the long roof poles at the bend, and narrower woven bands (*tizma*) are wound around each pole a little above this. Reed mats (*chii*) twined together with wool thread are placed around the outside of the yurt. The yurt entry supports a split wooden door (*erganak*). The Kungrat also make a door with a piece of felt tied to the frame with woolen rope, called a *charigich*, or use a *chii* mat with a felt lining.

Heavy felts keep yurts warm and cozy in the winter snows, and they are rolled up in the summer to let breezes pass through the mats. The outer covering consists of four or five large felt sections (*turlik*) around the walls. There are two semicircular dome mats (*uzuk*) with long laces of dark red wool on the front (*kizikbof*) and white wool on the back (*aqbof*) and a circular felt section (*tuinuk*) that closes the opening at the top of the dome. The round felt *tuinuk* has four wide woolen ropes (*tuinukbov*), which are usually made from twisted threads of light and dark goat hair. Wedges (*chalgai*) that seal the yurt from wind and dust are sewn onto the front-wall felts. The yurt is fixed in place with stakes (*kozik*) driven into the ground.[12]

When the yurt was a primary dwelling, women often stored their goods and prepared meals on one side, while men worked and rested on the other. But among the Lakai, there was not as strict a division into men's and women's sections as was common among some other yurt dwellers. A hearth was at the center, and domestic goods were stacked around the walls. There were heavy felt rugs and mats, food-storage containers made of the skins and stomachs of domestic animals, and cast-iron pots (obtained by trade) for cooking. Food was served on a special cloth called a *dastarkhan*. The Lakai diet was simple. Staples such as bread were supplemented with meat and milk from the flocks. The Lakai ate goat and mutton but little beef; they also ate horsemeat, often in sausages, but never killed a horse just for food. To preserve meat, they dried it in the sun or fried it. A favorite dish consisted of boiled melon flesh cooked to a paste and then dried; in the winter, women pounded this with sour-milk cheese, adding water and butter and then serving it warm.[13]

At night, quilts and blankets were spread around the fire for sleeping. If a young married couple did not yet have a new yurt, a section of the women's side might be curtained off for them. The yurt's earthen floor was usually covered with coarse felts (*takyamat* and *apran*), then flat-woven rugs with supplementary warp patterning (*gajari gilam*). Wooden trunks and coarsely woven wool bags stored staples, clothing, and tack, while utensils hung from the lattice in smaller bags. The *tor* — the place of honor in the yurt — was opposite the door; there, guests or the oldest people present would sit on felt mats or small carpets. In Lakai and Kungrat yurts, the *chuk*, an elaborately constructed stack of bedding, hangings, quilts, and blankets, was set against the back wall, behind the *tor*.

Chuk (or *djuk*) means load, and it refers to the bulkier items that transport animals would carry when the yurt was moved. The base of the *chuk* was a trunk or wooden frame supporting either a pile-woven or embroidered *mapramach* bag backed with plain or striped fabric and shaped to form a rectangular container. Decorative materials for the yurt — tent bands, plain and patterned braids, cords, and rugs not then in use — were stored in the *mapramach*. If the household was poor and had no additional decorative goods, the *mapramach* was stuffed with straw to make it look full.[14] The *mapramach* rested on a base of mud bricks, called a *sokirchek*. A *sokirchek* consisted, first, of forked pegs hammered into the floor; sticks were laid between the forks to form trestles, which were in turn covered with small planks or poles. After the Lakai became a settled people *sokirchek* were made from loam and planks.

Beneath the *sokirchek* was a niche for delicate teapots and bowls. *Mapramach* bags were placed atop the planks, and the bedding pile was placed atop that. The bedding consisted of pieced-cloth mattresses made

During the impoverished 1920s, few Lakai owned luxury textiles. In this home of a relatively prosperous Lakai farmer of the Badrak Ali tribe, the bedding pile (chuk) is mounted on adobe plugs and wooden boards. A bugzhoma *bag, used to store clothing, is seen at left. Tajikistan, 1929.*

A Lakai woman weaving a kilim strip.
Kainar village, Tajikistan, 1929.

TEXTILES AND RITES OF PASSAGE 61

Dasht-i-Kipchak chuk *decorations, such as this early twentieth-century example, represent an important tradition. Long strips of cross-stitched embroidery were used to bind together and decorate the bedding pile. This piece is virtually identical to* chuk *decorations made by present-day Lakai. Similar cross-stitched bands are made by other tribes as well. (2004.259.27a)*

from printed calico and stuffed with raw cotton. Stacked above these were more delicate quilts of pieced patchwork (*caroq*) and other fabrics and blankets, some decorated with embroidery.[15] In the middle of the *chuk* stack, a large envelope-shaped bag (*bugzhoma*), made of embroidered cloth or plain-woven wool fabric, held new clothing and bed linen.[16] Triangular fabric sections with embroidered flaps (also called *bugzhoma* in Uzbekistan and Tajikistan and *segusha* in Afghanistan) were tucked between layers of bedding. Long cloth bands about three to four inches wide and decorated with *caroq*, appliqué, and embroidery were tied across the bedding pile to stabilize and embellish it (see pp. 61, 73). Pairs of heavily tasseled decorations made of tapestry-woven and braided silk, called *bugzhoma kul*, were also tucked into the bedding stack.[17]

Kol, bands with silk embroidery and many tassels, hung on nearby latticework. Small square and shield-shaped embroideries (*ilgich* and *uuk kap ilgich*, respectively) were hung on the lattice walls on either side of the *chuk*. The number of trunks and overall size of the *chuk* were indications of social rank: poor families could only afford a single trunk and stack, while affluent families boasted three or four stacks. Today, the massive *chuk* is assembled inside the permanent dwelling, usually in the bedroom.

Some of the materials used to make these various textiles were domestically produced. Sheep were sheared both in the spring, when their wool was softer and of a higher quality, and in the fall, when wool was coarser and shorter. Cotton was also grown locally and spun by hand into thread. Synthetic dye materials were widely distributed throughout Central Asia by the end of the nineteenth century, but in remote areas inhabited by the Kungrat, natural dyes made from local plants are still used to dye wool for weaving.[18]

Felt made of wool from the coarser autumn shearing was the most common textile material; it was used for floor coverings, horse blankets, and yurt covers. Felt sections were vat-dyed in various colors and cut into large wavy, triangular, and ram's-horn shapes that were joined together to make long, narrow *caroq* rugs used on the floor on special occasions and hung as interior-wall decorations. For most floor rugs, a piece of plain felt would be partially rolled; then, tufts of varicolored wool were laid on to form a colored pattern, and the felt was rolled again. Multilayered felt bags tapering at the bottom were decorated with applied patterns, wool embroidery, plaited trim, and horsehair and wool tassels.

According to Belkis Khalilovna Karmysheva, before the Bolshevik Revolution the Lakai used a simple horizontal loom to weave striped fabrics for bags, tent bands, flat-woven rugs with supplementary warp float patterning, and *mapramach* with wool pile. She described one pile-woven Lakai *mapramach* as loosely woven with a wool warp, cotton weft, and wool pile. Separately woven rectangular sections formed the front and sides, which were then stitched together and backed with a "striped sacking." A second *mapramach* had a cotton warp and weft, with wool pile on the base, the front, and the sides. Both of these pile-woven bags bore the same design — three octagons enclosing hooked cruciform shapes, with diamond shapes at the center. In the 1950s and 1960s, when Karmysheva was conducting her research, Lakai carpet weaving in Tajikistan had almost ceased; only old women knew this craft, and all *mapramach* were embroidered. But despite the change in materials and technique (from wool pile to silk embroidery), the octagonal motif, called *mapramach guli*, remained the same (see p. 101).[19]

The Kungrat still weave extensively, especially during the summer, but the Kungrat in Uzbekistan no longer make knotted-pile carpets. Instead, they produce flat-woven wool rugs in various warp-faced

techniques, using a narrow loom that is staked in the ground so it can be easily moved. Plain-woven, striped strips are joined together to make *tumorcha tikish* rugs: supplementary warp-patterned wool bands are called *terme* or *gazhery*. A weft-faced rug, woven on a wider loom, with larger, repeating patterns across the entire width, is called a *takyr*. Perhaps the most distinctive Kungrat carpet is the *okenli-gilam*, which is made of strips of alternating embroidered plain- and pattern-woven wool or embroidered with large-scale designs similar to those encountered in *ilgich* wall hangings.[20]

In addition to all the textiles just described, the Kungrat and other Dasht-i-Kipchak peoples in Afghanistan also still weave small floor carpets and numerous forms of plain- and pile-woven bags and saddlebags. The most easily identified Kungrat weavings are the small *mapramach* bags that sit on the base of the *chuk*. The Kungrat prefer warm rather than bright colors, especially favoring an apricot-orange tone. The most characteristic Kungrat pattern is an eight-pointed star. A carpet design with polygonal medallions resembles a Turkmen *gul*, a type of carpet motif that shows tribal affiliation; it is not known if this pattern represents tribal identity when the Kungrat use it. Other carpet patterns seem to have been inspired by urban ikat designs. One barbell-like design is a symmetrical treatment of the cotton-flower (*paktagul*) motif found on early ikats from Bukhara. Some pile *mapramach* have a continuous pile, with a wide plain-woven band on the edges and ends. Another type, sometimes associated with the Durmen tribe, has three sections of pile forming a wide front and two almost square sides, with a plain-woven strip separating the pile sections. Distinctively Kungrat pile *mapramach* tend to be short and wide, with narrow plain-woven edges or ends. Other pile-woven articles include shield-shaped, double-sided *uuk kap* bags and square rugs with unfinished ends that cover charcoal braziers (*sandali*). Although very rare, there are also large Kungrat carpets with designs similar to those on *mapramach*.

Patchwork-cloth *caroq*, cross-stitched, V-shaped *segusha*, and other decorative textiles made for the yurt and permanent home are so common among the many Dasht-i-Kipchak tribes of northern Afghanistan and southern Uzbekistan and Tajikistan that specific tribes or locales cannot be identified on the basis of textile type alone. The Durmen, Kungrat, Lakai, and Semiz do, however, make the distinctive embroideries noted above: the square *ilgich* and the shield-shaped *uuk kap ilgich*. The highly abstract, often asymmetrical designs of *ilgich* distinguish them as some of the most original, dynamic, and artistically powerful textiles to be found anywhere in Central Asia.

The word *ilgich* means pouch or container, but among the Lakai it refers specifically to decorative embroidered pouches of pentagonal or rectangular shape that range in width from fifteen to thirty inches. The pentagonal *uuk kap ilgich* are similar in shape to the *uuk kap* tent-pole bags, household storage containers common to many Uzbek tribes.[21] Both types of *ilgich* are constructed with a backing cloth, but because they are too fragile to be used as containers, their top openings are usually tacked shut with a few stitches; sometimes, pats of dough hold the front and backing material together. Lakai and Kungrat *ilgich* are embroidered in silk thread on a cloth ground. Usually, the ground material is manufactured cotton or napped broadcloth; in rare instances, it is a hand-loomed cotton fabric. The Lakai bought silk from traders who came from Bukhara or local silk from Kuliab or Kabajan. If the silk was not dyed when they bought it, they purchased dyes from gypsies and dyed it themselves.[22] There are also Kungrat *ilgich* of hand-spun

A Kungrat ilgich with a pattern of four joined hexagons with double-horn and diamond motifs (often identified as a bow-and-arrow design), loosely embroidered on wool in a style characteristic of the nineteenth century (2004.259.93). The ethnographer Samuel Martinovich Dudin collected two similar ilgich from the Kungrat around 1900; they are now in the Russian Ethnographic Museum, St. Petersburg.

Overleaf:
Felts and kilim rugs cover the floor of this Kungrat yurt, as seen in two adjoining photographs, c. 1950. Two pile-woven mapramach bags and several envelope-shaped bugzhoma kilim bags form the base of the chuk.

This late-nineteenth-century Lakai uuk kap ilgich *has a stylized scorpion as its central motif. The long, sawtooth-edged patterns on the elongated double tail are characteristic of dynamic Lakai form and composition (2004.259.62). The rich, precise embroidery on a pieced ground cloth demonstrates the value that the Lakai placed on old cloth, which carried with it the traditions and good fortune of a particular family or clan.*

wool with wool embroidery. Among the Kungrat, the rectangular *ilgich* are sometimes called *ainak push*, or mirror bags — a term that is widely used in Uzbekistan and Tajikistan for a variety of small, rectangular embroideries, including those made by Tajiks.

In rural Afghanistan, the most common prestige items are textiles made by women of the household. Other status-enhancing possessions, such as horses, fighting camels, jewelry, and guns, are bartered for or purchased. In present-day Uzbekistan and Tajikistan, televisions and glass-fronted cabinets displaying porcelain knick-knacks are important signs of affluence, but homemade textiles remain crucial to family pride and social standing. A few textiles are always on display in the guest room (*mehmankhana*) — the public room of the house — where they demonstrate both family wealth and the skill of its women. Textiles are also prominently featured in traditional ceremonies, and rites of passage cannot occur without them.

The decorative usage of textiles can remain remarkably consistent, despite the move from yurt to permanent dwelling. In the 1960s, many Durmen Uzbek families in Babtag, Uzbekistan, hung calico or satin fabric across the corners of their guest rooms in order to create rounded walls like those of a yurt. *Ainak push* were hung up very high on the guest-room walls; in traditional yurts, they were hung at the top of the frame, just under the dome. The *chuk* was in the guest room, and the place of honor directly in front of it was laid with carpets and felt.

On a 2005 visit to Hissar, Tajikistan, we saw a massive traditional *chuk* in the home of Aimkhal Ernazarova, a Lakai matriarch. She apologized for the "small" size of the bedding pile of quilts and embroideries that covered an entire wall in her daughter-in-law's bedroom, which otherwise contained only a metal-frame bed and a table with a candle. During the many hours we spent interviewing Ernazarova about embroidery design and techniques, her daughters-in-law, when not doing housework or bringing us tea and sweets, were engaged in embroidery. She said that in the winter, when there was nothing to do but embroider and watch television, they completed twice as many pieces.

The *chuk* was a double stack of textiles at least eight feet tall and eight to ten feet wide (see p. 73). A family wedding had just taken place, and Ernazarova said the *chuk* was considerably smaller at the moment because she had lent a third of the family's textiles for display at the wedding. The *chuk* was formed as if it were in a Lakai yurt. At its base were chests covered with elaborate cross-stitched embroidery. Above them, the stacks of quilts, blankets, and cloth were bound with crisscrossing bands about three inches wide, completely embroidered in silk cross-stitch.[23] Triangular cloth sections with silk and cotton embroidery were tucked between layered quilts. The excellent workmanship was comparable to that found in the same types of textiles produced a century earlier, although the colors were sharp and the designs were quite stiff. Several pieces of Ernazarova's family embroidery bore new designs that had been integrated into traditional frames. For example, paired female figures adorned with Spanish combs and mantillas might be a design from a soapbox or inspired by a film the women had seen on television.

There were other contradictions, too. Ernazarova was fifty-five years old, a well-educated and articulate civil-service worker. Although she recited genealogies and told traditional stories with enthusiasm and facility, she also asserted emphatically that the Lakai had never lived in yurts. Apparently, the memory of the *chuk* as a functional element in a nomadic or seminomadic household was completely forgotten, as was the Lakai's nomadic past. Nevertheless, the skills, artistry, and dedication necessary to produce textiles remained vital.

This continuation of an earlier tradition into the modern world illustrates a source of the vigor and dynamism characteristic of early Lakai work. All women certainly did embroidery, and although not all of them were great artists, the society they lived in appreciated improvisation, individuality, and creativity rather than rote repetition or pure technique. The Lakai paid particular honor to fearless, aggressive men, and they valued tribal integrity and independence above comfort. In their women, they appreciated creativity and artistic independence. Today, many consider the embroideries of the Lakai to be the most artistically powerful examples of nineteenth-century steppe textiles. Lakai and Kungrat embroideries stand apart from the homogenized, generic embroidery work of their Tajik and Uzbek neighbors and even from those of their fellow Dasht-i-Kipchak tribes.

Religion and Household Magic

From birth to death, the lives of the Lakai and Kungrat contain many spiritual, magical, or simply traditional practices related to safeguarding the health of family and community. Ensuring healthy pregnancies and safe births through ritual practices is often the responsibility of the oldest women in the household, and only women take part in certain ceremonies. These practices have often been described as propitiating the spirit world or warding off demons, jinns, and the evil eye. From Soviet-era sociological studies in particular comes the impression of a women's sphere filled with irrational fears and estranged from a male world characterized by scientific thought. Officially, the Soviet state tolerated the observance of domestic "folk ritual" but was hostile to expressions of piety, especially those related to Islam. Thus, religious expression was curtailed in public. But women's rituals retained their power and became a "compensatory strategy for cultural self-preservation."[24]

Lakai and Kungrat Uzbeks consider themselves to be good Sunni Muslims. As with other Central Asian groups, their rituals and ceremonies often combine elements that are not part of formal Islam with prayers or invocations to Muslim prophets and saints. Some rituals may have originated in a pre–Islamic religion, while others stem from Sufi practice; certain more recent rituals may represent accommodations to official atheism.

The rites and rituals of the Lakai and Kungrat are deeply integrated into patterns of behavior shared by other farming and herding peoples in Central Asia. They are part of communal life and often require the presence of the entire local female population, not just family members. Participation in ritual reinforces a specific Kungrat or Lakai cultural identity, shows honor to ancestors and respect for tradition, and demonstrates community solidarity. In her work on the Chechka Uzbek in Afghanistan — who, like the Lakai and Kungrat, are of Dasht-i-Kipchak origin and considered part of the larger Qataghan group — the anthropologist Gabriele Rasuly-Paleczek lists five factors forming "the most important framework for self-representation: genealogical ties, common territory, language/dialect, costumes (especially women's dress), and customary practices (rites of passage)."[25]

Textiles play vital roles in rites of passage. Throughout Central Asia, children and women of childbearing age are considered especially vulnerable to evil influences from human and spirit contacts. The most dangerous of these are the evil eye, which is thought to cause sickness and death among small children, and evil female spirits, which are seen as particularly threatening to pregnant women and to nursing mothers and their small children.

The most common form of amulet found among people of various Central Asian ethnic and linguistic groups is the

This late-nineteenth–early twentieth-century Lakai uuk kap ilgich *has multiple designs combined in a less rigorous field pattern than is normally found in Lakai work (2004.259.85).*

triangular cloth *doga*, or *tumar*. Sometimes, the *doga* contains something — a scrap of paper on which Koranic verses have been written, a bit of salt or coal, a rag from the clothing of a powerful person, a piece of *dagdan* (wood with a particularly sacral character), or a few dried herbs. Frequently, amulets hold something unpleasant that the evil influence recognizes as similar to itself — and, therefore, will not attack the person wearing it.[26] People of all ages wear *doga*, which are also attached to horse harnesses, tied to cradles, and hung in houses and yurts. Those that are not containers are simply sections of triangular cloth decorated with embroidery. In Central Asia, the container for talismanic materials itself often becomes a talismanic item itself. This triangular shape is found as a design element in appliquéd, patchwork, embroidered, and woven materials as well as a discrete object in cloth, metal, beadwork, and wood.[27]

Marriage
For the Kungrat and the Lakai, the wedding is a community event as well as a family occasion. The ideal marriage partner is a close kinsman. The marriage alliance strengthens clan integrity, creates economic opportunities, and establishes reciprocal obligations between the two families. Most marriages are monogamous. Polygamy is outlawed throughout the independent states of the former Soviet Union, but it is occasionally practiced in Afghanistan. All Lakai and Kungrat communities frown upon divorce, which is quite rare in rural areas.

Weddings involve greater expense and longer preparation than any other rite of passage. Embroidered and woven textiles are made specifically for the bride's costume and dowry and to help furnish a new household. The rite begins with the arrival of the groom and his friends at the home of the bride after a journey beset with obstacles, such as feigned attacks arranged by the bride's relatives. At the bride's home, the men are given a special feast of nine dishes. The bride is veiled, and her garments are decorated with powerful patterns (to protect her from evil influences) and with bright, beaded silk tassels. There are embroidery patterns for good wishes and fertility symbols to encourage the birth of numerous children. (For more on auspicious embroidery designs, see Chapter Three.) In theory, the colorful costume will distract any evil influences, which will focus on the dress rather than on the bride.

The bride delegates authority to a maternal uncle to agree to the marriage, but it is considered polite for her to hesitate many hours before allowing him to give that assent. At last, a mullah performs the ceremony, called the *nikoh*. The couple sits behind the wedding curtain (*chimildik*), on a sheepskin or a *caroq* blanket. The groom's face is covered with a man's scarf sash, which is lifted when the bride's father presents him with a skullcap and a robe. As soon as the two are seated together, each tries to place a foot over the other's foot; the result determines who will rule in the family.

Several other rituals follow. The bride and groom see each other's faces reflected in a mirror; the groom takes the bride's hand; he smoothes her hair. After each gesture, he pays her a small cash ransom. Finally, their clothing is stitched together with a long, knot-free thread to signify the desire for longevity and an untroubled marriage. (Any knotting of string or secret closing of a lock in the presence of the couple is considered inauspicious, because it might result in failure to consummate the marriage.) The groom departs after paying an additional ransom to an elderly female family member, who lies down to block the threshold. Later, the bride bids a formal goodbye to her parents and is placed on a horse that carries her to the groom's home. Women from her household accompany her there; in the early twentieth century, the number of women equaled the number of

Opposite:
A contemporary chuk *in the home of Aimkhal Ernazarova, a Lakai woman, Hissar, Tajikistan, 2005.*

carpets and felts she brought as dowry, usually four or six.

A married woman with a large, healthy family meets the bride near the groom's home and, taking her by the hand, leads her between two bonfires. The bride's mother-in-law meets her at the entrance to the home and spreads a ram's skin under her feet. The bride then bows three times toward the yurt (or house), touching her forehead to the threshold. Early the next morning, her veil is lifted, usually by an adolescent to whom she presents a sash. Then come several ceremonies involving fat and flour, which symbolize abundance. Finally, the mother-in-law gives the bride a spindle and a little wool, to test her weaving abilities.[28]

Meanwhile, the entire community feasts for several days. When wedding guests leave for home, they are often presented with short lengths of cloth and with sweets. The gifts are shared with family members, and the cloth is used for making *caroq*.[29] In this way, those who are unable to attend the celebrations can honor and bless the joining of the couple in marriage, thus increasing the *qaum* connections of the couple and their families and reinforcing community solidarity.

A bride's dowry items do more than show her family's wealth and demonstrate her diligence and skill. They are understood to represent the communal endeavor of the women of her family who contribute to their preparation and, by extension, the entire network of that family. In the late nineteenth and early twentieth centuries, there was often a long hiatus (one to four years) between the *nikoh* and the time when the bride began living with her husband. Her chief occupation while she remained with her parents was preparing quilts, hangings, bags, pouches, and decorative embroideries.[30] The dowry also included at least one *mapramach* in which to store items she had made for yurt decoration. The *mapramach* had enormous symbolic importance, linking the new family to clan and community by evoking the nomadic tradition, even among long-settled families. A well-to-do Lakai or Kungrat bride would make several pairs of *ilgich* as part of her dowry. Although these small, elaborately embroidered hangings could be completed within a single month, other household tasks were also time-consuming; she might spend several months producing a single such embroidery.

Childbirth

The moment a child is born, Kungrat and Lakai women take propitiatory actions to ensure its health. In Kungrat families where children have died, the midwife assisting delivery passes a newborn through the dried, wide-open jaws of a wolf. Then she cuts the umbilical cord and washes the child's palate with the blood.[31] Before she begins to breast-feed, the mother winds the tip of her braid around her right forefinger and then circles the mouth of her child with this finger to "clean" it. While she does so, she says, "Let the mouth of my child be as strong as my hair."[32]

During the first forty days following the birth of a child, a period called *chillia*, both mother and infant are particularly vulnerable to supernatural forces that may cause sickness or death. A mother should not leave home during *chillia*, especially after sunset; if she must do so, she first draws off her breast milk three times, thus protecting the child.

Among the Kungrat, only women attend the ritual placing of the newborn into the cradle (*beshik*) for the first time. A mattress filled with wood shavings, millet, or barley is put into the cradle. Seven slim little blankets, often made of *caroq*, and one felt blanket (*pustak*) are laid over this mattress. A knife, an onion, and bread are put under the pillow. (At the end of *chillia*, the mother bites off a piece of this bread and gives the rest to a dog.) As the baby is

The pattern of this late-nineteenth-century Kungrat ilgich *includes spike-edged circular medallions in each corner and a ten-pointed star at the center (2004.259.49). This simple, relatively static design is characteristic of many Kungrat embroideries.*

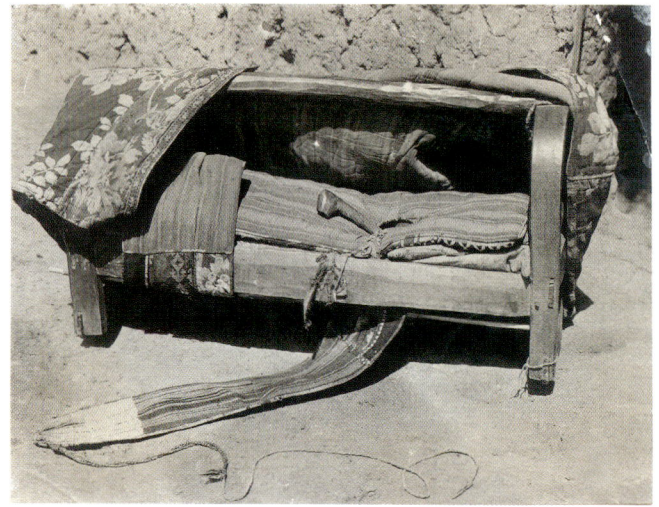

Top:
*A Lakai cradle (*beshik*) equipped with a straw mattress and a* sumak*, a wooden tube through which the male child can urinate. A swaddling band hangs from the cradle. Dagana Kiik village, Tajikistan, 1929.*

Bottom:
A contemporary Kungrat bugzhoma *made from hand-loomed, flat-woven wool fabric, Uzbekistan, 2005. The corner that forms the outer, closing flap is embroidered, and the top is decorated with tasseled straps.*

TEXTILES AND RITES OF PASSAGE   77

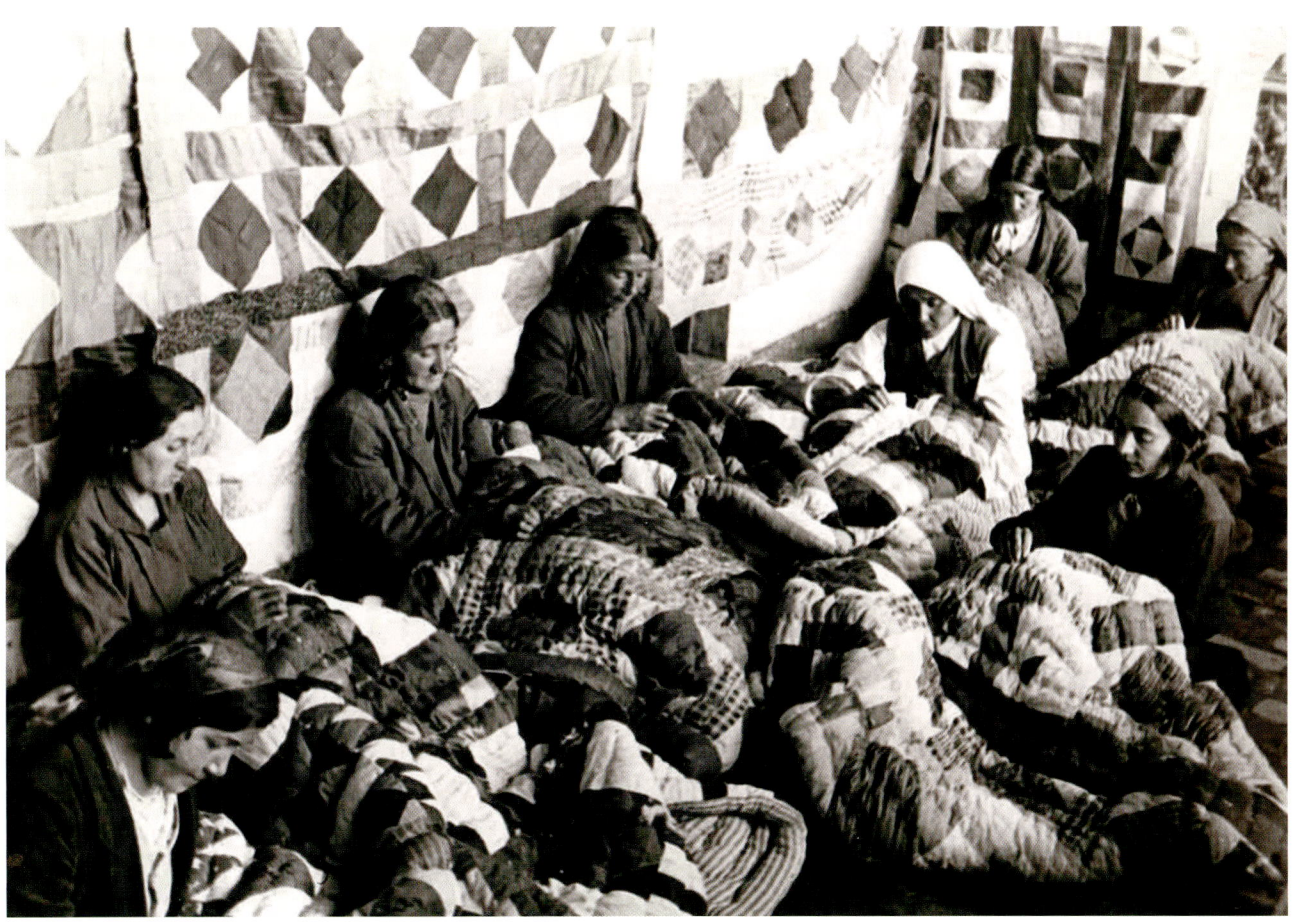

Uzbek women sewing quilts, Uzbekistan, c. 1930. The walls are covered with a traditional Uzbek-style caroq *patchwork.*

A little Kungrat girl wearing a quilted jacket that has an embroidered snake (a protective symbol) on its back, 2005.

put into the cradle, an older woman says: "When the parents swear at each other, don't be afraid. When a dog bays, don't be afraid. When the horses neigh, don't be afraid, when the sheep bleat, don't be afraid."[33] After each line, she touches the baby with a special twig, or *sabov*, that is used for teasing wool. Then she takes a thread and says, "Let him have the sleep of his father, let him have the sleep of his mother, let him have the sleep of his grandmother, grandfather," and so on until she names all the child's relatives. After each name, she makes a small knot on this thread. Then the knotted thread and a section of dried umbilical cord are wrapped in a piece of white material and attached to the right side of the cradle (see p. 76, top).

Each time the child is untied from the cradle, women say, "A back like cotton, *beshik* is from wool," an expression that accompanies cradle unbinding throughout Uzbekistan. When the baby is put to bed they say, "The master has come, put out the dog."[34] The child's hair and nails are not trimmed until the first birthday, when a respected family elder cuts them over a pile of banknotes to ensure the growing child's health. Some Kungrat do not cut all the hair on the back of the head; this is meant to encourage the birth of additional children into the family.

Textiles are seen as important protective objects for children. When a piece of cloth belonging to a person of dignity and strength is passed on to a child, positive personal attributes are transmitted from one generation to another. Soon after birth, shreds of cloth from the clothing of a famous *djigit*, or warrior, are tied to a newborn boy in hopes that he will become brave. Clothing is often an element of sympathetic or associative magic; therefore, the clothing of a child who died would never be passed down, and goods or clothing from a family without children lack auspicious qualities. The hems of children's clothing remain unfinished, a gesture to encourage the birth of more offspring and to ensure the continued growth of the child.[35] Women gather in the evening with friends and relatives to make multicolored *caroq* blankets, hangings, and shirts for their children.[36] According to one Kungrat woman interviewed by Binafsha Nodir, this activity encouraged friendly relations with other children; another said that the bright fabrics drew the attention of evil influences to the dress and away from the child.[37] The Kungrat from Afghanistan's Samangan province contend that the evil eye becomes tangled and confused in the complex *caroq* and thus cannot harm the wearer or enter the windows or doors of a home protected with it. Ailing people are also wrapped in *caroq*.[38]

Like other Turkic peoples in Central Asia, the Kungrat from the Surkhandarya region embroider a snake pattern in twisted black and white threads on the center-back of children's dresses and jackets (see opposite page). Black and white threads twisted together symbolize eyes to the Kungrat, who believe evil spirits (jinns, *adjina*, and others) can turn into snakes or other dangerous creatures. If, however, they see their image on a dress, these threats will turn aside and not hurt the child.[39] The right shoulder of a shirt or dress is the preferred location for a triangular amulet or a wolf's tooth or bird's claw.[40]

Costume

Scholars who have studied Central Asian culture have consistently pointed out the importance of traditional dress in establishing self-identity and differentiation among ethnic groups. A different set of rules applies to the distinctions between Uzbek men's robes and women's costumes. Some men's robes suggest an "urban" style — often worn over the shoulder and unbelted. These are made of subtly distinctive types of striped silk and cotton. Such robes identify the wearer by region or town and as

The central design of this late-nineteenth–early twentieth-century Kungrat ilgich *is comprised of four large, spiderlike elements with rosettes at their centers. Surrounding the central design is a border with smaller spiders that have* jillik bashi *designs at their centers (2004.259.46).*

*This late-nineteenth–early twentieth-century Lakai embroidered saddle cover (*da-our*) has a characteristic Lakai pattern that includes a double-tailed scorpion at the center, flanked by two other types of scorpion or pepper-shaped forms and surrounded by a border of wriggling spiders (2004.259.58).*

either an urban sophisticate or a hick. All one needs in order to change identities is the price of a robe in the bazaar.

By comparison, women's costume is conservative, expressing conformity and proper behavior. Among all Uzbek groups descended from steppe pastoralists, including the Kungrat and Lakai on both sides of the Amu Darya river, the more elaborate forms of traditional dress reflect a tribe-specific identity, an age-specific identity within family hierarchy, and social status — all by the quality of materials and degree of applied ornamentation. Formerly, a woman's skill at embroidery was also an important factor in her desirability as a marriage partner. Depending upon the amount of handwork required to produce the costume, a woman's dress demonstrated her skill as artist and artisan.

For example, the traditional everyday costume of a Kungrat woman is two wide, simple, long-sleeved shift dresses (*uima ekali koilak*) worn one atop another; underneath them are wide trousers, gathered at the top and narrow at the hem. Kungrat women preferred red and scarlet colors. Young women made clothes from very brightly colored material, while older women wore darker dresses. White and blue were considered mourning colors, and black was never used. The dresses of girls and unmarried women had a side closure at the shoulder; those of married women had a ten-inch-long vertical opening to facilitate breast-feeding. Early in the twentieth century, dresses with stand-up collars (*nugai burush koilak* or *it eka koilak*) became popular, followed by dresses with yokes (*kukrak burma koilak*). Nowadays, a plain scoop collar predominates.

The Lakai woman's costume was similar but without the elaborately wrapped headdress.[41] In the early twentieth century, Lakai women wore long, wide shirts, pants, and warm robes in winter. Older married women wore lightweight white scarves; young wives and unmarried women wore red ones. When they left their villages, they wore a light robe over their heads. Their leather shoes had sharply pointed toes. Wealthy women wore *ichig* — light, heelless half-slippers — when indoors, tucking them inside their other shoes during the winter.[42]

Even today, older Kungrat women wear padded robes (*chapan*) similar to those of men but with an open collar and rather short sleeves. Full festive dress includes a long-sleeved, unlined over-robe (*jelak* or *kurta*), worn atop the headdress. The most distinctive element of the Surkhandarya Kungrat costume is a turbanlike head covering (*bosh* or *sallabosh*, meaning head) consisting of multiple scarves wrapped around a small cap, called a *kiigich*.[43] The *kiigich* is first surrounded by a strip of red material; then, five to fifteen bright kerchiefs are tightly wrapped, one after another, into a herringbone pattern (*oikuchok*). The number of kerchiefs was a sign of social status; in the past, a rich woman might wrap twenty-five kerchiefs around a *kiigich* to create a headdress called a *boibosh*. A widow used white material instead of red. Women kept small items, such as thread, needles, and pins, in the folds of the headdress. According to some sources, the way the *bosh* was wrapped and the front strip was embroidered identified the clan of the wearer.[44]

Embroidery is used to embellish the dress, the robe collar and sleeves, and the headdress. A costume is incomplete without embroidered accessories and jewelry items consisting of layers of headbands, beadwork bibs (*halamat* or *hafamat*, protectors from sadness), multistrand bead-woven necklaces (*gulband*, protection against measles), and silver forehead ornaments of fine chain (*sinsileh*). Earrings with multiple pendants (*sirga*, *beshoek sirga*, or *ettioek sirga*) are still common. In the past, women also wore a single nose ring (*letiba*).

According to mid-twentieth-century research, Lakai men wore two robes, either

This Kungrat woman, shown playing a chang (Jew's harp) in 2003, wears an elaborately folded turbanlike headdress topped by a striped silk robe, a silk ikat dress from the early twentieth century, and several beaded necklaces.

This Kungrat woman is arrayed in full festive costume. Sherabad district, Uzbekistan, 2003.

TEXTILES AND RITES OF PASSAGE

striped or of a single color; a lightweight one was made of crude, homemade cotton cloth, and the other was quilted with cotton wadding. Beneath these, they wore wide broadcloth pants. In winter, they wore a sheep's-wool robe, called a *chekmen*, made of coarse, homemade cloth. Rich men wore shirts of striped cotton (*alacha*), while poorer men wore only lightweight robes against their skin. Men wore a thick, quilted, sharp-pointed skullcap (often made of felt) and wrapped a turban around it. A scarf served as a belt; in winter, this might be a cloth up to eighteen feet long. Men wore goatskin half-slippers with broad soles and sharp toes, and they used narrow strips of cloth as leg wrappings. Horse herders and riders playing *buzkashi* or *oglak-chakmog* (a horseback game in which riders vie to capture a large animal carcass and carry it to a distant goal) wore over their other clothing pants of bright yellow cloth or of a sturdy homemade cotton material. Their pants were slit at the bottom and covered with embroidery.

Horse Culture

The culture heroes of the Lakai are their warriors (*djigit*) and *cinchi*, men exceptionally skilled at raising and training horses.[45] Such characters are found not only in Lakai mythology but also among more recent historical figures. Apparently, when the Lakai were not battling with neighboring tribes, they fought one another. They went to war under four flags, one for each of the four brothers who founded the major clans, and they carried a red banner for war, a white one for peace. During battles, they would identify kinsmen through distinctive forms of costume — for example, wrapping their turbans around their bodies or braiding their horses' tails in unusual ways.

Originally, horse breeding was an essential part of the Lakai's occupation — that is, as warriors for their own clans or for hire. The region where they lived was known in ancient times as the source of the Khotal horse, the most prized in Central Asia. The horses that arrived along with the ancestors of the Lakai in the sixteenth century were probably Mongol ponies, which the Lakai soon replaced with local breeds.[46] According to Karmysheva, it was only after the late 1880s, by which time they had largely become settled, that the Lakai recognized horse breeding as an important commercial venture. Before that, they had probably engaged only in indirect long-distance trade, perhaps through the city of Bukhara.

Horses were pastured year-round, and the entire community moved with the herds from summer to winter camps. Pasturelands were considered the property of whole clans, and the appropriation of the finest grazing grounds by tribal chiefs is said to have compelled poorer people to raise crops instead of horses.[47] Because it was considered shameful to ride mares, the Lakai rode stallions, which they did not geld. Only horses that were to bear heavy burdens were shod, and the Lakai left blacksmithing to their Tajik neighbors.

Many ritual practices surrounded the care and protection of horses. The strongest oath a Lakai could take was sworn on a sheepherder's or a horse herder's staff. This entailed placing the staff on the ground, saying, "May I dry up as this staff has dried," and then jumping over it three times. The Lakai said jumping over the staff was the "oath of our grandfathers." When a herder accused someone of stealing a horse, he would throw his staff on the ground and command, "Jump!" If the accused were guilty, he usually would not dare to jump, fearing that such sacrilege could destroy him.[48]

Saddle covers were made of several layers of thick, dense felt. In cold weather, horses also wore a coarse, homemade cloth that was quilted with cotton wadding and decorated with multicolored wool threads; it was hand embroidered in chain stitch. A light, homemade flat-woven wool cloth was

Opposite, top:
A game of buzkashi *(also called* oglak-chakmog) *being played on the open steppe, c. 1900 – 1920. In it, riders vie to capture a large animal carcass and carry it to a distant goal.*

Opposite, bottom:
Lakai men in the Dushanbe bazaar, 1929.

worn as a saddle cover. Silvered metal plates decorated the harnesses, which could cost as much as a good horse. For example, the Russian traveler Rozhevitz described harnesses being made in the Baljuan bazaar in 1906; the leather was stamped, and silver plates with chiseled patterns and inlaid soft silver wire were set into the reins, stirrups, and bridle.[49] Women had their own prized saddles and tack, which were more ornately decorated than those of men. Women's saddles were placed with the bedding in the yurt, and women wove their own girth straps with wool pile on a cotton foundation.[50]

The Lakai especially prized racing and *buzkashi* horses. Wealthy parents would give a fully decorated horse to each son when he reached a mature age, bestowing it on one of the two major religious holidays. Following a game of *buzkashi*, it would be announced that a certain chief had made his son a horseman. The sons of the nobility had saddle covers, called *da-our*, which, according to Karmysheva, were made of a thick, coarse red cloth and heavily embroidered with a twisted silk fringe. They adorned the horse that brought the bride to the home of her groom and were used on other ceremonial occasions as well.[51]

Funeral Ceremonies

In the nineteenth and early twentieth centuries, horses also were an essential part of Lakai funeral ceremonies. If the man had died in an attack, he would be buried where he fell, unwashed and in his clothes. If all that remained were traces of his blood, then the bloody soil would be buried, and lamentations would proceed as if he had died in the village. Ordinarily, a wake for a deceased man lasted four days. On the first day, the corpse was placed inside a yurt, and the grieving survivors circled it in single file, wailing and beating their breasts. The women wore full-length white-muslin scarves over their heads, faces, and shoulders, and they wrapped turbans around their waists, using them as belts. Periodically, the wife, mother, and eldest sister of the dead man would break out of the circle, and one of them would sway from side to side and begin jumping; then the other women would hold her and lift her off the floor. Eventually, they would reenter the circle. The lamentations could continue all night, although at some point they would be conducted sitting down.[52]

If the deceased was a young man, mourners would tie up his horse in front of his house or yurt, and the circling ritual would take place there. The horse would be saddled and a bridle tied to its front legs. All the dead man's clothing would be thrown across the saddle, and, if he had been betrothed, all the gifts of clothing he made for his bride-to-be would be placed there, too. His relatives would start circling the horse, with the wife, mother, and sister breaking from the circle. One of those three would approach the horse, take it by the reins, and begin jumping from side to side. Then she would take hold of the stirrup and start jumping back and forth from the head of the horse to its side. After the ceremony, the dead man's belongings were given to those present; unfinished clothing was torn into little strips and distributed to all in the village, even babies.[53]

In northern Afghanistan, where many ritual elements of a traditional, seminomadic way of life remained intact, extensive textile production supporting this way of life continued up to the 1980s, when war impoverished and destabilized the region. Even in the former Soviet Union, a semblance of traditional dress and handicraft production remains, thanks to the formidable socializing influence of women — this in spite of the settlement of the Lakai and Kungrat, official calls to abandon the production of dowries, periods of economic hardship, and the general encroachment of the modern world. In large part, this is because these traditions are so closely tied to crucial rites of passage — birth, marriage, and death. Textile production is a striking example of constancy and resilience in ethnic identity, notwithstanding changing social and political circumstances that have altered other aspects of individual and group identity.

This late-nineteenth–early twentieth-century Kungrat ilgich *is of a relatively common type that includes a floral center and a spider-design border (2004.259.53).*

3. RENEWING ANCIENT FORMS: *ILGICH* AND THE ART OF EMBROIDERY

Ilgich
Lakai, late 19th century
2004.259.65 (detail)

The Lakai and Kungrat wall hangings known as *ilgich* and *uuk kap ilgich* form the core of the Jack A. and Aviva Robinson Collection at the Minneapolis Institute of Arts. These small embroideries were made to hang at either side of the *chuk*, the bedding pile that represented a family's textile wealth. Together with the *chuk*, *ilgich* formed the backdrop to the *tor*, the place of honor in the yurt. *Ilgich* were vital to the dowry a bride brought to her new home. More than any other element of the dowry, they demonstrated her technical and artistic skills. Making beautiful *ilgich* required these young girls to execute virtuoso embroidery, create vigorous, powerful designs, and use color in nuanced ways.

How did such sophisticated and original works come into being? The young women who embroidered *ilgich* were sometimes assisted by a *sizgich,* an older woman who marked the outlines of the design with chalk. But otherwise, *ilgich* were created solely by girls whose artistic sensibilities were honed by the beauty of their environment. Nomadic peoples must carry their belongings with them as they move from pasture to pasture. Many if not most household items are embellished and made beautiful by the application of pattern. Still, each object also serves some useful purpose — for example, as a container, as a tool, as bedding, or as a support for the framework of the yurt. *Ilgich*, however, were *not* utilitarian; their purpose was to display the talents of the new bride and to perpetuate and strengthen Lakai and Kungrat traditions.

Ilgich embroideries are only fifteen to thirty inches square, yet their compressed energy gives them tremendous artistic power. The imagination and intellect of the creator determine the caliber of the given *ilgich* design. The patterns of these hangings are not representational; rather, they express the energy of natural phenomena without replicating a specific object. Certain designs are derived from the animal world — scorpions, spiders, and snakes. At first glance, other designs resemble heraldic or totemic forms: birds of prey, rams' horns, and arrows fitted to bows. In *ilgich*, these are not associated with clan or ancestor worship; they are part of the flexible, often innovative Dasht-i-Kipchak vocabulary of pattern. Many fragmented geometric motifs are elaborated versions of pattern elements found in carpets, felts, and patchwork. Each design element is open to interpretation and alteration by the embroiderer, and patterns are often so intricate and convoluted as to appear kaleidoscopic. Of all the beautiful textiles made by the Dasht-i-Kipchak tribes, *ilgich* embroideries are considered true works of art — both by textile connoisseurs and by the Lakai and Kungrat themselves.

The range of embroideries made by Dasht-i-Kipchak tribes is not fully documented; only the Kungrat, Lakai, and closely related tribes (the Durmen, Marka, and Semiz) appear to make *ilgich* of outstanding artistic quality. (In fact, the word *ilgich* is found primarily among the Lakai. Other peoples call these decorative embroideries *ainak push*, or mirror covers.) Other Uzbek groups — the Kazakh, Kyrgyz, and many rural Persian speakers, or Tajiks — also make small, square embroideries with charming floral and geometric designs. However, these lack the imaginative design and quality of execution seen in Lakai and Kungrat *ilgich*; and while some are quite attractive, many are not worked with particular attention or artistic rigor.

The Lakai and Kungrat Embroidery Tradition

A brief description of decorated yurt and household furnishings should precede our detailed examination of *ilgich*. The materials collected by the Central Asian Museum of

A late-nineteenth-century cross-stitched Lakai ilgich *with a stylized scorpion in the center panel and horn-tipped diamond shapes — characteristic elements in Lakai work — in the surrounding border. The edging of the scorpion, normally electric, is here modulated and reduced to a series of free-floating paisley elements (2004.259.65).*

Distinctive Lakai-style graphic design and precise stitching are clearly evident in this twentieth-century segusha *(2004.259.89). The elaborate, multicolored fringe remains characteristic of much fine Lakai edging today.*

An early twentieth-century embroidery, representative of the wide distribution of cross-stitched segusha *among the tribes originating in the Dasht-i-Kipchak steppe, including the Lakai (2004.259.26).*

History and History of the Revolution (SAMIIR) expedition of 1930 contributed to the understanding of Lakai taste and sensibilities by permitting comparison of the humbler forms of yurt decoration, bedding, trim, and ceramics with the more sophisticated embroidered productions. For example, a pair of simple, rectangular cloth hangings with Russian chintz top sections has lower sections of pieced, multicolored cloth forming vertical stripes. There are definite parallels between these decorative hangings and the elaborately braided and tasseled fringes with multicolored stripes found on embroidered wall hangings. Likewise, the Lakai ceramics collected by the expedition are decorated with loose, sawtooth-edged hook and horn forms that closely resemble patterns found in embroidery.

The Lakai were well known for their embroidery skills and made decorated caps for their neighbors as well as for themselves. Lakai hats collected by the SAMIIR expedition are relatively tall, compared to other Uzbek hats, and are not completely covered with embroidery. The cotton ground is quilted, with ribs running vertically to the peak of the hat, which is embroidered with an eight-pointed star pattern in satin stitch. Some hats have additional, sharply defined geometric figures.[1]

Yurt furnishings form an important category of Dasht-i-Kipchak embroideries. The Lakai, Kungrat, and other tribes made a variety of bags for holding clothing, foodstuffs, utensils, and tools out of strips of patterned wool tent bands or out of striped, flat-woven fabric. Sometimes they embroider less sturdy cloth bags. The *bugzhoma* is a larger, envelope-shaped bag made from a rectangular piece of cotton cloth or wool flat weave; the corner that forms the outer, closing flap is embroidered. *Bugzhoma* are used to store clothing and are placed at the center of the bedding pile, or *chuk*.

Segusha (also called *bugzhoma* in Uzbekistan) are tucked into the middle of the bedding pile. They are made from two embroidered strips sewn into a V-shape, replicating the appearance of the triangular flap of the *bugzhoma*. Many Dasht-i-Kipchak tribes in Afghanistan make *segusha* embroidered with cross-stitched patterns; beyond this general designation, these cannot be differentiated according to tribal origin.[2] Most cross-stitched *segusha* have eight to twelve design repeats, and one side is slightly longer than the other. The simplest designs are highly abstract bird and swastika forms (see pp. 92–95). In more complex designs, a geometric figure encloses several other figures, one inside the other. Some chain- and blanket-stitched *segusha* can be identified as Lakai or Kungrat because those tribes employ distinctive stitching techniques and a characteristic design vocabulary. The designs of these *segusha* are commonly found as minor motifs on *ilgich*. Many other chain-stitched *segusha* with simple floral patterns cannot be linked to a particular Uzbek group.[3]

Sometimes a triangular panel of chain-stitched embroidery is inset into the V-shape of either cross- or chain-stitched *segusha*. In this form, the *segusha* resembles the triangular amulet, the *doga*, when it is tucked into the bedding pile. Plied-silk fringes are common, and the Lakai, especially, consider them to be necessary embellishments to all decorative hangings. Some fringes have beaded ends, and occasionally a seed-bead or two are stitched into the field, enhancing the embroidery's potency as a protective object.[4]

Shorter strips of cross-stitched embroidery in patterns similar to *segusha* are stitched together along the sides to form small pouches. Some of these *khalta* or *chai khalta* (bags for carrying tea leaves and other small personal items) are almost identical on the two sides; in others, the designs follow a similar theme or reverse the colors of the pattern.[5] A long string with a tassel at the end is attached to the

Opposite:
A contemporary triangular embroidered chuk *decoration, called a* segusha *or* bugzhoma, *on the bedding pile in the home of Aimkhal Ernazarova, Hissar, Tajikistan, 2005.*

RENEWING ANCIENT FORMS

Side 1

*The ground fabric for this late-nineteenth–early twentieth-century Kungrat or Lakai double-sided scissor bag (**kaichidon**) was pieced together from fabric in contrasting colors and then embroidered with chain stitch (2004.259.59).*

Side 2

top to close the bag or tie it to a belt.

Kaichidon, or scissor bags, are long, narrow pentagonal containers. Kungrat and Lakai scissor bags are often embroidered on both sides. The ground fabric may be of contrasting colors pieced in diamond and triangle patterns. A long silk tassel may decorate the base (see pp. 98–99).

Very small children are swaddled and bound into their wooden cradles with six-to-eight-foot-long strips of green or red flannel with embroidered designs or sections of *caroq* patchwork in cotton and silk.[6] There are rare examples of baby wrappers in solid silk cross-stitch with sequences of alternating geometric designs. A pair of much longer bands of the same thickness, often completely covered in cross-stitch, binds the stacks of bedding in the *chuk*, forming a cross along the diagonal. The 1930 SAMIIR expedition collected a long band, called a *chuk chari chuch*, made from strips of old *ilgich*.[7]

Aside from the *ilgich*, the *mapramach* bag is the most painstakingly decorated article of embroidery. *Mapramach* had a significant ritualistic function as well as a practical one. As essential furnishings for the yurt, they were placed at the base of the *chuk*. A poorly constructed, worn-out *mapramach* stuffed with straw did not have the cachet of a silk-embroidered *mapramach* filled with yurt decorations, but it was better than no *mapramach* at all. Only the visible front side of the object was finished with care. The multiple suspension loops were usually made of coarse cotton or wool; occasionally, elaborately braided trim was used. The loops fit over wooden poles to make a supporting frame for the mapramach. Frequently, pieces of old *ilgich* were cut and sewn to form the sides of embroidered *mapramach* bags.

The same designs appear on both pile-woven wool and silk-embroidered *mapramach*. According to Belkis Khalilovna Karmysheva:

The ground is filled in with three big patterns that differ from each other only in colors of single elements. These ornamental patterns are similar on all *mapramach* and are called "*mapramach guli*" — *mapramach* pattern. It is an octagon with more or less straight sides. A stepped rhomb is set in the center of the octagon; the rhombs' sides are edged with three rectangular hooks at each side. Another rhomb is set into the center, broken into four triangles by two lines that cross it diagonally. . . . One pair of hooks turned to each other and joined at their base are set into each of the four trapeziform spaces that are formed between the sides of the crosspiece. Thus, the background forms a typical Turk's ornament: a pair of ram's horns. The central rhomb, diagonally crossed with the crosspiece and ram's horns, is called *chakmak* — lightning.[8]

Even today in Tajikistan, this same pattern is rendered in cross-stitch in silk on a cotton ground on Lakai *mapramach* made for household use as part of the *chuk* ensemble.[9] Durmen, Kungrat, and other Dasht-i-Kipchak groups in Afghanistan and Tajikistan also still make cross-stitched silk *mapramach*. A pattern with three octagonal medallions is the most common design found in their *mapramach*, but a three-fold repeat of hooked diamond motifs is also seen.

Lakai and Kungrat horse trappings with the same design forms as *ilgich* are rare; only a few dozen are known to exist today. The design on Lakai saddle covers most often consists of three large paisley shapes, usually embroidered on a dark indigo blue or black ground to offset the brilliant colors of the embroidered motifs. (The Lakai and other people of nomadic descent identify this form as a scorpion. In urban contexts, it is called a *boteh* and is said to represent an almond or pepper; see p. 104.) Kungrat horse blankets often have floral field patterns with branching floral stems at each edge (see p. 107). As in Kungrat *ilgich*, spiders and scorpions are most often used

Opposite:
Aimkhal Ernazarova, a Lakai woman who lives in Hissar, Tajikistan, embroiders the front panel for a cloth mapramach, *utilizing a classic Lakai* gul *pattern, 2005.*

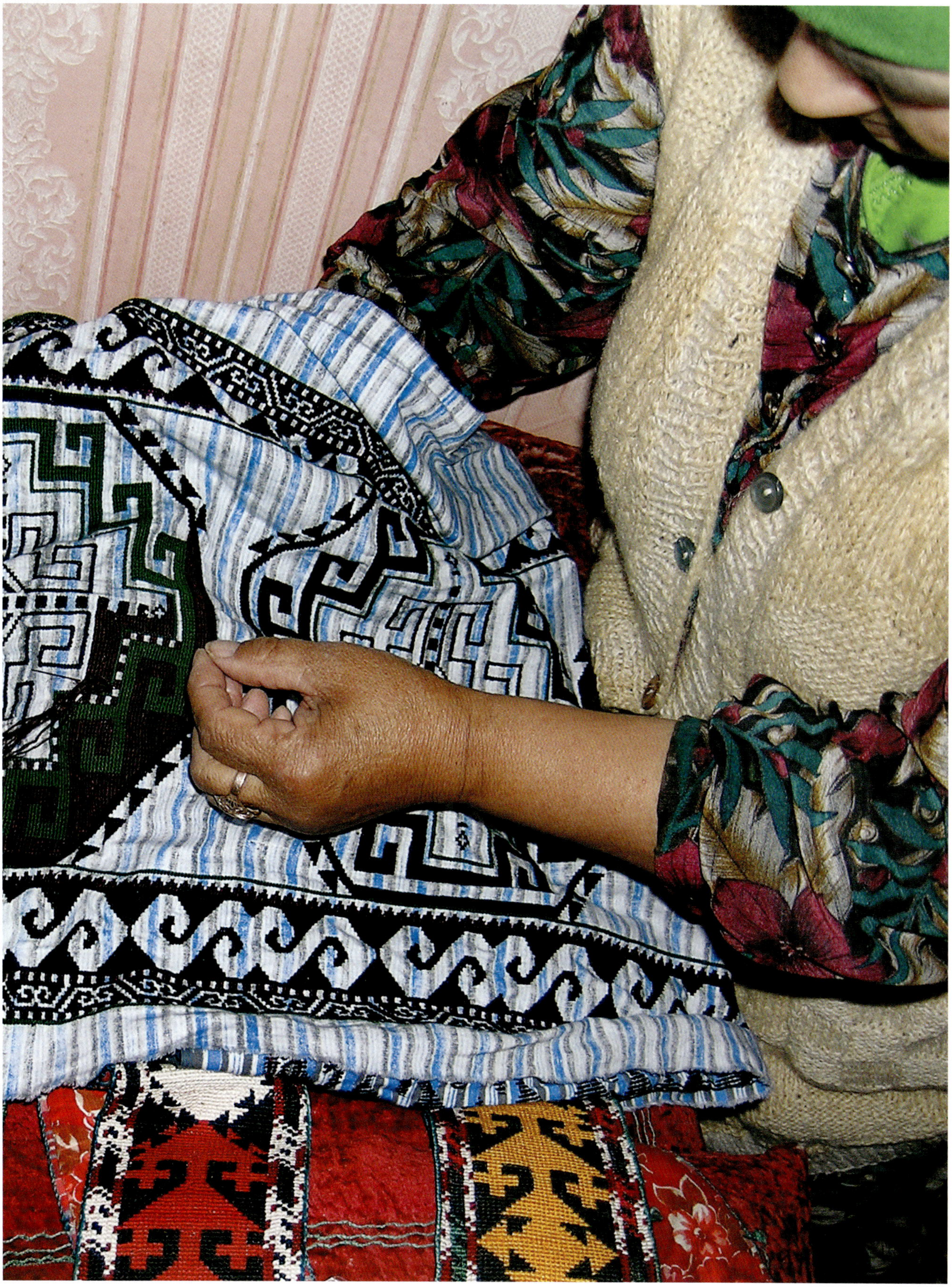

RENEWING ANCIENT FORMS   103

The pattern of this late-nineteenth–early twentieth-century Lakai at torba ilgich *includes four spike-edged elements surrounding a complex, edged circular form (2004.259.61; detail opposite). The placement of patterns on an uncluttered field and the exquisite detail of the discrete pattern elements are characteristic of Lakai design.*

as Kungrat border patterns. A widely distributed type of Dasht-i-Kipchak saddle cover has vinelike floral patterns edging larger vegetal, horned, or stylized scorpion shapes on a red ground. Covers for horses' heads are made of strips of embroidered red-ground cloth and have long horsehair tassels. Many Dasht-i-Kipchak tribes make horse-head covers, but those with distinctively Lakai or Kungrat patterning are quite rare.[10]

Ilgich

It is not known when *ilgich* left behind their utilitarian function as containers and became simply works of art. Like household storage bags, *ilgich* have cloth backs, but their construction is not sturdy, and the aperture at the top is almost always closed. The front and back fabrics are sewn shut or stuck together with bits of bread dough, a substance with sacred significance.[11] The ground fabric on the front side of Lakai *ilgich* is usually a napped wool flannel (*mogul*) or a plain-woven cotton cloth. Red and black are the preferred ground colors, but occasionally gray or khaki brown is used. The ground cloth may be pieced together from fabrics recycled from older clothing or bags. Since the silk thread for embroidery was by far the largest expenditure involved in making *ilgich*, the use of old, pieced fabrics may reflect community rituals of sharing cloth rather than economic concerns. "Similar pieces of old *ilgich* with much worn embroideries (mainly used *mapramach*) were met with more than once in Lakai families," Karmysheva noted. "All of them are embroidered with colored sewing silk on a red background using chain stitch or a combination of chain stitch together with buttonhole stitch."[12] Fabrics used to back *ilgich* are usually made from cotton cloth: a few have silk ikat linings. Border strips and fringes are made in a variety of woven and braided techniques. (For the techniques used to make the distinctive edgings and trims on these embroideries, see Frieda Sorber's appendix essay in the present book.)

Most of the *ilgich* embroideries in the Robinson Collection can be divided into categories of Lakai and Kungrat according to distinctive artistic styles, motifs, and techniques. Although many designs are common to all Dasht-i-Kipchak tribes of nomadic descent, it is the *treatment* of designs and the *use* of colors that characterize the work of the various tribes.

The Lakai, for example, excelled at using dynamic line and color to produce works that are often described as "electric." Their highly abstract, imaginative patterning does not include any recognizably floral motifs. Often, a single line of chain stitch or embroidery in imitation of a warp-twined trim outlines a pattern that is then filled with rows of fine, even, angled blanket or slanted buttonhole stitch in clear, saturated colors.[13] The consistent size of the lines of stitches and the intense color contrast between the embroidered sections and the open field reinforce the hard-edged appearance of Lakai material. Although the ground surface may be almost filled with embroidery, Lakai *ilgich* are composed so as to give the impression of a single, fully conceived design. Fringe, trim, and tassels are exceptionally well executed.[14]

Basic compositional forms may also be identified from each group. Karmysheva divided Lakai *ilgich* into three types: *tabaklau*, *torba*, and *uuk kap*. *Tabaklau* are square *ilgich* in an envelope shape, constructed with a false flap. All the edges, including those on the flap, are trimmed with patterned *chiraz* (trim) tape and a silk fringe, or *chachak* (silk fringe). The name *tabaklau* stems from the word *tabak*, which means cup. Karmysheva's Lakai informants said that the original *tabaklau* bags stored spoons and skimmers used daily for cooking. Square *torba*, or *at torba ilgich*, lack flaps; they were so named because of their similarity to horses' feedbags. (The Lakai also made special embroidered feedbags,

Opposite:
With its large, scorpion-based pattern elements, this central section of a classic saddle cover (da-our) *illustrates the rigorous abstraction and interplay of bold areas of color that are hallmarks of accomplished Lakai designs of the late nineteenth and early twentieth centuries (2004.259.64).*

called *at torba*, to hang over the horse's neck on ceremonial occasions.[15])

The pentagonal *uuk kap ilgich* was named after a bag used during seasonal migrations to decorate the *uuk*, the sheaf of curved wooden poles forming the roof of the yurt. The poles from the yurt were loaded on both sides of a horse or camel, and an embroidered cover, called an *uuk kap,* was put over the top.[16] Fringe often trims the base of the *uuk kap ilgich*, while several tiers of *pyopyok*, or tassels, adorn the three points of the base. Often silver beads are integrated into the tassels, and a silver cupola-shaped bead, a *shabak*, covers the top of the final tassel fringe.[17] Sometimes the maker of an *ilgich* would conceal a talisman included in the decoration inside a tassel or under a flap or fringe so that the casual viewer could not see it.[18] Functional *tabaklau* and *at torba* bags were still in use when Karmysheva was conducting her field research in the 1960s, but these were made from simple homespun sacking without embroidery. *Ilgich* did not serve a utilitarian purpose, as these bags did; they only carried their names.

Lakai embroideries also may be categorized in subgroups according to design. *At torba ilgich* often have cruciform-shaped central figures. In one type, the diamond and horn shapes form a single element, with a plump, curvilinear outline. In another, the center has a straight-edged diamond shape, and the horns have narrow, hatched bands. About this design, Karmysheva wrote: "The lines of the crosspiece are made with dotted lines of alternating white and dark (brown, black, sometimes dark red) narrow rectangles. This kind of decoration is called *ala kurt* — 'motley worm' (Lakai and Karluks more often call it *ala-kan* — 'motley blood'), and is very widely spread."[19] In another type of *at torba ilgich*, whirling sunlike images edged with wave or horn shapes fill the field. Variegated bands of embroidery are often used to outline large areas of color.

Smaller elements fill the corners and areas between the larger design elements.

In *tabaklau ilgich*, the field is sometimes divided into a grid or a central square that is outlined with stitching in contrasting colors. Each section may contain a whirling solar, horn-edged, or geometric rosette. In Lakai work, these designs remain restrained and balanced even if there is no imposed grid. In Kungrat *ilgich*, toothed disks or rosettes may be of different sizes and crowd the field. The overhanging flap at the top of the *tabaklau ilgich* closely resembles the overlapping flap of the *bugzhoma* storage bag. This style recalls that of the Turkoman bread bags (*bokche*) used on ceremonial occasions.

The shield-shaped *uuk kap ilgich* with central figures of scorpions are the most distinctive Lakai embroideries. Scorpions are depicted as symmetrical, double-horned forms with a surrounding border of zigzag or sawtooth-patterned arms that seem to vibrate with nervous energy. The scorpion may take up the entire field, or smaller designs may be scattered around it. Other *uuk kap ilgich* designs include *boteh* (almond/pepper) and diamond-shaped figures with various forms of horned surrounding elements (see p. 116).[20]

Many Dasht-i-Kipchak Uzbek groups make cross-stitched *mapramach*-size and square hangings and pillow covers in fairly regular geometric patterns. Certainly, some of the more subdued and repetitive older pieces are of Lakai manufacture; we have seen many with the classic *mapramach gul* still in use among the Lakai today. There is, however, a type of cross-stitched wall hanging that strongly resembles chain- and buttonhole-stitched *ilgich* in design, size, and shape. These *ilgich* share the dominant Lakai aesthetic of technical precision combined with an inspired and eccentric design. The most extraordinary and rare of these look almost deconstructed, like a jigsaw puzzle incorrectly assembled.

This late-nineteenth–early twentieth-century Kungrat da-our *has a typical design that includes two long-stemmed flowers set on a diagonal and surrounded by dozens of other floral forms, closely set together in the field (2004.259.35).*

A late-nineteenth–early twentieth-century Lakai at torba ilgich. *The borders of the central diamond shape, with its horned corners, enclose a ground pattern of alternating colors and a complex paisely fill pattern. The field patterns surrounding the central design contrast regular circle and star shapes with free-flowing, line-drawn spiral forms (2004.259.78).*

This nineteenth-century Lakai at torba ilgich *features an exceptionally detailed pattern of horn-tipped diamond shapes, surrounded by whirling-circle designs. The alternating sections of color fill are the most elaborately designed elements here (2004.259.84).*

A late-nineteenth–early twentieth-century ilgich, *possibly from the Durmen tribe. A flap covers an unadorned section at the top of a field of rosette designs. (2004.259.44). This piece is very similar to the* SAMIIR *expedition* tabaklau ilgich *on page 14.*

Karmysheva wrote that in cross-stitch embroidery, no *sizgich* is needed because the embroiderer works by counting threads, changing the patterns as her imagination dictates (see p. 126).[21]

Kungrat *ilgich* take the same three forms of *torba*, *tabaklau*, and *uuk kap* used by the Lakai, but Kungrat embroiderers employ a greater variety of stitches and different motifs (see p. 124). Continuous-thread couching, fishbone stitch, satin stitch, and blanket stitch are often combined in a single item of Kungrat embroidery, resulting in a textured, less consistent appearance than the smooth-surfaced Lakai embroideries. The Kungrat also embroider with both silk and wool yarns on a wool ground, and their *ilgich* often have elaborate braided and tasseled sections made from a variety of fibers.[22] While Kungrat coloration may be as fine as that of Lakai embroidery, many Kungrat pieces have a less even palette, mixing together a broad range of orange, peach, and other pastel tones.

Some examples of Kungrat embroidery reflect a degree of urban influence in their bouquetlike floral designs. The eight-pointed star, especially repeated in the border, is a characteristic Kungrat design, as are continuous border motifs of scorpions and spiders that appear in conjunction with floral field designs (see p. 87).[23]

Specific identifications for Kungrat designs are sometimes based on punning or amusing visual similarities to ordinary objects, such as the frequently occurring *burni kiyushik*, or "crooked nose," a hook or wave form that is sometimes fragmented and sometimes encircles circular designs. The *tarok gul*, or "comb," is an elongated hexagon with a simple comb outline on either end. An S-outline is called *tuyabuyin*, or "camel's neck," and a thicker S-shape is the *buryak*, or "kidney."

The *dombirakulok* design resembles an arrow, with stepped sides and curling hooks beneath; the *dumbira* is a plucked, two-stringed musical instrument used by semi-nomadic people, and *kulok* means ear. *Jillik*, which can be translated as bone marrow or "what grows bone," is the name given a geometric lozenge with a diamond center. The *jillik bashi*, or *jillik*-head, which resembles a cock's comb, is used as a fill design between multicolored, concentric circle forms or as a curling, vegetal-like ornament. Other patterns seem to be named for their protective qualities: a wavelike pattern surrounding a circle is called a snake design, as are other patterns with more realistic renderings of a snake with a diamond-shaped head and a tail. Concentric circles are "eyes" that distract the evil eye. The *oy tuyuk*, an uncompleted circular design surrounding a star or floral center, has beneficent qualities associated with animal designs; *tuyuk* means hoof.[24] These imaginative design names are considerably more recent than the designs themselves (see p. 118), some of which appear in steppe textiles dating back millennia.

The field decoration of Kungrat *ilgich* is often crowded, with thin arrow and line patterns forming simple geometric outlines scattered among star and circle patterns with colored fill. Around 1900, the ethnographer Samuel Martinovch Dudin collected two Kungrat-embroidered *ilgich* with a distinctive netlike appearance; this was created by leaving much of the ground cloth exposed. These objects closely parallel the unusually loose embroidery on a wool ground seen in the *ilgich* on page 124.[25]

Textile specialists have not yet been able to distinguish Lakai and Kungrat *ilgich* clearly from *ilgich* produced by the Durmen and Semiz tribes.[26] Some scholars in Tajikistan and Uzbekistan say these two tribes are part of the Lakai group.[27] And a distinct group of *ilgich* in the Robinson Collection bears strong stylistic and design similarities to both Lakai and Kungrat embroidery. (See, for example, 2004.259.32, p. 122.) Most feature a circular motif with

In this unusual nineteenth-century Lakai at torba ilgich, *the diamond-shaped central figure is lighter and less elaborate than the pattern encircling it (2004.259.63).*

This nineteenth-century Lakai ilgich *is worked in fine cross-stitch. The repeating pattern of rows of horn-tipped diamond shapes is rendered in contrasting colors against a black background (2004.259.76). Similar sharp-edged, geometric patterns are often found in small, rectangular Lakai tent decorations.*

A late-nineteenth–early twentieth-century Lakai uuk kap ilgich *featuring a scorpion motif with sawtooth-edged, spiraling forms (2004.259.86).*

RENEWING ANCIENT FORMS *115*

A late-nineteenth-century Lakai uuk kap ilgich *with an unusual composition that features two large, abstract figures placed one above the other (2004.259.87).*

The central design element of this twentieth-century Lakai uuk kap ilgich *is a scorpion, set on a black field and tightly enclosed by trim-patterned borders (2004.259.69).*

hooked or sawtoothed edges familiar from Lakai *ilgich* as well as vibrant, striking designs that are associated with the Lakai. However, these compositions are also close to those of the Kungrat in three ways: the frequent use of a fingerlike floral design with hooked ends as a minor motif; the way the designs are crowded into the field; and the minimal use of contrasting edgings. A fragmentary *ilgich* of similar type (but without tribal identification) is among the early materials in the collection of the Museum of Ethnography in Dushanbe.

There are, however, several similar pieces in the State Historical Museum, Tashkent, that the SAMIIR expedition collected in 1930 from peoples identified as "Uzbek-Lakai from the Durmen clan." The textiles, rugs, ceramics, and other household goods gathered then provide the most solid basis for chronology and tribal identification prior to Karmysheva's data from the 1950s and 1960s. S. T. Rusyaikina designated most of the textiles collected as "Uzbek Lakai" and captioned them with source, village, and clan when known. In these 1930 accession records, the names Kungrat and Durmen are used as clan identities within the Lakai group. Rusyaikina wrote that Lakai *ilgich* were no longer being made, that embroidery was then in a parlous state, and that almost all the *ilgich* collected predated 1914. That year marked the beginning of a period of increasing economic hardship for many Central Asian Uzbeks, who were affected by the distant World War I and by the struggle between White Russian and Bolshevik forces for control of Central Asia. The materials collected by the M. S. Andreev expedition to Tajikistan of 1925, also in the State Historical Museum, were ragged, damaged, and of very poor technical and artistic quality. The existence of provenanced and generally well-documented materials bolsters the case that better-quality Lakai and Kungrat *ilgich* were produced prior to 1914 in regions that later came under Soviet control. Photographs of Lakai settlements taken in 1929 by the ethnographer Jurabaev confirm that impoverished economic conditions prevailed in the Lakai regions at that time — lending further support to Rusyaikina's conclusions.

The economic situation in Afghanistan during the early Soviet period was substantially better than it was in Uzbekistan and Tajikistan. Massive immigration into the country for economic, political, and religious reasons occurred between 1914 and the closing of the Soviet borders, around 1930. It is quite possible that embroidery of high artistic and technical quality continued to be made on the Afghanistan side of the border for several decades.

The immediate antecedents to *ilgich* embroideries are unknown. Certainly, the Lakai were not novice embroiderers in the late nineteenth century, but what ground cloth did they use for embroidery before they obtained commercially made fabrics? One possibility is a super-fine felt similar to *mogul* (napped wool flannel), a popular ground cloth for Lakai and Kungrat *ilgich*. Urban fabrics have always been available to Central Asian nomads through trade, but the original inspiration for these wall hangings probably lay in embroidered and appliquéd felts. Karmysheva did note a few rare examples of Lakai textiles embroidered on felt.[28] But because so few examples of embroidery on hand-woven fabrics remain — possibly due to the recycling of worn *ilgich* into new decorative items — it seems unlikely that any known Lakai and Kungrat materials can be firmly dated to before the mid-nineteenth century.

Another indication of the relatively recent age of most *ilgich* is that few have been made with all-natural dyes. A characteristic purple color that probably was achieved with synthetic dyes is found even among the early collections of Lakai and Kungrat embroideries. These materials showed substantial age at the time they

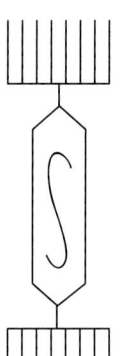

Tarok gul: "comb" (an elongated hexagon with a simple comb outline on either end)

Burni kiyushik: "crooked nose"

Tuyabuyin: "camel's neck" (an S-outline)

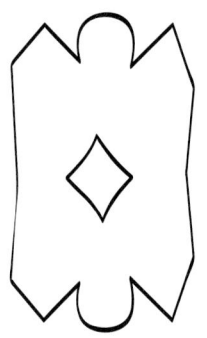

Jillik: bone marrow, or "what grows bone" (geometric lozenge with a diamond center)

Buryak: "kidney" (a thicker S-shape)

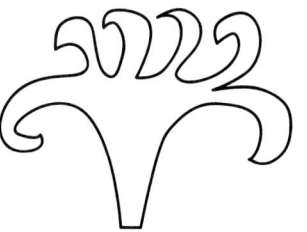

Jillik bashi: *jillik* head (resembles a cock's comb)

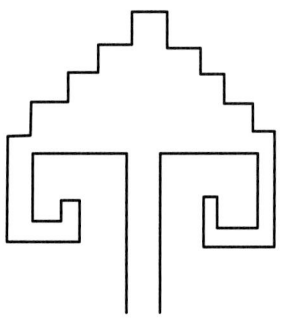

Dombirakulok: resembles an arrow, with stepped sides and curling hooks beneath (The *dumbira* is a plucked, two-stringed musical instrument, and *kulok* means ear.)

Oy tuyuk: "hoof" (uncompleted circular design surrounding a star or floral center)

This late-nineteenth-century Kungrat ilgich *has circular, sawtooth-edged figures with* jillik bashi *patterns set between them (2004.259.38).*

This nineteenth-century Kungrat ilgich *has a multicolored, pieced ground cloth and three elaborate, spiderlike patterns at its center (2004.259.34).*

Although the scorpion motif is prominent among Lakai uuk kap ilgich, *a combination of smaller forms, as seen in this late-nineteenth–early twentieth-century example, can be equally effective in expressing the dynamic qualities of Lakai design (2004.259.77).*

This late-nineteenth–early twentieth-century Kungrat or Durmen ilgich is one of a group of embroideries in the Robinson Collection that combine Lakai and Kungrat design features. This type of ilgich is often marked by a relatively loose composition and crowded-together field elements (2004.259.32).

were collected, and several were made from cut sections of other, apparently older objects. This purple is found in many of the older items gathered by the SAMIIR expedition, where it is used in conjunction with what appear to be natural vegetal dyes.[29] Synthetic dyes became rapidly available on the market in Central Asia, and this factor, combined with the fact that the Lakai are said to have purchased dyes or already-dyed silk threads, may suggest the creation of *ilgich* with synthetically dyed silk threads as early as the 1880s or even the 1870s.

Origins of Design

The source of Dasht-i-Kipchak design, best exemplified by the embroidered art of the Lakai, is rooted in the ancient art of the steppe. Many of the most important elements of the steppe style originated in the earliest settled civilization of the Bronze Age in Central Asia. Although they were capable of naturalistic rendering, the artists of 2000 BCE favored abstract animal and floral forms, and they frequently evoked an animal's potency and strength by depicting a feature of its body. The ram's horns, the scorpion's tail, and the falcon's claw and beak became independent elements that were linked and multiplied to form medallionlike motifs. In Bronze Age artifacts, stylized human, animal, and floral forms were usually framed within a medallion, and the tendency toward reticulation was pronounced. This arrangement of opposing and four-fold figures within a medallion became one of the most enduring conventions in Central Asian art, and it occurs frequently in later carpets and textiles.

Central Asian nomadism evolved only after the collapse of the Bronze Age cities, when a pastoral way of life provided the best means of taking advantage of steppe lands unsuited to agriculture. Gradually, groups of nomads organized to form military structures capable of dominating settled peoples in the region. Some nomad organizations were able to control trade routes, obtaining luxury goods from both China and the West. They were far more interested, however, in developing their own native arts. The artifacts found in the mid-first-millennium BCE Pazyryk tombs of the Altai Mountains demonstrate a kinship between design in wood and metal and more fragile felts and woven fabrics.[30] In stylistic terms, the art of the Lakai and Kungrat is directly descended from that of these ancient steppe peoples. There are remarkable similarities between the powerful rhythm, vigorous line, and loosely reticulated form of the wave-edged patterns on an appliquéd felt from Pazyryk Barrow 5, for example, and of Lakai and Kungrat *ilgich* design. The assertive color relationships and fill patterning in another Pazyryk felt with a scalloped design from the same site are mirrored in the patchwork felts of many present-day Dasht-i-Kipchak tribes.[31]

The needs and resources of pastoral peoples determined their choices of materials and forms of decoration. Flocks provided wool and leather, and textiles were better suited than wood or metal to withstand the rigors of travel and hard use. The early steppe artists maintained a delicate balance among exuberance, improvisation, and restraint. The surface of virtually every functional object was embellished with pattern, but designs were not over-elaborated. Craft never became an end in itself, and sentiment is refreshingly absent in the work.

The finest nineteenth- and early twentieth-century steppe-tradition textiles utilize the same artistic approach as the animal-style art of the ancient nomads: their designs are based on abstract forms derived from the natural world, on powerful rhythm and vigorous line, and on the contrast between brilliant colors and negative and positive space. Some viewers attribute the menacing qualities of the spider and scorpion motifs to the remnants of shamanic tradition. But

This late-nineteenth–early twentieth-century Kungrat ilgich, *with its starlike, geometric central form and scattered designs in the field, is loosely embroidered on wool in a typical nineteenth-century style (2004.259.30). Around 1900, the ethnographer Samuel Martinovch Dudin collected two similar Kungrat* ilgich; *they are now in the Russian Ethnographic Museum, St. Petersburg.*

Kungrat ilgich *often combine purely decorative pattern elements with traditional steppe designs, such as spiders, snakes, and scorpions, as in this late-nineteenth–early twentieth-century example featuring floral and spider shapes (2004.259.47).*

This nineteenth-century Lakai ilgich has an exceptionally free-form geometric composition (2004.259.82). The central design is an elaboration of the horn-tipped diamond shape found in many Lakai ilgich, but the alterations of color and fragmentation of patterns within such a complex composition are of exemplary quality.

the true power of these images lies in their rigorous forms and the ways they are combined, not in any symbolic or talismanic function. Similarly, designs that in other circumstances act as talismans — as prophylaxes against harm — are not actually talismans within the context of *ilgich*. In *ilgich*, these same designs assert and reinforce tribal identity.

Ilgich do not represent an idealized urban garden, as *suzani* embroideries do among long-settled peoples; rather, they represent Nature as a powerful and uncontrolled force. The placement of motifs depends not on a horizon line, as a more naturalistic representation would, or even on symmetrical organization, although many *ilgich* are composed around a dominant central figure. The design vocabulary is a visual language, not a symbolic one. The harmonies it expresses are artistic, based on a common visual understanding rather than on a literal meaning of design. As in the case of ancient steppe art, the smaller elements of a composition are as essential as the larger ones. No matter how complex or irregular, the design registers visually as a compositional whole.

Each embroidered *ilgich* reflects this remarkable unity of design and expression — and every one is unique, a fresh formulation of Lakai or Kungrat identity as defined by its maker. *Ilgich* proclaim the ability of the individual embroiderer to work creatively within a design tradition and to express her own understanding of its forms. As an artistic genre, they represent the highest point of Lakai and Kungrat material culture, the pride of the family, and the reputation of the tribe.

A Kungrat woman wearing a high, wrapped headdress, 1960.

4. URBAN EMBROIDERY: SHAHRISABS AND *SUZANI*

Suzani
*Probably Kitab, late 19th–
early 20th century*
2004.259.13 (detail)

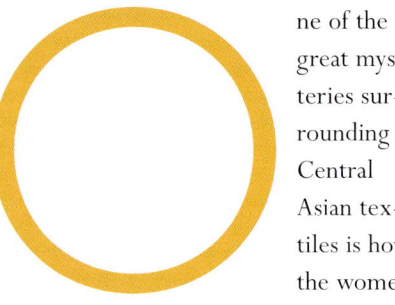

One of the great mysteries surrounding Central Asian textiles is how the women of each urban center developed unique and highly sophisticated artistic styles of embroidery. Women were cloistered, with few opportunities to interact outside the family circle. Often, their education was limited to instruction by older members of their own households. Yet an elegant and original embroidery style, through which women expressed their artistic creativity, emerged from each region.

There are three major types of nineteenth- and early twentieth-century embroideries from the Shahrisabs region: large *suzani* wall hangings with silk embroidery in floral patterns on a white cotton ground; *suzani* embroidered with eccentric, abstract forms on colored silk or ikat ground; and cross-stitched embroidered robes, saddle covers, hangings, and accessories. Each type offered its makers different artistic and technical challenges. The scale of the large *suzani* wall hangings permitted those who made them full artistic expression, and the importance of *suzani* in domestic ritual encouraged women to devote considerable time, energy, and thought to their construction. Smaller items used as daily or ceremonial clothing and accessories lent themselves to improvisation and experimental design. Large-scale cross-stitched embroidered pieces were the most prestigious and expensive of all the costumes and horse trappings made in the khanates, and they were also the most time-consuming to produce: the sale of smaller cross-stitched and other embroideries contributed substantially to the income of needy families.

The varied styles and purposes of embroidered textiles and the different ways they were distributed and used complicate any analysis of women's embroidery activities. Although time, distance, and the region's tumultuous political and social history have limited the number of documentary materials available, enough remain to form a picture of the art of Shahrisabs embroidery.

The types of embroideries designated as "Shahrisabs" in the literature on textiles include those from neighboring Kitab, a major silk-producing and textile center, and from the surrounding region. Shahrisabs and Kitab were situated close to rural populations that had vigorously maintained their pastoralist traditions. Many people in those two cities had stronger ties to Uzbek tribal identity than did the populations of other Central Asian towns.[1]

Shahrisabs and Kitab

Shahrisabs, the "green city," has also been known as Shahr and Kish. Writing in the sixteenth century, the Timurid prince Babur (1483–1530) noted, "Since the countryside, city, roofs, and walls all turn beautifully green in the spring, the town is also called Shahrisabs."[2] The town's most famous native son, the conqueror Timur Leng (known in the West as Tamerlane, c. 1336–1404/5), established his capital in Samarkand, but he was determined to make his birthplace beautiful as well. He built a *medresse* (Muslim school), a tomb, and a court, of which Babur wrote: "Few such superb arches can be pointed out in the world. They say that it is more splendid than Chosroës' Arch."[3]

During the nineteenth century, the name Shahrisabs often referred to both Shahr and the city of Kitab, which were just a few miles apart. A single wall enclosed both cities, and lush flower gardens and fruit-tree orchards linked them as well. Shahrisabs lay in marshy lowland near the Kashkadarya river. Kitab, which was on higher ground, had a drier, healthier climate. The cities shared a common history,

Kitab and *Shahrisabs* suzani share numerous similarities. The embroideries of both cities are characterized by wide borders and loose, slightly irregular compositions, as in this late-nineteenth–early twentieth-century example, which is probably from Kitab (2004.259.13).

economy, and culture but were administered separately, and each was ruled by its own *beg*.

Shahrisabs is a hundred miles south of Samarkand, at the northern end of the Kashkadarya Valley. To reach it from Samarkand, one had to traverse the Takhta Karachi pass in the Zarafshan Mountains or, from Bukhara, to cross the waste of the Karambchul and Karshin steppes. Officially, the city was under the suzerainty of the Bukharan emirs and ruled by their appointees. However, because of its relative isolation, it had a history of periodic uprisings and only a tenuous alliance with Bukhara.

Shahrisabs was the third-largest city in the Bukharan khanate, after Bukhara and Samarkand. In 1877 the American scholar and diplomat Eugene Schuyler put its population at twenty thousand inhabitants and of Kitab, at fifteen thousand.[4] The region's cultural and social structure was unusual; slavery, for example, was never permitted there. During the nineteenth century, Shahrisabs, besieged by numerous forays from Bukhara and Samarkand, struggled to remain independent of Bukharan rule. Capable local rulers from the Keneges Uzbek tribe alternately fought back and negotiated for independence. They sent gifts to the Bukharan emir each year and supplied him with troops but did not allow outside interference in local affairs. The cities lost their independence in 1870, when an attack by bandits on a party of Russians who were traveling through provided an excuse for the Russian governor general of Turkestan, K. P. von Kaufman, to order a major offensive. Kitab was taken after a hard fight, Shahrisabs surrendered, and the *begs* fled to Khojent. Von Kaufman immediately transferred authority over Shahrisabs to the emir of Bukhara so as to show that Russia had no interest in further conquest.[5]

The ethnic composition of Shahrisabs and Kitab strongly reflected that of the rural and seminomadic Dasht-i-Kipchak Uzbek population of the surrounding Kashkadarya and Surkhandarya regions.[6] Many neighborhoods had Persian names, but according to the ethnographer Olga Aleksandrovna Sukhareva, the Persian-speaking population was greatly outnumbered and had become assimilated into Uzbek political and social configurations. She contended that Shahrisabs's population should be considered as having been almost entirely Uzbek by the nineteenth century. Unfortunately, early census data are unavailable, and those provided after the Soviet period are unreliable.[7] Certainly, daily contact reinforced the connection between steppe and town. Urban and steppe people interacted with one another at many levels, participating in artistic as well as economic and political exchange. Nomads relied upon the wealth of the cities for the sale of domestic products and for finished goods, while the cities depended on the nomads for animal products and for their military skills as mercenaries and allies. In the case of Shahrisabs and Kitab, close and mostly friendly communications were based on centuries of common history in the region and on not-too-distant connections to a pastoralist way of life.

Kitab was an important producer of textiles and other crafts and the likely source of most textile materials identified today as "Shahrisabs." More than a thousand looms in Kitab and the surrounding region produced silk and half-silk (cotton-weft) fabrics. There were twenty-eight cocoon-boiling and silk-winding establishments. Kitab silks, mostly striped fabrics, were exported from Shahrisabs to Samarkand and beyond, where they were designated "Shahrisabs fabrics."[8] Goods from Hissar and the Surkhandarya region (home to the Lakai, Kungrat, and other seminomadic peoples) were also sold in Shahrisabs, the largest marketplace in the Kashkadarya Valley.

Raw materials, food, and locally made cotton, silk, and woolen textiles were exported from Shahrisabs to the cities of Bukhara, Samarkand, and Urgut.[9] Large

A professional male worker uses a hooked iron tool and hoop to embroider in chain stitch, apparently on leather. Tashkent or Samarkand, Uzbekistan, 1870.

URBAN EMBROIDERY *133*

A hat seller's wares are displayed on the wall behind him, 1870.

A man holding a horse with a luxurious gold-embroidered saddle cover, 1870.

wholesale merchants operated from caravanserais, small shopkeepers were organized by specialty in the bazaars, and neighborhoods were usually populated with workers in the same crafts. Shahrisabs was divided into fifty-two residential neighborhoods, with a street running through the center of each one. There were neighborhoods of potters, ironsmiths, copper and bronze casters, oil pressers, hatters, furriers, and butchers. Only one family wove silk textiles, several wove turbans, and a dozen families wove cotton *alacha* (striped fabrics) and *karbaz* (undyed, plain-woven cotton fabric).[10] Eugene Schuyler, after a visit to the Shahrisabs bazaar in the 1870s, wrote:

> I saw no English goods except a few thin muslins for turbans, but I saw many Russian prints and calico and other cotton goods, although most of the fabrics on sale were of native manufacture. The only things special to the place were skull-caps, embroidered in silk in the same cross-stitch used by our ladies.[11]

Commercial Embroidery

Compared to other Central Asian regions, the Shahrisabs area produced an astonishing variety of embroidered fabrics. There is also circumstantial evidence that an extensive professional, as well as domestic, embroidery production existed in the area. Most sources on Central Asia separate professional male textile crafts from female domestic production. The textual and photographic evidence of the period for commercial embroidery done by men is from other cities in Central Asia (see p. 132). Nonetheless, the existence of both male and female professional embroiderers appears plausible. We discount the possibility that an extensive, male-dominated system of professional embroidery operated in Shahrisabs because there is no historical evidence for it, as there is for other cities, and because women of the region continued to maintain their own successful, independent commercial-embroidery tradition throughout the twentieth century.

Katalog Turkestanskovo Otdela (Catalogue of Turkestan Manufacturers), which documents an 1871 exhibition at the Polytechnic Institute in Moscow, contains details of embroidery work done by men in Central Asia. According to the catalogue, male professional embroidery evolved in Bukhara and was brought from there to Khojent sometime between 1820 and 1830 by Ishan Isa Khodja, who taught as many as six hundred pupils. His students then brought the trade to Tashkent, where it rapidly expanded following the arrival of the Russians, who created a market for embroidered jackets, tablecloths, and napkins. Mir Safar, an embroiderer who gave demonstrations of his craft at the exhibition, embroidered on a hoop (*gardich*) with a hooked iron tool (*bigiz*), using a silk thread on wool or hide. He criticized the quality of women's embroidery, saying they preferred to work with a needle, while men used embroidery hooks to produce a more even stitch. Mir Safar made his patterns from memory, drawing a simple chalk outline on his ground material and then embroidering a larger flower or leaf, which to him was the "mother" and from which came smaller branches and leaves, or "children." He also described how he invited other embroiderers to drink tea with him, so he could secretly copy features of their new designs for his own use.[12]

A separate section of the catalogue contains descriptions of ordinary domestic textiles and luxury items collected by or presented to high-ranking Russian officials from the Turkestan protectorate. On view in the exhibition were displays with costumed mannequins and re-created interiors that included a replica "embroidery store" and a "ready-made clothing store," which contained "all types of men's and women's clothing, shoes and hats, shirts, wide trousers, turbans, belts, shawls, even horse-

cloths, quilted things, and pillows." The materials exhibited were based on those found in the clothing bazaar, an "entire sarai of the same articles." The catalogue lists prices for many of the garments: less than two rubles for a full summer costume, two rubles for a quilted robe of *alacha*, eight rubles or more for the least-expensive robes of *kanaous* (an all-silk, plain-woven ikat fabric), and considerably more for robes of *atlas* (a silk-satin ikat fabric), "Kashmir" wool, Russian brocade, and wool embroidered with silk. The most expensive robes are "completely embroidered in silk, that which is called Shahrisabs. The last demands very much work and is therefore expensive, from eighty to one hundred rubles."[13]

According to the catalogue, Mir Safar said that women embroidered bedspreads, hats, and shawls. The items described in the catalogue correlate with traditional household embroidery and also include the distinctive Shahrisabs cross-stitched hats and other clothing accessories, saddle covers, and robes as well as hangings and furnishings worked in couching stitch and chain stitch.

The Social Life of Embroidery

The presentation of robes and horse trappings was an important social ceremony in Central Asia, as it was in the rest of the Islamic world.[14] Social status was bestowed and confirmed through gifts of robes of honor; this practice went back to both Mongol and ancient Sogdian traditions in Central Asia.[15] During the nineteenth century, the largest and most magnificent embroidered articles were made for gift-giving and for ostentatious display. Robes were frequently given to visitors at family celebrations, a bride and groom exchanged sets of clothing, warriors received payment in robes, and soldiers and male servants were annually furnished with complete suits of clothing. A robe, belt, horse, harness, and horse trappings completed a proper set of gifts for a distinguished guest. Writing in 1885, the American traveler Henry Lansdell described receiving a horse as a present from the Bukharan emir in Kitab:

> Nor was my charger sent without saddle or bridle, for it had both, as well as a saddle-cloth, covering him from mane to tail, and hanging down on either side, two feet from the withers and three feet behind. The saddle-cloth is the handsomest I have ever seen, and is of crimson velvet, embroidered with gold and silver thread and silk of various colours, in seven large foliate patterns, surrounded by a scroll border of similar workmanship, and edged with wide amber and crimson fringe, the whole being adorned by spangles of silver and gold.[16]

Only the wealthiest and most powerful people could afford to give — or would be fortunate enough to receive — cross-stitched coats and saddle covers. For example, the Bukharan emir Mohammed Alim Khan (1880–1944) sent more than a dozen cross-stitched robes and very large, twelve- to twenty-foot-long cross-stitched wall hangings to Czar Nicolas II.[17] The emir's summer palace in Bukhara also contained several large wall hangings with cross-stitch patterns in designs reminiscent of *suzani*, tile work, and Persian and Turkish carpets. Most of the larger wall hangings appear to have been embroidered using a counted-stitch technique in which a sequence of colors is repeated again and again; geometric and floral patterns sometimes stop abruptly when an edge is reached. Saddle covers, robes, and smaller cross-stitched articles made for domestic use display more improvisational patterning and finer, more delicate stitching, often on a black or dark indigo-blue embroidered background. These include belts (sometimes with knife holders), *ainak push* (small embroideries on cloth known as mirror bags) about a foot square, bags for carrying tea, and hair bands. Elaborately

Opposite:
In this 1890 photograph, a man wears a robe entirely covered in silk cross-stitch embroidery. Such robes were among the most highly valued garments made in Central Asia.

colored and fantastic floral and vegetal designs and geometric patterns are characteristic of the smaller embroideries. The dynamic style and imaginative rendering of abstracted figures in these smaller cross-stitched items have sometimes caused them to be confused with the equally vigorous embroidered art of the steppe. There is frequent use of cross-stitch in embroidery by the Lakai, Kungrat, and other Dasht-i-Kipchak groups. (For descriptions of cross-stitch techniques in items made by these groups, see pp. 106 and 188–89.)

The most important social function of embroidery was related to marriage and domestic decoration. Embroidery was a communal activity — from the arrival of the professional designer (*kalamkash*), who sketched the outlines of the design directly onto the cloth, to the choice of colors, addition of details, and edge binding and backing of the completed embroidery. Making embroideries served as an outlet for family creativity and gave the bride a reassuring memento of her family of origin. Embroidery represented fashion and tradition, luxury and labor.

Suzani were not devoid of talismanic properties; superstition is as prevalent in Central Asia as anywhere else. But when Central Asians needed a talisman, they made a specifically talismanic object.[18] When the ethnographer Sukhareva asked why a *suzani* was held above a bride as she entered the marriage chamber, the reply was that it had "good properties."[19] There are designs incorporated within *suzani* that represent talismans, but while these enhance the positive aura of the wall hanging, they do not transform it into a talisman. Objects become auspicious when age and custom sanctify their use in rites of passage. In a circular way, the long history of using *suzani* in ceremonies reinforced and enhanced their "good properties" and made their presence necessary in family ritual.

Soviet authors generally agreed that specific articles, their number and type differing slightly from town to town, were essential components of a young woman's trousseau. This is confirmed by our field research in Central Asia and by that of others in recent decades. Even today, a bride in Shahrisabs is expected to embroider twenty hats for her husband and thirty to forty kerchiefs for her husband's friends, lest she be considered "lazy."[20] Small (one- to one-and-a-half-foot-square) embroideries in *suzani* style with a single vegetal element and simple vine border (*ainak push*) appear to be common dowry components in Shahrisabs (see opposite page). Photographs from the nineteenth century indicate that there was a preference for rich and plentiful household decoration, with large wall hangings and curtains, even though several detailed descriptions of interiors from that era do not mention the presence of such hangings in private homes.[21] Instead, rooms were painted in bright geometric and floral patterns, and elaborately molded niches were set into the plastered walls. Wall paintings, however, echoed the shapes and, sometimes, the patterns of textile hangings. Only on special occasions, such as circumcisions and weddings, when pavilions were put up in courtyards, was a family's entire textile wealth displayed both inside and outside its residence.

Dowry textiles included at least one large *suzani*. Several medium-to-large-size hangings (*chaishab*) were needed to cover niches and decorate the home. Arched alcoves of various sizes were set into the walls of guest rooms and bedrooms; these contained open shelves with teapots, plates, and bowls, or they held bedding and clothing. Embroideries with arched borders and an empty central field were often used to cover niches.[22] Some Soviet sources describe arch-shaped *suzani* as *jainamaz* (literally, prayer place) and state that they serve the same purpose as a prayer rug; however, our field research does not

Opposite:
Small, rectangular decorative embroideries on cloth, called ainak push, *were often like miniature* suzani. *They were widely distributed, among urban and rural communities alike, in Central Asia. This late-nineteenth–early twentieth-century example from the Kashkadarya region has a single, elaborately embroidered central element and a simple stripe-and-leaf border (2004.259.25).*

support this assertion. Smaller arched embroideries may have been used during prayer, but many others are far too large for this purpose. A large *suzani* or an arched hanging (*ruijo*) served as a bedcover for the wedding night, although a smaller embroidery, described as a nuptial towel, might be placed there instead.[23] Well-to-do families would also prepare additional hangings to conceal household goods, to curtain doorways, and to partition areas of a room. The *zardevor*, or *dorpech*, was a narrow embroidered strip, sometimes long enough to circumscribe a room at ceiling height. Smaller dowry items included rectangular pillow and bolster covers (*bolin push*, and in Shahrisabs, *yastik push*), small square *ainak push* that, though known as mirror bags, were used for various decorative functions, and embroidered kerchiefs, belts, and headbands.[24]

Embroidery Production and Technique

Most sources note that, before the 1880s, urban embroideries were done on handspun, handwoven, white-cotton *karbaz* (also called *buz*) and that embroidery on silk cloth was a later phenomenon.[25] But in 1902, a well-provenanced Shahrisabs-style embroidery on a silk ground with an embroidered date of 1809 was discovered; and for that matter, *karbaz* is still being made today.[26] One should be cautious, therefore, in dating materials based on the type of ground cloth.[27] Both professionally wound and lightly twisted floss-silk threads in a wide range of colors were used for embroidery. Occasionally, an import from India appears — red wool thread dyed with cinnabar. The use of cinnabar wool supposedly ended in 1880, although that date is probably based only on the official closing of imports from India after the establishment of the Russian protectorate.[28]

The implements used for embroidery are needles (*igna nina*), a thimble (*angish*), a chain-stitch tool consisting of a curved iron hook set in a wooden handle (*bigiz*, or *daraush*), an embroidery hoop (*chambarak*), and a sewing machine for chain stitch (*popuk mashina*). The lengths of needles depend on the fabric being embroidered. The *ninaduz*, a larger needle, secures the embroidery as the work progresses and stretches the fabric on the embroidery frame.

Large embroideries from urban areas throughout Central Asia generally combine several stitches in a single article. *Basma*, done with long threads couched with small, slanted securing stitches, is especially common in *suzani* embroideries. The *kanda-khayol* stitch, popular in the Shahrisabs region, is similar to *basma*, but its couching stitches are longer and diagonal to the stitch being held down. The *khomduzi* is a simple, double-sided straight stitch. *Iurma* (chain stitch) is often used to outline large areas filled with couching stitch and also to work the borders of *suzani*. *Iroki* is a full cross-stitch. And *kuklyama* is a half cross-stitch in which the base thread is drawn diagonally along a row; crossing stitches are then laid over it in a regular pattern to replicate the appearance of a full cross-stitch.[29]

No sources have yet been located describing, firsthand, the domestic embroidery practices of the women of Shahrisabs during the nineteenth century, but it seems likely that they followed customs similar to women in other large urban centers. They began preparing dowry materials soon after a daughter was born. Girls started doing embroidery when they were very young and presented their first work (an embroidered hat or braided ribbons, for instance,) to "a good and healthy teacher, and sometimes to a respected old woman, so that she herself [might] become a master artisan and live to old age."[30] It was common for local female relatives and friends to assist in the preparation of dowry textiles. Women came to such gatherings (called *kashkar*) to chat, embroider, and sew clothing and quilts. Since the work was divided among several women, embroi-

Opposite:
This nineteenth-century Sharisabs-style cross-stitched wall hanging, with its well-matched Kungrat-style border, was collected in Afghanistan in the early 1970s (2004.259.55).

deries done on narrow panel fabrics were sewn together only after the panels were completed. Often, the different panels of an article of embroidery reveal differences in handiwork, likely evidence that more than one person worked on it.

Sources describing urban areas other than Shahrisabs note that wealthier women did needlework to pass the time, poorer women to earn a little money.[31] Few women had substantial time to do embroidery, since domestic duties were very demanding. Unless they worked by contract (as women did in carpet weaving), the cost of raw materials for a large piece of embroidery would be prohibitive. They could, however, complete smaller articles quickly and reinvest the money earned. By the 1880s, many women in the Ferghana Valley, for example, were selling their embroidery.[32]

Professional designers (*kalamkash*) often helped local women create patterns for embroideries.[33] They brought to the task both skill and vast repertoires of memorized designs. Using charcoal or ink, the *kalamkash* drew patterns freehand directly onto the fabric; a designer might also make suggestions for the general color scheme. Female *kalamkash* were paid for their services, with fees ranging from a few bread cakes for a cap design to five kopeks for a belt-scarf and more for a larger embroidered article.[34]

History and Design

Historical data on *suzani* and other embroidered textiles dating to the eighteenth century and earlier are limited because there was no Central Asian tradition of preserving textiles in court treasuries. Furthermore, the Central Asian economy was at low ebb during the seventeenth and eighteenth centuries, increasing the likelihood of a major gap in luxury-textile production. Nonetheless, the vital role *suzani* play in women's dowries and in family ceremonies argues for a lengthy tradition of embroidery production of this type. So, too, does the wide distribution of fully developed, specialized forms of *suzani* throughout Central Asian cities and among urbanized ethnic groups.

The taste for using colorful textiles as wall decoration dates back at least to the Sogdian period (third–eighth centuries CE). Popular fabrics such as *zandanaji* had large roundels in horizontal rows, alternating with smaller interstitial designs and surrounded by decorative borders. There are many striking similarities between Sogdian textiles and the patterning of carpets and embroideries from later periods. The scale and texture of urban fabric design changed over time in Central Asia, but each period offered a new exploration of the same subjects or a fresh stylistic approach. In recent years, an extraordinary early embroidery has come to light — carbon dated to the fourteenth century — that bears a remarkable resemblance to nineteenth-century *suzani* in its cotton ground cloth, floral medallions, stitching technique, and coloration.[35] The discovery of this and other, more fragmentary works suggests the existence of a lengthy and vital embroidery tradition. It remained only for the embroiderers of the eighteenth and nineteenth centuries to focus intently on a single theme — the living landscape of the paradise garden — that became the primary subject of the urban textile arts.

There is no identifiably Uzbek or Tajik style of *suzani* on cotton *karbaz* cloth because design is regionally, not ethnically, based. Typically, *karbaz* cotton-ground *suzani* have highly stylized floral and vegetal patterns in which a central field of intertwining rosettes, leaves, lattices, bouquets, and medallions is surrounded by borders of vines and flowers. *Suzani* from the Nurata region, near Samarkand, are probably the easiest to identify (see p. 146). They are embroidered in silk on white or light-brown handwoven cotton cloth, using various types of stitches, including *kandakhayol*, *basma*, *ilmoq*, and *iurma*. Most Nurata

This 1880 photograph of a Central Asian home shows a suzani *being used as a bedding-pile cover. It also shows a* sandali, *the frame built to cover a brazier and support a layer of felts, kilims, and, here, a suzani. In the winter, the family gathered around the* sandali, *warming their feet and legs beneath the covers. A silk-velvet ikat robe hangs from a peg on the back wall.*

In this 1870 photograph, taken in Samarkand, we see a Kitab or Shahrisabs-style suzani, *with a four-to-one floral pattern in the field, used in a sukkah — the shelter put up for the weeklong Jewish harvest festival of Sukkot. Although it is not known whether a family member made this* suzani, *there is strong evidence that Jewish women and girls in Central Asia created embroideries for home use and for dowries.*

*This 1870 photograph of Uzbek nuptials shows the bride, groom, and guests standing beneath a raised wedding curtain (*chimildik*) made of a Shahrisabs-type* suzani *and a block-printed fabric. One woman holds a mirror before the couple, the other, a bowl of clear water. The sewing of the* chimildik *was begun by an old woman who had many grandchildren. After the wedding, the* chimildik *would be used to make a cradle blanket for the couple's children.*

suzani have four large, densely embroidered bouquets of flowers, one in each corner of the field, with smaller bouquets arranged around a central rosette or bouquet and smaller floral elements scattered through the field. Generally, the designs lack the strong compositional symmetry of *suzani* from other regions, although the borders are quite regular. More often than other types of *suzani*, those from Nurata contain small figures of people and animals, but these are not integral to the overall design. This is the most precious and sentimental (that is, over-elaborated and repetitive) style of *suzani*, and it is also the one most within the bounds of Persian artistic tradition.

Karbaz suzani from the Tashkent region represent another tradition. In an example from the Robinson Collection, eleven large circles fill almost the entire space (see p. 148). The design is bold, with strong reds and yellows, but each circle differs slightly from the one opposite it. Embroideries with these circular motifs are called *palak* (sky) *suzani* and are said to represent moons or planets. Tashkent *suzani* may have only a single large circle or dozens of smaller ones, usually surrounded by a dark-green border that suggests vines or leaves. In many Tashkent *suzani*, *basma* and *ilmoq* stitches cover the backing fabric entirely, although a little of the white *karbaz* backing may show (see p. 149). Their visual effect is dense, heavy, and physical. Except in the leaflike patterns surrounding the large circular medallions and in their pomegranate-to-rose-red coloration, these *suzani* do not evoke the garden motif in the manner of other urban *suzani* in Central Asia; instead, they recall the large roundel designs of early Islamic *zandanaji* fabrics.

Bukhara *suzani*, like Shahrisabs *suzani*, are not limited to a single design group. The rosettes and other floral forms have a wider palette and more delicate colors than Nurata *suzani*, and there is often a compositional arrangement of a diamond lattice, worked in the *iurma* and *basma* stitches. Both the field and the border design are well coordinated. Samarkand embroideries seem closer in style to those of Tashkent, with bold compositions of large rosettes and thick, vinelike tendrils in a more limited palette. Later pieces use even fewer colors.

Shahrisabs, Kitab, and the surrounding region are major production centers of *karbaz suzani* and *suzani* on colored (often purple) silk fabrics. Distinctive elements of the Shahrisabs style are the extensive use of the *kanda-khayol* stitch and a broad, boldly applied palette that often juxtaposes a vibrant yellow with a cinnamon or apricot orange.[36] Shahrisabs *suzani* design is often freer and more exuberant than other urban *suzani* styles; borders are wide in proportion to the field, and the so-called *char-chiroq* motif (discussed on page 151) appears frequently. However, there were *suzani* made in and around Shahrisabs that lacked any of these characteristics, just as there were *suzani* produced outside Shahrisabs (especially in Bukhara) that exhibited some or all of them.

The metaphor of the garden gives a nuanced, multilayered meaning to *suzani* designs. Central Asians have long been known for their passion for gardens. Raising fruits and flowers in a harsh continental climate demanded dedication; and the formal structuring of the garden in order to create beauty from very limited resources took on an almost spiritual significance.[37] Early Arab invaders admired Central Asian gardens. So did the Chinese traveler Ch'ang-Ch'un, who visited Samarkand in 1222 and compared its gardens favorably to those of China.[38] The Central Asian garden tradition differed from that of Persia, where, typically, the garden was viewed from a raised path or platform. Beginning with the reign of the Ilkhanids in the fourteenth century, the Central Asian ideal was to live in the garden. All the Timurids were avid gardeners, and rulers from Timur to Babur were personally engaged

Opposite:
A Nurata-region suzani, *made in the third quarter of the nineteenth century, with characteristic bouquet arrangements in the center panel and wide, densely embroidered borders (2004.259.10).*

A Tashkent suzani, *done in the exuberant style that was popular at the turn of the twentieth century. Its field composition is relaxed, and the circular design elements show substantial variation in both size and pattern (2004.259.22).*

in creating large walled gardens. Rulers held court in tents erected in gardens; a well-designed green space was seen as being even more important than a palace.

Although gardens were not as grand in the nineteenth century as they had been in earlier times, they remained vital to peoples' social and spiritual lives. In the drab environment of urban Central Asia, the desire for color and natural beauty was intense, and considerable effort was expended to maintain the three components of a formal garden — plants, walls, and watercourse. Shahrisabs's location, near the Kashkadarya river, made it possible to cultivate more extensive urban gardens there than in other oasis towns.

As representations of idealized, not real, gardens, *suzani* are a perfect domestication of nature.[39] Although most *suzani* designs are floral, they rarely depict specific flowers. Embroideries, like other forms of Central Asian art, are more concerned with the abstract qualities of nature than with its details. The best of the floral *karbaz suzani* express the energy of spring in the steppe oasis. In their form, sentimental character, color, and design, they are distinctly urban and more closely related to wall painting than to tent decoration. The architectural harmonies established between painting, niche decoration, and arched forms are expressed in *suzani* through the construction of lattices and interlocking motifs. In essence, *karbaz suzani* belong to the universal style of Islamic art — the "endless repeat" in which patterns are linked and can be repeated and enlarged infinitely. *Suzani*, like other forms of wall decoration in the Islamic world, depict a predictable universe of beauty, symmetry, and order.[40] This direct, even simple approach to *suzani* design is rooted not only in long-standing regional taste and character but also in the immediate interests of the women who made them. The gardens surrounding Central Asia's cities were oases of freedom for urban women; inside their walls, women could enjoy the beauty of nature in the company of friends and family, unencumbered by heavy veils.

Arguments for pre–Islamic, ancient design sources for Central Asian *suzani* are less convincing. One popular but flawed interpretation is the identification of a common *suzani* design as a *char-chiroq*, or four-wicked lamp; it is actually a four-to-one floral arrangement. The lamp is said to be what is represented in various floral configurations of four stems radiating from a central rosette or disc. This identification was proposed by Sukhareva, who tied it to Zoroastrian rites associated with the protective and purifying qualities of fire; however intriguing this interpretation might be, it is entirely subjective and has no basis in anthropology.[41]

Rather, this four-to-one organization of design elements is a compositional device shared by both urban Shahrisabs and the nomadic Dasht-i-Kipchak tribes. The relationship between the nomadic tradition and the urban tradition is particularly clear in the silk and colored-ground *suzani* from Shahrisabs and Kitab (see pp. 131, 159). Each has a series of borders that enclose a rectangle with a central motif from which four symmetrical elements radiate. Three Lakai embroideries collected by the 1930 SAMIIR field expedition have the same design — a central disc with flame or tooth-edged shapes surrounding it. The Lakai embroideries are far smaller, suitable for display in yurts rather than in houses. But their four-to-one configuration closely resembles Shahrisabs *suzani*. Other correlations between nomadic and Shahrisabs designs may be found in the thin strips of alternating tiny stitches in contrasting colors that edge many design elements in Shahrisabs silk-ground *suzani* (see p. 159). Of course, designs and pattern treatments have been exchanged between steppe and town for centuries, and the flow of ideas

URBAN EMBROIDERY 151

Newlyweds stand behind a block-printed wedding curtain (chimildik) *with a* suzani-*like pattern. Uzbekistan, 1870.*

It is often hard to determine the region
where a given embroidery was made.
Although the floral elements of this
nineteenth-century suzani are executed

URBAN EMBROIDERY 155

Left:
A classic Kitab or Shahrisabs white cotton-ground **karbaz suzani**, with a four-to-one pattern in the field, dating to the mid-nineteenth century (30.23.27). This type of free-flowing design is often considered to be characteristic of individually made embroideries, produced for personal use. The existence of numerous similar embroideries may mean there was an organized commercial trade even at that early date.

Above:
This late-nineteenth-century cross-stitched **ainak push** from Kitab or Sharisabs has an open backing of cotton cloth (2004.259.16). Commonly called mirror bags, **ainak push** were small, embroidered pouches that also held such personal items as combs and cosmetics.

moves in both directions. Silk-ground Shahrisabs and Kitab *suzani* also incorporate floral elements similar to those found in *karbaz suzani*, but the animation and verve of their design owe much to the continuing influence of embroidery designs found among neighboring rural and pastoralist peoples.

Other theories about the origins of Central Asian *suzani* designs are based on the influence of foreign arts. The art historian Ernst Grube rejects the identification of the *char-chiroq* design with a lamp, suggesting instead that it stems from seventeenth-century blue-and-white Chinese porcelain patterns.[42] Although the design does appear to be strikingly similar, Chinese pottery very rarely made its way into Central Asia; the sea trade that carried vast quantities of Chinese ceramics to the Islamic West bypassed Central Asia, traveling from South China into Near Eastern seaports in Persia, Egypt, and present-day Iraq.[43] Because land transport was so difficult, the few ceramics that reached Central Asia belonged to the nobility and the wealthy and had little to no effect on domestic embroidery. In any case, Chinese blue-and-white ceramic production began as a style for export to the Islamic Near East during Yuan/Mongol rule in the early fourteenth century and largely followed Muslim taste in design (including Arabic inscriptions) and form. Only later did the style become popular in China itself.[44]

The art of India's Mughal empire is often cited as an inspiration for Central Asian textile art, based on a shared visual aesthetic and close historical ties. The artistic exchanges that took place, however, largely originated in Central Asia. Central Asians ruled India for seven centuries, first under the Delhi sultanate (1206–1526) and then under the Mughals (1526–1858). The rulers' taste was Central Asian, and their patronage reflected that stylistic preference.[45] Trade records indicate that there was little export of luxury fabrics from India to Central Asia. No surviving Indian luxury textiles in Central Asia predate the mid-nineteenth century, and there is very little after that.[46] The chief textile export from India was *chit*, an inexpensive block-printed cotton cloth used as a lining fabric. (Most block-printed fabrics from Central Asia were locally made and almost identical to the Indian fabrics, and a local *chit* industry has existed in Central Asia since at least the sixteenth century.[47]) Some textile technology, such as batik, may have passed from India to Central Asia. Over-all, however, indigenous Indian design has not influenced Central Asian embroidery in any substantive way.

The relationship between women's traditional production and nineteenth-century commercial embroidery is just beginning to be examined. A Shahrisabs *karbaz suzani* at the Minneapolis Institute of Arts (but not part of the Robinson Collection) illustrates the challenges of determining the circumstances in which *suzani* were made (see p. 154). The field pattern of this *suzani* is asymmetrical, loose, and flowing. One pair of rosettes with radiating stems and buds (the four-to-one design discussed above) is evenly spaced: each forms a large circular design. Two other floral arrangements in the field have been compressed in order to fit within the borders, which are of even width and balanced composition. One minor interior border stripe extends beyond the framing square. Apparent improvisations such as these give Shahrisabs embroidery much of its charm. Yet the same compression of identical field elements occurs in a *suzani* in the private Ignazio Vok Collection and in a very similar *suzani* that is part of the Caroline and H. McCoy Jones Collection at San Francisco's de Young Museum.[48] There are many small variations in the three *suzani*; the smaller design elements are different, and differently arranged, but the Vok *suzani* even has the same "accidental" overlap of a minor border as the Minneapolis museum's example. An "improvisational" approach now appears to

This bird's-eye view of Samarkard from about 1900 shows a section of the city's bazaar.

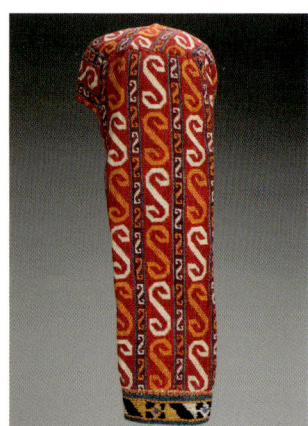

Above:
This late-nineteenth–early twentieth-century Kitab or Shahrisabs woman's hat is constructed of three embroidered cloth sections sewn together: a circular crown, a band forming the front and sides, and a wide band extending down the back (2004.259.2).

Right:
The Shahrisabs region was noted for its small cross-stitched accessories as well as for its inventive designs. Embroiderers preferred a dark blue or black ground color and made occasional use of a red wool. Belts are generally wider than similar forms of robe trim. The ends of the warp-twined edge trim on this nineteenth-century **kamarband** have been used to create the small tassel visible at the center of one short side (2004.259.20).

Right:
A nineteenth-century robe trim made in Kitab or Shahrisabs (2004.259.18). Trims for the front edges of robes and for the collars of women's dresses were tacked lightly to garments and removed for washing.

Dating to the third quarter of the nineteenth century, this embroidery from Kitab or Shahrisabs exemplifies suzani *whose central fields contain the four-to-one composition (2004.259.12). Imaginative treatment of floral forms, refined juxtaposition of colors, and detailed patterning and edging distinguish the highest-quality colored-ground* suzani *produced in that region.*

160 URBAN EMBROIDERY

In this Samarkand home, photographed sometime between 1885 and 1892, are elaborate wall paintings, arched niches, and carved, colored plaster.

be a calculated design. Is this the work of a *kalamkash* who spread the same design from household to household while preparing dowry textiles? Or does this indicate organized commercial production of multiple versions of the same *suzani*?⁴⁹ William Eleroy Curtis, writing in 1911, supported the latter conclusion:

> A well-known Chicago gentleman, who has visited Turkestan twice and is a recognized authority on matters pertaining to that part of the world, carried home with him from his last trip a very handsome specimen of Bokhara embroidery. A few weeks after his return he was astonished to find an exact duplicate hanging upon the wall of a friend in Evanston, who had purchased it at a department store in Chicago. My friend went to the store the next day and found fifty pieces precisely like his own, offered for sale at a less price than he had paid in Bokhara.⁵⁰

Technically, the three nearly identical embroideries just noted have all the characteristics of women's work, as they are needle-embroidered in a variety of stitches rather than executed in chain stitch in the prevalent style of men's embroidery work. Seen together, these embroideries argue for a reconsideration of women's influence as professional embroiderers during the nineteenth century.

Soviet and Contemporary Embroidery

After the Bolshevik Revolution, women continued to hand-embroider *suzani* for home use and local sale, but the quality of materials, workmanship, and design declined. Soviet policy on textile production supported the organization of men and women into factorylike craft associations. Officials celebrated folk art, but only selectively, and encouraged craft, not creativity; the results were devoid of both artistry and emotion. A few specialists became famous as "people's artists" whose virtuoso needlework blended Central Asian motifs with European styles commemorating Soviet social programs and the cult of cotton.⁵¹ New Soviet designs were promoted in newspaper articles as part of the *hujum* campaign to liberate women from traditional family and community structures. Many men and women were employed in craft factories, with names such as the Andijan First of May Embroidery Guild, that made *suzani* with sewing machines for the mass market. Publications celebrated the labor-saving, efficient production of these chain-stitched *suzani* for workers' homes.⁵² Outside of officially sanctioned art production, there was little time or money to invest in the making of beautiful textiles.

Among the most remarkable developments during the post–Soviet years has been the revitalization of many textile arts in Central Asia. In the mid-1990s, Central Asian scholars initiated a revival of lost skills and traditional patterns by bringing antique designs to weavers and embroiderers and asking them to replicate long-unused techniques.⁵³ Local entrepreneurs quickly recognized the commercial potential of contemporary ikat and *suzani* based on nineteenth-century models. Within a few years, brand-new embroideries and ikats had attained such quality that they were often assumed to be antique treasures. But by 2002, this new production had expanded exponentially and could be more easily identified.⁵⁴ Today, these embroidery projects have evolved into creative as well as commercial enterprises. Antique models are elaborated upon and given individual interpretation. It is heartening to know that the skills and artistry needed to create extraordinary textiles still exist and that *suzani* retain their value as part of Central Asian identity.

Interviews with embroiderers in Shahrisabs in September 2004 challenged the notion that nineteenth-century embroiderers worked by rote repetition and did not really understand or appreciate the designs they used. Women were happy to discuss improvisation and "meaning" in highly abstract motifs. For instance, they agreed that a scorpion design and the *gulibadam* (almond flower) design had talismanic qualities but said that other patterns, such as tulips, were without symbolic meaning.[55]

Even today, textile production continues to reinforce familial, cultural, and national identity. There is less focus on replicating specific regional and clan traditions than in the past and more on expressing a broader Central Asian cultural identity. Although handmade textiles are not as necessary in daily life as they once were, they are still sources of individual and family pride, and their production continues to link members of a community, who incorporate their *suzani* in rites of passage. The essential "meaning" of Central Asian embroidered *suzani* is found in this multiple, many-layered role.

The same flexibility, willingness to adapt, and innovation that are seen in textiles have historically characterized all the Central Asian arts. The trade that passed along the Silk Road and between India, Russia, and Persia carried artistic concepts and technical information in every direction. The geography of Central Asia has made the region subject to frequent and sometimes dramatic political and social change, yet there has also been a remarkable continuity within the arts from one period to the next. The influx of peoples who came for conquest or refuge brought styles and skills that were incorporated within existing art forms or inspired new artistic endeavors. New economies created new needs and fostered the creation of both original materials and ideas.

Individual improvisation within boundaries set by tradition sustained and enlivened the textile arts in both urban Shahrisabs and in the steppe communities of the Lakai and Kungrat. It is this vitality and freedom of expression, rather than mere craft or laborious exercise, which we value most in Central Asian embroidery today.

CHAPTER NOTES

1. Epics and Heroes: The Steppe Uzbek

1. The name Chagatai has a complex history and has been used as an identifying term by disparate groups in Central Asia. Although it was associated with the Arlat, Barlas, Djalayir, and Kauchin tribes up to the fourteenth century, by the fifteenth century it also referred to all the Turkic-speaking inhabitants of southern Central Asia east of Balkh. The name was later used to distinguish earlier inhabitants of Central Asia from the newly arrived Uzbeks under the aegis of the Shaibanid confederation. In the nineteenth and twentieth centuries, it referred to groups comprising about 40 percent of the highland Tajiks living in the same area as the Lakai.

2. Mansura Haidar, *Central Asia in the Sixteenth Century* (New Delhi: Manohar Publishers and Distributors, 2002), 41.

3. Before that, the tribe's name was Togmaq. The historian Vasilii Vladimirovich Barthol'd wrote that the terms *Uzbek* and *Uzbek ulus* were used in Central Asia to distinguish this military and tribal unit from the Chagatai until the breakup of the Golden Horde in the fifteenth century. Hasan B. Paksoy, "Z. V. Togan: The Origins of the Kazaks and the Ôzbeks," Central Asian Survey 11, no. 3 (September 1992), n. pg. This article can also be found at www.turkiye.net/sota/origins.html.

4. Haidar, Central Asia, 46.

5. Ibid., 47, citing MS. no. 4330, Oriental Institute Library, Tashkent, 132–33ff., and other sources.

6. Today the Durmen form the majority population in the settlements of the Kafirnigan Valley in southern Tajikistan. Most Durmen work at the giant Kalinin state farm. N. G. Borozna, "Material'naia kul'tura uzbekov Babataga" [Material Culture of the Uzbeks of Babtag], in *Materialnaya kultura narodov srednei azii i Kazakhstana* [Material Culture of the Peoples of Central Asia and Kazakhstan] (Moscow: Academia Nauk SSSR 1966), 93.

7. Belkis Khalilovna Karmysheva, *Uzbeki-Lokaitsi Iuzhnovo Tadjikistana* [Uzbek-Lakai of Southern Tajikistan] (Stalinabad: Akademii Nauk Tadjikskoi SSR, Institut istorii, arkheologii, i etnografii [Academy of Science of the Tajik SSR, Institute of History, Archaeology, and Ethnography], 1954), 19.

8. Haidar, Central Asia, 46.

9. Yuri Bregel, ed. and trans., Munis Khorezmii (1778–1829), *Firdaws al-iqbal: History of Khorezm / Shir Muhammad Mirab Munis and Muhammad Riza Mirab Agahi* (New York: E. J. Brill, 1999), n. 504 (citing Gladyshev and Muravin, 533–34).

10. Among other sources with this characterization, see K. Sitnyakovskii, "Rodoslovnaia tablitsa sem'i kungradov" [Genealogical Table of the Kungrad Family], *Bulletin of the Imperial Geographic Society* (Tashkent) 7 (1907): 26.

11. Gunnar Jarring, writing in 1939 and citing one Khanikov, placed the Kungrat (Qungrad) in Russian Turkestan but added that there were Kungrat in Afghanistan and that in Kunduz (Qunduz) and Tashkurgan (Tashqurghan) the Uzbeks mainly belonged to the Qataghan. Jarring estimated the population of Uzbeks in Afghanistan at that time to be five hundred thousand. Our field observations in Afghanistan during the 1970s indicated that many Kungrat lived in and around the town of Haibak (Samangan). Jarring, *On the Distribution of Turk Tribes in Afghanistan* (Lund, Sweden: Hakan Ohlsson, 1939), 53, 57, 64.

12. Jonathan Lee, *The Ancient Supremacy: Bukhara, Afghanistan, and the Battle for Balkh, 1731–1901* (New York: E. J. Brill, 1996), xix–xxi.

13. Of all the Central Asian rulers, only the emir of Bukhara retained control over his capital; administration of the eastern territory of the Bukharan khanate and the city of Samarkand passed to the Russian protectorate.

14. Karmysheva, *Uzbeki-Lokaitsi*, 43.

15. Jurabaev, photograph album prepared for the Central Asian Museum of History and History of the Revolution (SAMIIR), 1929.

16. Since independence in 1991, popular sentiment and official policy in both Uzbekistan and Tajikistan have reversed to accord heroic status to the *basmachi* movement, prompting captioning changes in historical-museum displays.

17. For more on the retention of tribal hierarchies within collective work and rural political organization, see Pauline Jones Luong, "Economic 'Decentralization' in Kazakhstan," in Jones Luong, ed., *The Transformation of Central Asia* (Ithaca, N.Y.: Cornell University Press, 2004), 207.

18. Olivier Roy, *The New Central Asia: The Creation of Nations* (New York: New York University Press, 2000), 24.

19. *Turk* is used here as a general term for Turk, Barlas, Kalmuk, and other Turkic-language-speaking tribes that inhabited southern Central Asia before the Uzbeks arrived.

20. For example, the ethnographer M. S. Andreev noted the rapid spread of the family name Jalayeer between 1917 and 1921. Presumably, people who took the surname did so in hopes that Jalayeer's gang would not attack its chief's relatives. Andreev, "Certain Results of an Ethnographical Expedition to the Samarkand Region in 1921," paper presented to the Turkestan Division of the Russian Geographical Society, Tashkent, January 27, 1922. Photocopy in the authors' possession.

21. Binafsha Nodir, e-mail to authors, September 18, 2005. For details about rituals connected with birth and childhood, see Chapter Two.

22. Since Uzbekistan became independent, in 1991, cultural "production" there has been tightly controlled, just as it was in Soviet times. Academics, along with state-supported cultural workers, such as writers, actors, and musicians, are expected to provide products that further and enhance government policies. For example, in Uzbekistan professional dancers have crafted a "national dance" repertoire that unites regional styles of varied ethnic groups and European balletic influences under the rubric of "Uzbek dance"; this is performed in "traditional costume," another hodgepodge of ethnic and invented styles. Until the mid-1990s, schools did not teach in Uzbek or Persian languages, but a new government-supported "Uzbek literature" is rapidly being developed by authors who, a decade ago, were writing exclusively in Russian. Under the Soviets, general-purpose ethnic identities were forged for each titular nationality that underscored cultural differences among the various Soviet Socialist Republics. This policy has continued, as national governments stress a Tajik identity in Tajikistan, Uzbek identity in Uzbekistan. For more about the government's direction of cultural activity, see Laura Adams, "Cultural Elites in Uzbekistan," in Jones Luong, ed., *The Transformation of Central Asia,* 97.

23. The region had settlements of "Tadzhik, Karluq, Qongrad, Arab, Moghul, Laqay, Mami, Hazara, Qauchuin, and Timaz." Gabriele Rasuly-Paleczek, "Kinship and Politics among the Uzbeks of Northeastern Afghanistan," in Ingeborg Baldauf and Michael Friederich, eds., *Bamberger Zentralasienstudien: Konferenzakten escas IV* [Bamberg Central Asia Studies: Conference Documents IV] (Bamberg, October 8–12, 1991), series: Islamkundliche Untersuchungen [Investigations in Islamic Art] (Berlin: Klaus Schwarz, 1994), 12.

24. This situation continued throughout the twentieth century. Sons and relatives of *begs* were integrated into the Afghan governing authority, and gifts from *begs* to government officials established ties of obligation that could be called upon later. Local alliances for the purpose of representing regional interests grew to include not only Tajik and Turk inhabitants but also Pashtuns who had settled earlier in the region, prior to the population transfers that took place under Abdur Rahman Khan in the 1880s and Nadir Khan in the 1930s. Gabriele Rasuly-Paleczek, "Tribe and State: The Afghan and Central Asian Example," MESS — *Mediterranean Ethnological Summer School* 3 (Piran, Slovenia, 1997–98): 274–75.

25. Gabriele Rasuly-Paleczek, "Ethnic Identity versus Nationalism: The Uzbeks of North-Eastern Afghanistan and the Afghan State," in Touraj Atabaki and John O'Kane, eds., *Post–Soviet Central Asia* (London and New York: Tauris Academic Studies, 1998), 221.

26. In the Kunduz bazaar one day about thirty years ago, we had an encounter with a Lakai in which we found ourselves insisting that he was an "Uzbek," while he stoutly maintained that although he spoke Uzbeki, he was a Lakai, not an Uzbek. See also Roy, *The New Central Asia,* 12.

27. A *qaum* can be expanded or reduced according to circumstances. It can be as small as one's immediate lineage group, but when tied to language or religious affinity, it often crosses national borders. The centuries of highly fluid political and social alliances in Central Asia demonstrate this malleability. Rasuly-Paleczek, "Tribe and State": 277.

28. Ibid.: 269.

29. Cynthia Werner, "Women, Marriage, and the Nation-State," in Jones Luong, ed., *The Transformation of Central Asia,* 89.

30. Roy, *The New Central Asia,* 17.

2. Textiles and Rites of Passage: The Rhythms of Life

1. An *aq atau*, another type of white yurt similar to the *aq oy*, was traditionally presented to newlyweds among the Durmen, Kazakhs, Khorezm, Kungrat, and Lakai Uzbeks. It was made of white or gray felt and had a white-cotton ribbon braided over its dome. N. G. Borozna, "Material'naia kul'tura uzbekov Babataga" [Material Culture of the Uzbeks of Babtag], in *Materialnaya kultura narodov srednei azii i Kazakhstana* [Material Culture of the Peoples of Central Asia and Kazakhstan] (Moscow: Academia Nauk SSSR, 1966), 94.

2. The Uzbekistan scholar Binafsha Nodir collected this saying from B. G., a fifty-two-year-old Kungrat woman from Hijabulgon village, Baisun district, in 2005. Kungrat and Lakai yurts are identical to those widespread among other Dasht-i-Kipchak-region groups, although Karmysheva noted that hearths in these yurts have a distinctive shape. The details about yurt names and construction presented here are from Binafsha Nodir, e-mail to authors, September 10, 2005. For more on Lakai dwellings, see Belkis Khalilovna Karmysheva, *Uzbeki-Lokaitsi Iuzhnovo Tadjikistana* [Uzbek-Lakai of Southern Tajikistan] (Stalinabad: Akademii Nauk Tadjikskoi SSR, Institut istorii, arkheologii, i etnografii [Academy of Science of the Tajik SSR, Institute of History, Archaeology, and Ethnography], 1954), 21.

3. Belkis Khalilovna Karmysheva, "On the History of Population Formation in the Southern Areas of Uzbekistan and Tajikistan," paper presented at the Seventh International Congress of Anthropological and Ethnological Sciences, August 1964 (Moscow: Nauka, 1964), 6. Photocopy in the authors' possession.

4. Before the Bolshevik Revolution, large-scale sheep herding was in the hands of tribal chiefs, who employed herdsmen to move sheep to pasture, treat them for disease, and supervise birthing. In addition to more conventional veterinary methods, there was magic involved in safeguarding the herd's health: charms, talismans, and spells were used. Sick sheep were brought to shrines for healing and rituals undertaken to purge and purify the flock symbolically. The

shepherd's staff had particular importance. If a shepherd was unhappy with his position, he could throw down his staff and be quit of it, but he would never be allowed back. Karmysheva, *Uzbeki-Lokaitsi*, 105–15.

5. The area of Afghanistan between the upper Amu Darya and the city of Balkh, which was home to the Lakai and the Kungrat in the sixteenth century, is today occupied by the Kungrat, Lakai, Qataghan, and other Dasht-i-Kipchak groups.

6. Karmysheva, *Uzbeki-Lokaitsi*, 43–50, 149–57.

7. After extensive contact with nomadic peoples and the adoption of the yurt, Tajik women also began weaving bands of red wool with embroidery, and even pile-woven items, for their yurts. Karmysheva, "History of Population Formation," 12.

8. *Lochik* are similar to yurts, with a latticework base arranged in a round, square, or rectangular shape and roof poles forming a vault or dome. There is no roof wheel at the top. Borozna, "Material'naia kul'tura uzbekov Babataga," 102.

9. *The Encyclopaedia of Islam*, 2nd ed., s.v. "Özbegs" (Audrey C. Shalinsky) (Leiden: Brill, 2005) 233–34.

10. Agricultural Uzbeks commonly cultivate cotton, wheat barley, sorghum, alfalfa, spinach, beans, and fruits (including melons, peaches, and plums). They also grow mulberry, which provides fruit as well as leaves for silkworms. They raise sheep, goats, cows, and horses. Ibid., 233.

11. The Marka (a Dasht-i-Kipchak group closely related to the Lakai and Kungrat) are said to have been the finest yurt craftsmen; both the Durmen and the Lakai bought their yurts from them. Also according to Borozna, two latticework walls were placed atop one another in Durmen, Marka, Lakai, and Kungrat yurts, making the yurt walls very high. But this is not confirmed by other sources. Borozna, "Material'naia kul'tura uzbekov Babataga," 94.

12. Nodir, e-mail, September 10.

13. Karmysheva, *Uzbeki-Lokaitsi*, 144.

14. Borozna, "Material'naia kul'tura uzbekov Babataga," 96.

15. *Caroq* making is so widespread that it is not often possible to link specific types with particular tribal groups. However, a thin *caroq* blanket collected from Lakai tribesmen during the Central Asian Museum of History and History of the Revolution (SAMIIR) expedition of 1930 (now in the State Historical Museum, Tashkent, inv. no. 219) has a grid pattern with a cruciform shape composed of five squares with small diamond centers that is also found on many cross-stitched *segusha*.

16. Borozna, "Material'naia kul'tura uzbekov Babataga," 96–99.

17. Collected during the SAMIIR expedition of 1930, this item is now in the State Historical Museum, Tashkent (inv. no. 184).

18. Natural dyes are still in use in Gumatak village, although the colors obtained are not strong and do not last. Dyestuffs include wild mushrooms, nut fruits, poplar and apricot tree roots, and madder. Elmira Gul', "Kovri kungradov" [Carpets of the Kungrats], *Moziydan Sado* (Tashkent) 21, no. 1 (March 2004): 10–12.

19. In the carpet world, this design is generally known as a Memling gul. Belkis Khalilovna Karmysheva, "Lokaiski mapramatchi i ilgichi" [Lakai *Mapramach* and *Ilgich*], in *Soobshchenii Respublikanskogo istoriko-kraevedsheskogo musea Tadjikskoi SSR* [Report of the Republican Historical-Folk Arts Museum of the Tajik SSR] (Stalinabad: n.p., 1955): 121–34.

20. Gul', "Kovri kungradov": 10–12.

21. *Uuk kap* storage bags are often tasseled, as are their *ilgich* counterparts, and are made of pile-woven or embroidered and appliquéd felt. Called tent-pole bags in much of the literature on Central Asian textiles, they are suitable only for the decoration of a few poles on the outsides of bundles during transport. More often, *uuk kap* are used as household containers. The pile-woven *at torba* bag, which has the same pentagonal shape, is hung over the horse's breast on ceremonial occasions.

22. Karmysheva, "Lokaiski mapramatchi i ilgichi": 147.

23. Piles of bedding stacked on trunks were traditional features of many rural and urban dwellings. However, in comparison to the household decoration of settled populations in Ferghana, the Lakai *chuk* most closely resembled a traditional yurt bedding pile.

24. Deniz Kandiyoti and Nadira Azimova, "The Communal and the Sacred: Women's Worlds of Ritual in Uzbekistan," *Journal of the Royal Anthropological Institute* 10, no. 2 (June 2004): 331.

25. Gabriele Rasuly-Paleczek, "Ethnic Identity versus Nationalism: The Uzbeks of North-Eastern Afghanistan and the Afghan State," in Touraj Atabaki and John O'Kane, eds., *Post–Soviet Central Asia* (London and New York: Tauris Academic Studies, 1998), 218.

26. A Kungrat *tumar* that Binafsha Nodir saw in a village in the Surkhandarya region was made of felt; it held dried dog feces and seven seeds of *garmal*, a plant burned for ritual purification and to ward off the evil eye. Nodir, interview by authors, Tashkent, Uzbekistan, May 2005.

27. Amulets made for the house or yurt are intended to protect the entire family. For example, many of the fences in Hujaulkan village in the Surkhandarya region have impaled skulls of sheep or bulls as protective objects. The

ubiquitous *doga* hangs in homes along with more specialized amulets, such as *mehrgie*. According to Z. A., a seventy-two-year-old woman of the Kushtamgali clan, Kalamozor village, Baisun district, *mehrgie* are made from sheep intestines and look like small stones. According to T. B., a seventy-six-year-old woman of the Kushtamgali clan, Kalamozor village, Baisun district, *mehrgie* are caplike pieces of fur that occur in an abnormal sheep's birth. She said that rich and noble Kungrat make sleeve cuffs from *mehrgie*; their belief was that if they were given poisoned food, the cuffs would sparkle and flare up. Binafsha Nodir, e-mail to authors, September 5, 2005.

28. Nodir, interview.

29. Cousin and Dupaigne, *Afghan Embroidery,* 14.

30. Karmysheva, "Lokaiski mapramatchi i ilgichi": 124, n. 9.

31. The Uzbek word for wolf is *buri*. Newborn girls for whom this ritual is performed are named Buritosh, Burigul, or Burihol, while the boys are named Buriboi, Burikul, or Burihol. The source for this information is Z. Ch., a sixty-six-year-old Kungrat woman of the Tortuvli clan, Omonhona village, Baisun district. According to a gynecologist in the Kumkurgan district, old women still ask the doctors to perform this ritual. Nodir, e-mail, September 5.

32. Nodir, e-mail, September 10.

33. Ibid.

34. Nodir, e-mail, September 5.

35. According to Gleb Pavlovich Snesarev, Khorezm Uzbeks left the hem unsewn to help ensure a long life for the child. G. P. Snesarev, *Remnants of Pre–Islamic Beliefs and Rituals among the Khorezm Uzbeks,* pt. 4, chap. 2: "The Magic of Family and Household Ritual," *Soviet Anthropology and Archaeology* (Winter 1971–72): 271–72.

36. Françoise Cousin and Bernard Dupaigne, *Afghan Embroidery* (Lahore, Pakistan: Ferozsons, 1993), 14.

37. Nodir collected this information from I. O., a seventy-six-year-old Kungrat woman of the Kushtamgali clan, Egarchi village, Sherabad district; and P. D., a sixty-four-year-old Kungrat woman of the Totuvli clan, Dashtigoz village, Baisun district. Nodir, e-mail, September 10. Nodir added that economy was a factor in the choice of used patchwork fabrics, as the pieces were taken from material left over from the manufacturing of adult clothes.

38. In Central Asia, patchwork textiles have a time-honored association with certain spiritual qualities. For example, patchwork clothing was worn by religious mendicants during the Buddhist period of the first millennium CE and by Sufi dervishes during the Islamic period up to the nineteenth century.

39. Snesarev also mentioned the embroidery of a snake on children's dress, adding that the evil eye or spirit is not repelled by its own image or smell but instead becomes "confused" and distracted. Snesarev, *Remnants of Pre–Islamic Beliefs and Rituals:* 30, n. 23.

40. Among the Turkoman, embroidered or appliquéd snake images are placed on children's talismanic garments, called *elek.* See Kate Fitz Gibbon, "Turkoman Embroidery and Women's Magic," paper presented at the Textile Society of America Annual Conference, September 19–23, 2000; typescript.

41. The Durmen wore a wrapped headdress that was similar to the Kungrat type but shorter and wider. Borozna, "Material'naia kul'tura uzbekov Babataga," 116.

42. Karmysheva, *Uzbeki-Lokaitsi,* 146–47.

43. Nodir, interview.

44. The form of the *bosh* differed according to region. For example, in the Baisun district, it was broader at the top than at the base. In the Shurchi and Denau districts, Kungrat women wore a cylindrical *bosh.* Nodir, interview.

45. *Cinchi* understood the routine as well as the magical methods of caring for, healing, and training horses. Talismans were used as much for horses as for people, and the healing of ailments involved prayers and the sprinkling of holy soil. Karmysheva, *Uzbeki-Lokaitsi,* 105–12.

46. Belkis Khalilovna Karmysheva, "Etnograficheskii ocherk zhivotnovodstva u lokaitsev" [Ethnographical Essay on Animal Husbandry among the Lakai] (Leningrad: Academia Nauk SSSR, 1951), 9–10.

47. Ibid., 15. It is important to bear in mind that Karmysheva was adhering to a basic Soviet party line here.

48. According to Karmysheva, in the early twentieth century, when a favorite horse was sold, four hairs would be torn from its forelock and hidden. When buying a horse and leading it home, one would take a stone and knock it against the ground and against the horse's hooves to help ensure that the hooves and the legs would be strong. When a horse was lost, its owner would fashion reins from a length of thread and hide them under a piece of felt on the floor of the house. Mullahs would say prayers for lost horses intended to close up wolves' mouths — wolves being the major predators of horses and livestock. Karmysheva, *Uzbeki-Lokaitsi,* 105–12.

49. Ibid.

50. A brand-new girth of this type was purchased for the Museum of History and Ethnography, Dushanbe, Tajikistan, from its weaver and original owner, an elderly woman from Burdan-Gel village, but we were unable to locate it when

viewing the museum's textile-storage area. This girth is cited in Karmysheva, *Uzbeki-Lokaitsi*, 47–55.

51. Ibid.

52. Ibid., 105–12. To compare these circling rituals with those of the Khorezm Uzbeks, see G. P. Snesarev, *Remnants of Pre–Islamic Beliefs among the Khorezm Uzbeks*, pt. 6, chap. 3, "Vestiges of Early Forms of Religions and Zoroastrianism in Burial Rituals," *Soviet Anthropology and Archaeology* (Spring 1973): 348.

53. Karmysheva, *Uzbeki-Lokaitsi*, 47–55.

3. Renewing Ancient Forms: *Ilgich* and the Art of Embroidery

1. This observation is based on the authors' examination of six Lakai hats for men and young boys (inv. nos. 229–34) and a cloth cap with a long black flap worn by married women over fifty years old (inv. no. 223) in the collection of the State Historical Museum, Tashkent.

2. *Segusha* are still made today by Dasht-i-Kipchak Uzbeks in Afghanistan. See also Pierre Centlivres, "Les Uzbeks du Qattaghan," *Afghanistan Journal* (Graz, Austria: Akademishche Druck-u. Verlagsanstalt) 2, no. 1 (1975): 2–36 and fig. 7.

3. Ibid., 32–36.

4. Aimkhal Ernazarova, interview by authors, Hissar, Tajikistan, May 2005. Ernazarova is a Lakai woman.

5. Because the market values of *khalta* are often greater than those of *segusha*, the latter are often cut and sewn into bags. Typically, these are narrower than true *khalta*, and their patterns wrap around the base.

6. Centlivres, "Les Uzbeks du Qattaghan": 33, fig. 13.

7. This piece was purchased in Abdali Sultanski jamiyat. See State Historical Museum, Tashkent, inv. no. 199.

8. Belkis Khalilovna Karmysheva, *Uzbeki-Lokaitsi luzhnovo Tadjikistana* [Uzbek-Lakai of Southern Tajikistan] (Stalinabad: Akademii Nauk Tadjikskoi SSR, Institut istorii, arkheologii, i etnografii [Academy of Science of the Tajik SSR Institute of History, Archaeology, and Ethnography], 1954), 137.

9. Authors' observations in Hissar, Tajikistan, May 2005.

10. According to Karmysheva, there were two elaborate saddle covers, which she called *da-our*, in the collection of the Andreev Museum (now the Museum of Ethnography, Dushanbe, Tajikistan), one acquired in Kazakh village, Sovietski district, and the other in Abikik village, Dagankik district. Karmysheva, interview by authors, Moscow, 1995. We were unable to locate either of these items in the Museum of Ethnography in 2005, possibly because they had been moved. For an illustration of a distinctive Lakai horse-head cover, see *Hali: The International Journal of Oriental Carpets and Textiles*, no. 75 (1994), cover.

11. Bread is never thrown away, and it cannot be dropped on the ground or otherwise treated disrespectfully. Each meal is begun by tearing off and eating a small piece of bread, signifying that it alone would make a sufficient meal. When a guest partakes of bread, an obligation of hospitality (which includes physical protection) on the part of the host is created.

12. Belkis Khalilovna Karmysheva, "Lokaiski mapramatchi i ilgichi" [Lakai Mapramach and Ilgich], in *Soobshchenii Respublikanskogo istoriko-kraevedsheskogo musea Tadjikskoi SSR* [Report of the Republican Historical-Folk Arts Museum of the Tajik SSR] (Stalinabad: n.p., 1955): 147.

13. For details on the techniques used to make edge and trim decorations, see Frieda Sorber's appendix in this book.

14. According to Aimkhal Ernazarova, the fine working of fringe and tassels was more important to the Lakai than to other Uzbek groups. She believed that attaching beads to the end of each strand of a silk fringe was a characteristically Lakai technique. Ernazarova, interview. We believe this technique to be widely distributed among Dasht-i-Kipchak Uzbek groups but also acknowledge that beaded fringe is found very often in Lakai work.

15. Karmysheva, "Lokaiski mapramatchi i ilgichi": 146.

16. Such embroidered covers were also used by the Turkoman, Kazakhs (who called them *uuk bas*), and other Turkic Central Asian peoples.

17. Karmysheva, "Lokaiski mapramatchi i ilgichi": 146.

18. Ernazarova, interview.

19. Karmysheva, "Lokaiski mapramatchi i ilgichi": 137.

20. Karmysheva illustrated an *uuk kap ilgich* bearing a design very similar to that of an unusual *ilgich* with embroidery on a green ground in the Robinson Collection. "Lokaiski mapramatchi i ilgichi": 152, fig. 24.

21. Ibid., 147.

22. For a detailed review of edge and trim treatments, see Frieda Sorber's appendix essay in the present book.

23. "Cloud-band" patterns, which appear in several Kungrat *ilgich*, are probably borrowed from carpet designs. See Kate Fitz Gibbon and Andrew Hale, "Lakai: Bad Beys of Central Asia," *Hali: The International Journal of Oriental Carpets and Textiles*, no. 75 (1994): 73, ill. 9.

24. Binafsha Nodir, e-mail to authors, September 10, 2005.

25. Two Kungrat *ilgich* of this type that Dudin collected are in the Russian Ethnographic Museum, St. Petersburg.

26. Karmysheva included Semiz embroideries in the same group as the Lakai. The early twentieth-century expeditions also collected materials from the Durmen and the Semiz that were indistinguishable from materials collected from the Lakai, nor is there any obvious difference between these materials and Lakai materials collected in Afghanistan. See Karmysheva, "Lokaiski mapramatchi i ilgichi": 155–56.

27. Saodat Marafova and Nadezhda Vasitova, Museum of Ethnography, Dushanbe, Tajikistan, interview by authors, May 17, 2005.

28. Unfortunately, according to officials at the Museum of Ethnography, Dushanbe, no felt embroidered items cited by Karmysheva could be located in the museum's collections. Marafova and Vasitova, interview. However, "a *mapramach* from the collection of Republican Historical Ethnographical Museum 506 . . . does not have a registration certificate, i.e., the information on the collector, place and time of acquisition is not available. But, without any doubts, it belongs to the Lakai tribe and is a very rare specimen of *mapramach*, made from felt. We have not met any other specimens of Lakai *mapramach* made from felt before. The embroidery with twisted silk threads on the red cloth, completely reproducing the ornamental pattern of fleecy *mapramach*, is embroidered on its front side. The pieces of old embroidered bags are sewed on its lateral sides." Karmysheva, "Lokaiski mapramatchi i ilgichi": 133.

29. No dye analysis has been done on embroideries in these earlier collections, nor, at this writing, is any such analysis available for materials in the Robinson Collection.

30. Fredrik T. Hiebert, "Pazyryk Chronology and Early Horse Nomads Reconsidered," *Bulletin of the Asia Institute*, no. 6 (1992): 117–29. Excavations in the Altai Mountains point to a local origin for almost all the material remains unearthed as well as to the development of a regional style that was largely influenced by Central Asian (rather than Greek, Persian, or Chinese) fashion.

31. Sergei I. Rudenko, *Frozen Tombs of Siberia: The Pazyryk Burials of Iron Age Horsemen* (Berkeley and Los Angeles: University of California Press, 1970), figs. 160, 161 (n. pg.).

4. Urban Embroidery: Sharisabs and *Suzani*

1. Olga Aleksandrovna Sukhareva, "Shahrisabs," in *K istorii gorodov Bukharskogo khanstva* [History of the Bukharan Khanate], Istoriko-etnograficheskie ocherki [Historical-Ethnographic Studies] (Tashkent: Izd-vo Akademii nauk Uzbekskoi SSR, 1958), 132–33.

2. *The Baburnama: Memoirs of Babur, Prince and Emperor*, trans. Wheeler M. Thackston (New York: Oxford University Press, 1996), 87.

3. Ibid.

4. Sukhareva thought Schuyler's figures were too high; she estimated that in 1926 Shahrisabs had a population of some eighteen thousand, with about six thousand in Kitab — this following substantial growth in the 1900s and 1910s. Sukhareva, "Shahrisabs," in *Bukharskogo khanstva*, 131.

5. For more on the Russian capture of Shahrisabs, see Eugene Schuyler, *Turkestan*, 2 vols. (New York: Scribner, Armstrong, 1877), 1: 72–79, 241.

6. The largest group of Uzbeks living in Shahrisabs and Kitab claimed to belong to the Keneges tribe. However, the name Keneges may mainly have served to represent a solidarity group, or *qaum*, rather than reflecting the population's true ethnic background. According to Sukhareva, the Russian scholar Alexander Kun wrote that many neighborhoods in the two cities were dominated by Mangit, Sarai, and Kungrat Uzbeks. Kun's survey, published in 1880, noted that the population was made up of the following groups: Chagatai, Ming, Mitan, Sayat, Achamaili (a Keneges subgroup), Kipchak, Kirgiz, Kalmak, and Mogul. Sukhareva wrote that even though the Keneges were not the majority inhabitants of Shahrisabs, her interviewees there insisted that all the city's residents should be called Keneges. Sukhareva, "Shahrisabs," in *Bukharskogo khanstva*, 133.

7. Sukhareva's detailed demographic research in other urban areas and evenhanded treatment of ethnic issues lend credence to her argument with respect to Shahrisabs. In other Soviet-era sources, population numbers sometimes reflect the Kremlin's interest in presenting the image of a homogenous Uzbek state. Within two decades of the national delimitation of Turkestan into Uzbek and Tajik Soviet Socialist republics, the "official" Tajik population had dropped by 50 to 75 percent in many urban areas. The people remained, but their official ethnic identity had changed.

8. Sukhareva, "Shahrisabs," in *Bukharskogo khanstva*, 138.

9. Ibid., 128.

10. Ibid., 138.

11. Schuyler, *Turkestan*, 70.

12. *Katalog Turkestanskovo Otdela* [Catalogue of Turkestan Manufacturers], exh. cat. (Moscow: Polytechnic Institute, 1871), 59.

13. Twelve robes were on view in the exhibition's robe store, several of which belonged to Turkestan's governor general, K. P. von Kaufman; these were made of gold-embroidered and silver-embroidered velvet, Kashmir shawl material, marten fur, and astrakhan. There were also "wide trousers of Shahrisabs, embroidered in silk." *Katalog Turkestanskovo Otdela*, 61.

14. Lisa Golombek, "The Draped Universe of Islam," in *Content and Context of Visual Arts in the Islamic World: Papers from a Colloquium in Memory of Richard Ettinghausen* (Institute of Fine Arts, New York University, April 2–4, 1980), ed. Priscilla P. Soucek (University Park, Pa.: Pennsylvania State University Press for the College Art Association, 1988), 28.

15. The eleventh-century Central Asian writer Narshakhi, of Bukhara, related a story about the presentation of gifts by the eighth-century Sogdian queen Khatun. She "issued orders and prohibitions, and gave a robe of honor to whomsoever she wished and punishment to whom she wished." Abu Bakr Muhammad ibn Jafar Narshakhi (899–959), *The History of Bukhara*, Richard N. Frye, ed. and trans. (Cambridge, Mass.: Mediaeval Academy of America, 1954), 9.

16. Henry Lansdell, *Russian Central Asia* (London: Sampson Low, 1885), 29.

17. These articles are in the Russian Ethnographic Museum, St. Petersburg, but nearly all of them were damaged when the dyes ran during a flood in the 1920s.

18. Only two types of textiles have primarily talismanic functions: *caroq*, a pieced-patchwork fabric; and *tumar*, pendants (generally triangular) that enclose a magical object or inscription.

19. The words Sukhareva heard, "khosiiat doran," can also be translated as "happy properties." Olga Aleksandrovna Sukhareva, "The Design of Decorative Embroidery of Samarkand and Its Connection with Ethnic Ideas and Beliefs," *Soviet Anthropology and Archeology* (Winter 1983–84): 26.

20. Marifat Mirzaeva, interview by authors, Shahrisabs, Uzbekistan, September 2004. Mirzaeva is a professional embroiderer.

21. A detailed description from the 1880s of guest rooms in the homes of affluent Uzbeks in Ferghana, eastern Uzbekistan, does not mention the presence of embroidery on the walls. Instead, there were large and small niches set into the walls; the small ones had patterned-stucco decoration. The ceilings and upper cornices were delicately carved and painted in bright reds, yellows, blues, and greens, and they were accented with gold leaf. On the floors were felts, quilted blankets, and pillows. The regular living quarters, which were less elaborately decorated, included trunks with piles of brightly colored blankets among the furnishings but no textile wall decorations. Vladimir Petrovich Nalivkin and [his daughter] Nalivkina, *Essay on the Everyday Life of Women of the Settled Indigenous Population of Ferghana* (Kazan: n.p., 1886), 75–84. For another description of interior decorations during this period, see Ole Olufsen, *The Amir of Bokhara and His Country: Journeys and Studies in Bokhara (*Copenhagen: Gylendal, Nordisk Forlag, 1911), 328.

22. While doing field research in Afghanistan, we often saw embroideries in everyday use as niche covers, curtains, and doorway hangings, especially in women's quarters. During wedding preparations and celebrations, embroideries and carpets were collected from relatives and used to construct and decorate pavilions in which male visitors would eat and listen to music. Women guests gathered inside the home.

23. It is impossible today to determine which types of embroideries were used as nuptial bedcovers in Central Asia during the nineteenth century. Textile dealers in Afghanistan and the United States have identified stains on various large embroideries as bloodstains. It seems most likely that different types of *suzani* were used to decorate the nuptial bed as well as to embellish the home for the wedding celebration and that no *suzani* were made solely and specifically as bedcovers. Nineteenth-century *suzani* bearing an arched *mihrab* design are often identified in the literature as bedcovers. This pattern certainly resonates with Islamic tradition and thereby projects a benevolent image — and such suzani would be appropriate wedding-night decorations — but so would other decorative embroideries.

24. Compare these items to ones made in the nearby region of Baisun, Uzbekistan, hailed by Soviet and Uzbek ethnologists as a models of textile-craft preservation. Common forms of embroidery there include: *suzani*, *borpush*, or *bugzhoma* (triangular embroidered-cloth sections for decorating bedding piles), *zardevor*, *jainamaz* (embroideries with an arched or *mihrab* shape), *bolinpush* (pillow covers), *belbog* (embroidered scarf-belts), *aina khalta* (mirror covers), and *chai khalta* (small bags for tea or personal items). Akbar Hakimov, "Baisun Khalq Sanati: Folk Art of Baisun," *Moyzidan Sado* (Tashkent) 21, no. 1 (March 2004): 4–7.

25. Plain-woven cotton *karbaz*, or *buz*, has been known for millennia. It was extensively produced during the nineteenth century. Besides being a common and inexpensive trade item, it was used in Turkestan as ground cloth for embroidery, woodblock stamping, and other textile applications. For a concise history of the *karbaz* trade since the sixteenth century, see Audrey Burton, *The Bukharans* (New York: St. Martin's Press, 1997), 365–66.

26. Now in the Rickmers Collection at the Museum für Volkerkunde, Berlin, this embroidery is catalogued there as being from Bukhara. But it is far more likely to be from the Shahrisabs region. Johannes Kalter and Margareta Pavaloi, *Uzbekistan: Heirs to the Silk Road* (London: Thames and Hudson, 1997), 275, pl. 555.

27. G. L. Chepelevetskaya wrote that, after 1880, embroidery was done on locally produced silk ground cloth. The vast majority of Soviet-period embroideries were made using machine-manufactured cotton. Chepelevetskaya,

Suzani Uzbekistana [Suzani of Uzbekistan], Institut Iskusstvoznaia AN UZSSR [Institute of the Arts of Uzbekistan], Gosudarstvennii muzei vostochnih kultur [State Museum of Eastern Culture] (Tashkent: Gosudarstvennoe izdatelstvo khudozhestvennoi literature [State Publisher of Artistic Literature], UZSSR 1961), 23. We have found that this is only partly true; there are many late-nineteenth- and early twentieth-century embroideries in which handmade cotton cloth was still employed. A handwoven ground cloth is often used for new, commercially produced *suzani*.

28. In the 1880s, the government of the Russian protectorate established a customs barrier to keep Indian goods out of Russia. But the barrier was not effective until 1894, when Russia became powerful enough to demand the creation of a trade agreement with Bukhara and closed its border with Afghanistan, ending illicit trade with India. Ian Murray Matley, "Industrialization (1865–1964)," in Edward Allworth, ed., *Central Asia: 130 Years of Russian Dominance; A Historical Overview* (Durham, N.C.: Duke University Press, 1994), 322.

29. Irina Bogoslovskaya and Larisa Levteeva, "Embroidered Skullcaps of Uzbekistan," *Ornament* 23, no. 3 (2000): 32–35.

30. A. Mardonova, "Customs and Rituals of the Childhood Cycle among the Tadjiks of the Upper Zeravshan Valley in the Past and Today," *Soviet Anthropology and Archeology* 24, no. 2 (1985): 51.

31. Our observations in Afghanistan in the 1970s indicated that this was done by wealthy and poor women alike there. Moreover, we noticed that women used the money they earned from embroidery for their own and communal expenses.

32. Skullcaps that took four to five days to embroider were sold for one and a half rubles; women who embroidered headscarves and sashes could earn eighty silver kopeks a week — the sale price minus the cost of the muslin and silk. Nalivkin and Nalivkina, *Women of the Settled Indigenous Population of Ferghana*, 109–45. In conversations with professional embroiderers in Shahrisabs in 2004, we were told that two to three days of full-time work were needed to embroider one square foot of cross-stitch.

33. While doing field research in Tashkurgan, Afghanistan, in the 1970s, we worked with the local male silk dyer, who also drew designs for the local women to embroider. In the late 1970s and early 1980s, his female relatives and other women in Tashkurgan embroidered copies of Lakai *ilgich* for the market.

34. Nalivkin and Nalivkina, *Women of the Settled Indigenous Population of Ferghana*, 118. Given that the cost of silk used to make a *suzani* was likely to be greater than that of female labor to do the embroidery, the lower production cost of Nurata-style *suzani* relative to other regional *suzani* types may be a reason why, despite the Nurata region's small population, a comparatively greater number of nineteenth-century Nurata *suzani* remain today. The sentimental bouquet design appealed strongly to Western buyers, and the open field meant that less time and fewer silk threads were required to produce these embroideries.

35. Francesca Galloway, conversation with authors, 2002. For more on very early examples of Central Asian *suzani*, see Ernst Grube, *Keshte, Central Asian Embroideries: The Marshall and Marilyn R. Wolf Collection* (London: Marcuson Publishing Services, 2003), 3.

36. Despite what is found in much of the literature, the *kanda-khayol* stitch, one of many variants of the *basma* stitch, was not exclusive to Shahrisabs. Embroidery stitches migrated throughout the khanates, and while certain ones were preferred in certain places, there were no hard-and-fast rules governing their distribution.

37. The spiritual symbolism of the garden is still important in Central Asia. Soviet ethnologists rarely discussed Islamic origins of folk beliefs, preferring to focus on possible pre–Islamic origins for religious concepts surrounding a "tree of life." G. P. Snesarev, "Remnants of Pre–Islamic Beliefs and Rituals among the Khorezm Uzbeks," *Soviet Anthropology and Archeology* (Spring 1974): 15.

38. Jeannette Mirsky, ed., *The Great Chinese Travelers* (Chicago: University of Chicago Press, 1964), 151.

39. There is an intriguing possible connection between the integration of different flower types depicted in *suzani* and wedding rites involving the cutting and stripping of a tree and decorating it with candies, apricots, and apples. Young women stand on the roof of the house where the wedding is taking place and try to snatch the fruits from the tree. As well, bouquets are tied to the wedding curtain when it covers the cart carrying the bride to her new home. Snesarev, "Remnants of Pre–Islamic Beliefs and Rituals": 18–19 and (Winter 1971–72): 258–59.

40. Eva Baer, *Islamic Ornament* (New York: New York University Press, 1998), 2–3.

41. Sukhareva stressed the pre–Islamic and Zoroastrian grounding for this identification. She pointed to the "apotropaic role" of fire in ancient and modern Central Asian ritual: a lit lamp was passed around the heads of newlyweds and was kept burning in their room on the wedding night. "The same significance was doubtless attached at one time or another to the image of a lamp on nuptial embroideries. Its example was the oil lamp with four wicks, facing different directions." Sukhareva, "Design of Decorative Embroidery of Samarkand": 29–31.

42. Grube, Keshte, *Central Asian Embroideries*, 7, pl. 21.

43. Nishapur is a northern Iranian archaeological site that produced vast quantities of ceramic bowls and shards. Only seventeen pieces of Chinese pottery were found there in excavations covering a period from the ninth century to 1221 CE. See Charles K. Wilkinson, *Nishapur: Pottery of the Early Islamic Period* (New York: Metropolitan Museum

of Art and Greenwich, Conn.: New York Graphic Society, 1973), 254–55. See also Ludmila Sokolovskaia and Axelle Rougeulle, "Stratified Finds of Chinese Porcelains from Pre–Mongol Samarkand (Afrasiab)," *Bulletin of the Asia Institute*, no. 6 (1992): 87–98. One hundred years of excavation at pre–Mongol Samarkand yielded only three dozen shards.

44. John Carswell, "Archaeology and the Study of Later Islamic Pottery," in D. S. Richards, ed., *Islam and the Trade of Asia* (Oxford, England: Bruno Cassierer; Philadelphia: University of Pennsylvania Press, 1970), 63–65.

45. For example, the Taj Mahal, India's best-known Mughal monument, was built by an Ottoman architect. The chief draftsman on the project was from Samarkand, and the head sculptor was from Bukhara. The building's style is Timurid, reflecting its patron's heritage. Richard Foltz, *Mughal India and Central Asia* (New York and Karachi: Oxford University Press, 1998), 88.

46. Scott Levi, e-mail and phone conversation with authors, October 2005. Levi is a noted historian of Central Asia, specializing in trade.

47. The historian Roziia Galievna Mukminova noted several workshops in sixteenth-century Samarkand where *chit* woodblock printing was done but none in Bukhara. The earliest recorded Central Asian textile-trade guild was that of *chit* makers. Three late-eighteenth-century guild texts, or *risolas*, of the *chit* woodblock printmakers have been studied. Mukminova, interview by authors, Tashkent, Uzbekistan, Spring 1995. For a listing of textiles in early records of the Russian-Central Asian trade, see Burton, *The Bukharans*, 367

48. Ignazio Vok, *Suzani: The Textile Art of Central Asia; Vok Collection*, introduction and catalogue text by Jakob Taube (Munich: Edition Vok, 1994), pl. 28. Regarding the de Young Museum embroidery, C. M. Cootner wrote, "It is unlikely that the drawing in this example was by an experienced embroideress or a local professional designer." Cootner, "Gardens of Paradise," *Hali: The International Journal of Carpets and Textiles*, no. 30 (1986): 46–51.

49. "Not only women, but also, or even predominantly, men are engaged in silk embroidery." Franz von Schwarz, *Turkestan: Die Wiege der Indogermanischen Volker* [Turkestan: The Cradle of the Indo-Germanic Peoples], 1900, cited in Vok, *Suzani*, 9. Von Schwartz wrote that these embroideries were made for sale to foreigners, and he listed many types that were available.

50. William Eleroy Curtis, *Turkestan: The Heart of Asia* (New York: Hodder and Strouton, 1911), 172–73.

51. Under Soviet rule, Central Asia was transformed from an economically self-sufficient region with diverse farming and herding into a single-crop economic zone, producing raw cotton for textile manufacture in the Soviet Union. Forced settlement of Central Asians on collective farms was justified by the Soviet and Internationalist need for textiles. Artistic treatments of cotton farming in painting and the depictions of cotton motifs in artisan crafts and textiles attempted to romanticize this economic manipulation and it make more palatable.

52. A. Morozova, *Uzbekistanda iurmaduzlik* [Embroidery of Uzbekistan], (Tashkent: Uzbek Academy of Arts, 1960), 12–14.

53. Sayora Mahkamova, interview by authors, Tashkent, Uzbekistan, Spring 1995. Mahkamova is a textiles scholar.

54. Present-day textile artisans who copy antique pieces are remarkably skilled. Some of them read textile publications to find technical hints and see authentic early designs. For example, we have seen exact copies of published ikats from the Guido Goldman Collection, formerly in Massachusetts and now dispersed among a dozen U.S. museums. We have also have noted that some embroiderers create wear on fabrics and make sparing use of a red wool described in writings on textiles in order to mimic works produced before the 1880s.

55. According to these Shahrisabs embroiderers, certain designs have life-affirming qualities, and though they are not talismans per se, they help create a positive environment. "The power of scorpions make bad powers run away," one of them said. Scorpion designs are used often on hats. The *gulibadam* design is said to encourage happiness and health. Other designs are perceived as neutral. Asked why black backgrounds are no longer common, one embroiderer said, "Tourists don't like the black." Thus embroidery traditions are retained but continually adapted to market demands. Marifat Mirzaeva and other embroiderers, interviews with authors, Shahrisabs, Uzbekistan, September 2004.

THE JACK A. AND AVIVA ROBINSON COLLECTION OF CENTRAL ASIAN EMBROIDERIES

Notes to Reader

Identification information for each object is based on standard museum practices that indicate cultural and geographic origins as well as technical considerations.

All embroidery-stitch names are as given in Mary Thomas, *Dictionary of Embroidery Stitches* (1934; reprint 1977), except for references to couching stitches and slanted buttonhole stitches.

The use of a hook or needle in reference to chain stitching is noted only if the stitch could be verified by analysis of the reverse of the fabric.

A cotton backing cloth is present, except where noted.

Edge indicates an integral element that has no life independent of the object.

Band indicates an element that was made separately and later applied to the object.

Cloth band refers to a fabric strip applied as an outer edging. Often, it is visible on the face and reverse of the object and is a basis strip of fabric.

LM indicates loop manipulation.

Newly lined indicates a lining presumably added after the object left Central Asia.

Measurements are in inches and centimeters; height precedes width and excludes fringes or tassels, except where noted.

Suzani
Southern Uzbekistan, 20th century
Silk, cotton; continuous-thread couching, chain stitch, satin stitch, machine embroidery
74-1/2 x 49-1/2 in. (189.2 x 125.7 cm)
Cloth band
Pieced, printed lining
2004.259.1

Woman's hat
Kitab or Shahrisabs, late 19th–early 20th century
Silk, cotton; cross-stitch, chain stitch, checkered chain stitch
16 x 6 x 5-1/2 in. (40.6 x 15.2 x 14 cm)
Embroidered band, warp-twined (LM) edge
Printed lining
2004.259.2

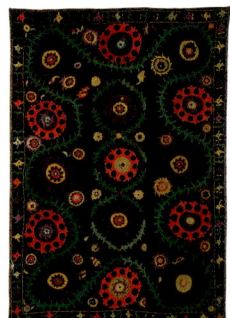

Suzani
Samarkand, c. 1930
Silk, cotton; continuous-thread couching, hook chain stitch, cross-stitch
105 x 75-1/4 in. (266.7 x 190 cm)
Warp-twined edge (LM) with cross-stitch embroidery
Ikat band on reverse edge
2004.259.3

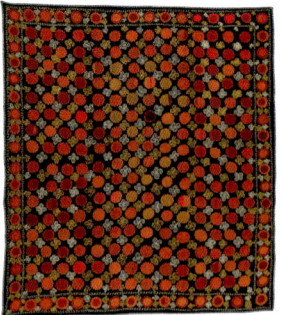

Suzani
20th century
Cotton; continuous-thread couching, machine chain stitch
95-1/2 x 86-1/2 in. (242.6 x 219.7 cm)
Commercially woven band with warp-faced patterning
2004.259.4

Decorative band for clothing
Shahrisabs, late 19th century
Silk, cotton; cross-stitch
38 x 2-3/4 in. (96.5 x 7 cm)
2004.259.5

Kamarband
Shahrisabs, late 19th century
Silk, cotton; cross-stitch
47-1/8 x 3-3/4 in. (119.7 x 9.5 cm)
Warp-twined band
Pieced ikat lining
2004.259.6

Decorative band for clothing
Shahrisabs, late 19th–early 20th century
Silk, cotton; cross-stitch
32 x 3-1/4 in. (81.3 x 8.3 cm)
Warp-twined (LM) band fragments
Pieced ikat and printed lining
2004.259.7

Suzani
Bukhara, Kitab, or Shahrisabs, 19th century
Silk, cotton; hook chain stitch
62-1/2 x 45 in. (158.7 x 114.3 cm)
Cloth band
Newly lined
2004.259.8

Suzani
Urban Uzbek, early–mid-20th century
Silk, cotton; continuous-thread couching, machine chain stitch
92 x 86 in. (233.7 x 218.4 cm)
2004.259.9

Suzani
Nurata, third quarter of the 19th century
Silk, cotton; continuous-thread couching, open chain stitch, chain stitch, stem stitch
101 x 75-1/2 in. (256.54 x 191.8 cm)
Newly lined
2004.259.10

Tent hanging
Dasht-i-Kipchak Uzbek (probably Lakai), 19th century
Silk, cotton; cross-stitch
9-1/2 x 6-1/4 in. (24.1 x 15.9 cm)
Printed cloth bands
Printed lining
2004.259.11

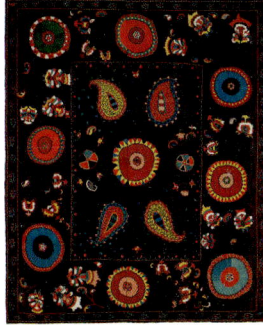

Suzani
Kitab or Shahrisabs, third quarter of the 19th century
Silk, cotton; chain stitch, checkered chain stitch
85-1/2 x 73 in. (217.2 x 185.4 cm)
Ikat band
2004.259.12

Suzani
Probably Kitab, late 19th–early 20th century
Silk, cotton; chain stitch
57-3/4 x 69 in. (146.7 x 175.3 cm)
Ikat and printed lining
2004.259.13

Suzani
Kitab or Shahrisabs, late 19th–early 20th century
Silk, cotton; hook chain stitch
76-3/4 x 54 in. (194.9 x 137.2 cm)
Printed lining with ikat band on reverse edge
2004.259.14

Suzani
Kitab or Shahrisabs, 19th century
Silk, cotton; hook chain stitch, checkered chain stitch
83-1/2 x 63-1/2 in. (212.1 x 161.3 cm)
Printed cloth band
Pieced, printed lining
2004.259.15

Ainak push
Kitab or Shahrisabs, late 19th century
Silk, cotton; cross-stitch
17-1/4 x 14 in.; 2-1/2 in. fringe (43.8 x 35.6 cm; 6.3 cm fringe)
Fringe with warp-twined heading, warp-twined (tablet) band
Bag back: printed, with a printed lining
2004.259.16

Kamarband
Shahrisabs, late 19th century
Silk, cotton; cross-stitch
38-1/2 x 3-1/4 in. (97.8 x 8.3 cm)
Leather lining
2004.259.17

Robe trim
Kitab or Shahrisabs, 19th century
Silk, cotton; cross-stitch
46-1/8 x 3 in. (117.1 x 7.6 cm)
Warp-twined (LM) edge
No backing cloth
2004.259.18

Kamarband
Shahrisabs, late 19th century
Silk, cotton; cross-stitch
Warp-twined (LM) band fragments
32-1/2 x 4 in. (82.6 x 10.2 cm)
Striped lining
2004.259.19

Kamarband
Kitab or Shahrisabs, 19th century
Silk, cotton; cross-stitch
33 x 3-1/2 in. (83.8 x 8.9 cm)
Warp-twined (LM) edge
Printed lining
2004.259.20

Suzani
Tashkent, late 19th–early 20th century
Silk, cotton, linen; continuous-thread couching, open chain stitch
100 x 80-1/2 in. (254 x 204.5 cm)
Newly lined
2004.259.21

Suzani
Tashkent, late 19th–early 20th century
Silk, cotton; continuous-thread couching, open chain stitch
110 x 80 in. (279.4 x 203.2 cm)
Cloth band
2004.259.22

Suzani
Tashkent, 19th century
Silk, cotton, linen; continuous-thread couching, chain stitch, open chain stitch
104 x 82-1/2 in. (264.2 x 209.6 cm)
Newly lined
2004.259.23

Uuk kap ilgich
Lakai, early 20th century
Silk, cotton, metal; cross-stitch
22-1/2 x 3-1/2 in.; 11–14 in. tassels
(57.1 x 8.9 cm; 27.9–35.6 cm tassels)
Printed lining
2004.259.24

.27 a) .27 b)

Ainak push
Kashkadarya region, late 19th–early 20th century
Silk, cotton; hook chain stitch, needle chain stitch
15 x 14-1/2 in.; 4 in. fringe
(38.1 x 36.8 cm; 10.2 cm fringe)
Fringe with warp-twined heading, ikat band
Pieced, block-printed lining
2004.259.25

Segusha
Dasht-i-Kipchak Uzbek, early 20th century
Silk, cotton; cross-stitch
20 x 29-1/2 in. with fringe (50.8 x 74.9 cm with fringe)
Warp-twined (LM) edge
Fringes with warp-twined and plain-weave headings
Pieced, printed lining
2004.259.26

Djuk-chari-chuk (chuk decoration)
Dasht-i-Kipchak Uzbek, early 20th century
Silk, cotton, metal, glass, plastic; cross-stitch, chain stitch, machine embroidery
a) 103-1/2 x 3-1/2 in.; 3 in. tassels
(262.9 x 8.9 cm; 7.6 cm tassels)
b) 100-1/2 x 3-1/4 in.; 3 in. tassels
(255.3 x 8.3 cm; 7.6 cm tassels)
Embroidered band
Pieced, printed lining
2004.259.27a,b

Ilgich
Dasht-i-Kipchak, late 19th–early 20th century
Silk, cotton; cross-stitch, chain stitch
23-1/4 x 23 in.; 1-3/4 in. top fringe
(59.1 x 58.4 cm; 4.4 cm top fringe)
Braided-net fringe, embroidered bands
Pieced, striped, and printed lining
2004.259.28

Ilgich
Dasht-i-Kipchak Uzbek (probably Kungrat), late 19th–early 20th century
Silk, wool, cotton; chain stitch
21 x 21 in.; 3 in. fringe (53.3 x 53.3 cm; 7.6 cm fringe)
Pieced, printed lining
2004.259.29

Igich
Kungrat, late 19th–early 20th century
Wool, silk; blanket stitch, needle chain stitch, continuous-thread couching, spaced button-hole-filling stitch, outline stitch
25-1/2 x 26 in.; 3/4 –2-1/2 in. fringe (64.8 x 66 cm; 1.9–6.3 cm fringe)
Fringe with warp-twined (LM) heading
No backing cloth
2004.259.30

Ilgich
Kungrat, late 19th–20th century
Silk, wool; needle chain stitch, cross-stitch
26 x 28-3/4 in.; 3 in. fringe with tassels (66 x 73 cm; 7.6 cm fringe with tassels)
Braided-net fringe, embroidered and warp-twined (LM) bands
2004.259.31

Ilgich
Kungrat or Durmen, late 19th–early 20th century
Silk, wool, cotton; chain stitch
22-1/2 x 22-1/4 in. (57.1 x 56.5 cm)
Ikat band at top only
2004.259.32

Ilgich
Kungrat, early 20th century
Silk, wool; chain stitch
19-1/2 x 20-1/2 in.; 3-1/4 in. fringe (49.5 x 52.1 cm; 8.3 cm fringe)
Pieced fringe with warp-twined (tablet) heading and cloth band
Pieced, block-printed lining
2004.259.33

Ilgich
Kungrat, 19th century
Silk, wool; needle chain stitch
28-3/4 x 16 in. (73 x 40.6 cm)
Warp-twined (LM) band
2004.259.34

Da-our
Kungrat, late 19th–early 20th century
Silk, wool, cotton, metal; chain stitch, cross-stitch
48-1/2 x 59 in.; 4-1/2 in. band and fringe with tassels (123.2 x 149.9 cm; 11.4 cm band and fringe with tassels)
Braided-net fringes with tassels, warp-twined (LM) and embroidered bands, assumed LM braid
Pieced, printed lining
2004.259.35

Ilgich
Kungrat, early 20th century
Silk, wool, cotton; hook chain stitch
19 x 21-1/2 in. (48.3 x 54.6 cm)
2004.259.36

Ilgich
Kungrat, late 19th–early 20th century
Silk, wool, cotton; chain stitch
21-3/4 x 21-3/4 in.; 2–4 in. fringe (55.2 x 55.2 cm; 5.1–10.2 cm fringe)
Fringes with warp-twined headings (LM and tablet), warp-twined (LM) edge
Printed lining
2004.259.37

Ilgich
Kungrat, late 19th century
Silk, wool; chain stitch
23-1/2 x 23-1/2 in.; 3 in. fringe (59.7 x 59.7 cm; 7.6 cm fringe)
Fringe with warp-twined (LM) heading, warp-twined (LM) band
2004.259.38

Ilgich
Kungrat, early 20th century
Silk, wool; needle chain stitch
18-1/2 x 18-3/4 in. (47 x 47.6 cm)
2004.259.39

Ilgich
Kungrat or Durmen, late 19th–early 20th century
Silk, wool, cotton; chain stitch, cretan stitch
20 x 22 in.; 2-1/4 in. fringe
(50.8 x 55.9 cm; 5.7 cm fringe)
Fringe with warp-twined heading, embroidered and cloth bands
Pieced, printed lining
2004.259.40

Ilgich
Kungrat or Durmen, late 19th–early 20th century
Silk, wool, cotton; chain stitch
19-3/4 x 20-1/2 in.; 2-1/2 in. fringe
(50.1 x 52.1 cm; 6.3 cm fringe)
Fringe with warp-twined (tablet) heading, warp-twined (LM) edge, cloth band
Two printed linings
2004.259.41

Ilgich
Kungrat, 20th century
Silk, wool; chain stitch
25 x 21-3/4 in. (63.5 x 55.2 cm)
2004.259.42

Ilgich
Kungrat, 19th century
Silk, wool; continuous-thread couching, cross-stitch, outline stitch, chain stitch, spaced buttonhole-filling stitch
21-1/4 x 21-1/4 in. (54 x 54.6 cm)
2004.259.43

Ilgich
Possibly Durmen, late 19th–early 20th century
Silk, wool, cotton; chain stitch
21-1/2 x 21-3/4 in.; 3 in. fringe with tassels
(54.6 x 55.2 cm; 7.6 cm fringe with tassels)
Braided-net fringe, fringe with warp-twined (tablet) heading, warp-twined (LM) edge, cloth band
Pieced ikat and printed lining
2004.259.44

Ilgich
Kungrat, 20th century
Silk, cotton; open chain stitch, fishbone stitch
24 x 17-1/4 in. (61 x 43.8 cm)
Cloth band
Bag back: cotton with printed lining
2004.259.45

Ilgich
Kungrat, late 19th–early 20th century
Silk, wool, cotton, metal; needle chain stitch
20-1/2 x 20 in.; 1–1-1/4 in. fringe
(52.1 x 50.8 cm; 2.54–3.2 cm fringe)
Crocheted fringe, cloth and ikat bands
Pieced, printed lining
2004.259.46

Ilgich
Kungrat, late 19th–early 20th century
Silk, wool, cotton; chain stitch
23-1/2 x 24-1/2 in.; 4–5 in. fringe
(59.7 x 62.2 cm; 10.2–12.7 cm fringe)
Wrapped and knotted lattice treatment on pieced fringe with warp-twined (tablet) heading
Pieced, printed lining
2004.259.47

Ilgich
Kungrat, early 20th century
Wool, cotton; chain stitch, checkered chain stitch, continuous-thread couching, outline stitch, back stitch, fishbone stitch
26 x 26 in. (66 x 66 cm)
Cloth bands on reverse edge
No backing cloth, lining fragments
2004.259.48

Ilgich
Kungrat, late 19th century
Silk, wool, cotton; chain stitch
24-1/4 x 22-1/4 in.; 2-1/2 in. fringe
(61.6 x 56.5 cm; 6.3 cm fringe)
Fringe with warp-twined heading, warp-twined bands
Pieced, printed lining
2004.259.49

Ilgich
Kungrat, 20th century
Silk, wool, cotton; chain stitch
23-1/4 x 23-1/2 in.; 3-1/2 in. fringe
(59.1 x 59.7 cm; 8.9 cm fringe)
Braided-net fringe with tassels, cloth band
2004.259.50

Ilgich
Kungrat, 19th century
Wool, silk; double chain stitch, chain stitch, continuous-thread couching, outline stitch, detached chain stitch, stem-stitch filling, spaced satin stitch
24-1/2 x 23-3/4 in.; 2-3/4 in. fringe
(62.2 x 60.3 cm; 7 cm fringe)
Fringe with warp-twined (LM) heading
No backing cloth
2004.259.51

Tent hanging
Kyrgyz or Kazakh, early 20th century
Wool, silk; needle chain stitch, double chain stitch, detached chain stitch, cretan stitch
26-1/2 x 27 in. (67.3 x 68.6 cm)
No backing cloth
2004.259.52

Ilgich
Kungrat, late 19th–early 20th century
Silk, wool, cotton; chain stitch
19-1/4 x 18-3/4 in.; 2-3/4 in. fringe with tassels (48.9 x 47.6 cm; 7 cm fringe with tassels)
Braided-net fringe
Bag back: striped cloth, lined
2004.259.53

Ilgich
Kungrat, late 19th century
Silk, wool, cotton; needle chain stitch
20 x 20 in. (50.8 x 50.8 cm)
Ikat band
Bag back: striped cloth, printed and woven linings
2004.259.54

Wall hanging
Uzbek, 19th century
Silk, wool, cotton; cross-stitch, chain stitch, detached chain stitch, continuous-thread couching, fishbone stitch
24-1/2 x 23-3/4 in.; 3-1/2–4 in. fringe (62.2 x 60.3 cm; 8.9–10.2 cm fringe)
Fringes with warp-twined (LM) heading, wide embroidered bands
2004.259.55

Ilgich
Kungrat or Durmen, early 20th century
Silk, wool, cotton; chain stitch
21-1/2 x 22-1/2 in. (54.6 x 57.1 cm)
2004.259.56

Ilgich
Kungrat, 20th century
Silk, wool; chain stitch
21 x 20 in. (53.3 x 50.8 cm)
2004.259.57

Da-our
Lakai, late 19th–early 20th century
Silk, wool, cotton; chain stitch
46-1/2 x 61 in.; 7 in. fringe with tassels (118.1 x 154.9 cm; 17.8 cm fringe with tassels)
Braided-net fringe
Pieced, striped lining
2004.259.58

Kaichidon
Kungrat or Lakai, late 19th–early 20th century
Silk, cotton, wool, metal; patchwork ground; slanted buttonhole stitch, chain stitch, cretan stitch, fishbone stitch
14-1/2 x 5 in.; 6-3/4 in. tassel (36.8 x 12.7 cm; 17.1 cm tassel)
Cloth band at top
2004.259.59

Kaichidon
Dasht-i-Kipchak Uzbek, 19th century
Silk, wool, cotton; needle chain stitch
18-1/2 x 6 in. (47 x 15.2 cm)
Overcast stitching attaches front to back, cloth band at top
Striped lining
2004.259.60

At torba ilgich
Lakai, late 19th–early 20th century
Silk, wool; slanted buttonhole stitch, chain stitch, cretan stitch
22-3/8 x 22-7/8 in. (56.8 x 58.1 cm)
2004.259.61

Uuk kap ilgich
Lakai, late 19th century
Silk, wool, cotton, metal; hook chain stitch, needle chain stitch
24-1/4 x 14 in.; 13-1/2 in. tassels (61.6 x 35.6 cm; 34.3 cm tassels)
Embroidered bands
2004.259.62

At torba ilgich
Lakai, 19th century
Silk, wool; chain stitch, double chain stitch
15-3/4 x 15-1/2 in. (40 x 39.4 cm)
Cloth band
2004.259.63

Da-our fragment
Lakai, late 19th–early 20th century
Silk, wool, cotton; hook chain stitch, needle chain stitch, detached chain stitch
21-1/4 x 48-1/8 in. (53.4 x 122.2 cm)
Embroidered band at top
Pieced ikat lining
2004.259.64

Ilgich
Lakai, late 19th century
Silk, cotton; cross-stitch
23-1/4 x 22-3/4 in.; 3-1/2 in. fringe with tassels (59.1 x 57.8 cm; 8.9 cm fringe with tassels) Braided-net fringes, ikat band
Bag back: pieced, printed stripes and woven lining
2004.259.65

At torba ilgich
Lakai, late 19th century
Silk, wool, cotton; slanted buttonhole stitch, needle chain stitch
20-7/8 x 22-1/2 in. (53 x 56.5 cm)
Printed cloth band
2004.259.66

Uuk kap ilgich
Lakai, late 19th century
Silk, wool, cotton; chain stitch, double chain stitch
22 x 13-1/2 in. (55.9 x 34.3 cm)
Warp-twined (LM) edge
Pieced lining
2004.259.67

Ilgich
Possibly Durmen, late 19th–early 20th century
Silk, wool, cotton; chain stitch
22-3/4 x 22-3/4 in., including fringe (57.8 x 57.8 cm, including fringe)
Braided-net fringe, ikat band at top
Bag back: pieced, striped cloth and printed lining
2004.259.68

Uuk kap ilgich
Lakai, 20th century
Silk, cotton; chain stitch, double chain stitch
23 x 13-3/4 in.; 3 in. fringe (58.4 x 34.9 cm; 7.6 cm fringe)
Fringe with plain-weave heading (machine made), warp-twined band
Lined
2004.259.69

At torba ilgich
Lakai, late 19th–early 20th century
Silk, cotton, wool; cross-stitch, slanted buttonhole stitch, double chain stitch, chain stitch
24-1/2 x 24-1/2 in.; 3 in. fringe (62.2 x 62.2 cm; 7.6 cm fringe)
Fringe with plain-weave heading, cloth band, one Jacquard-woven band, three wide embroidered bands
Pieced, printed lining
2004.259.70

At torba ilgich
Lakai, late 19th–early 20th century
Silk, wool, cotton; slanted buttonhole stitch, chain stitch
24-1/2 x 26-1/2 in.; 2-1/4 in. fringe (62.2 x 67.3 cm; 5.7 cm fringe)
Fringe with warp-twined (LM) heading, cloth band
Pieced, printed lining
2004.259.71

At torba ilgich
Lakai, late 19th–early 20th century
Silk, wool, cotton; needle chain stitch, slanted buttonhole stitch, cretan stitch
18-1/4 x 17 in. (46.4 x 43.2 cm)
Cloth band
Pieced, printed lining
2004.259.72

At torba ilgich
Lakai, late 19th–early 20th century
Silk, wool, cotton; chain stitch, slanted buttonhole stitch
18-1/4 x 17-1/2 in. (46.4 x 44.4 cm)
Pieced, printed lining (also forms edge finish)
2004.259.73

Uuk kap ilgich
Lakai, late 19th century
Silk, wool, cotton; slanted buttonhole stitch, chain stitch
22 x 13-3/4 in. (55.9 x 34.9 cm)
Cloth band
Pieced ikat lining
2004.259.74

At torba ilgich
Lakai, late 19th–early 20th century
Silk, wool, cotton; chain stitch
21 x 21-1/2 in. (53.3 x 54.6 cm)
Handwoven band
Printed lining
2004.259.75

Ilgich
Lakai, 19th century
Silk, cotton; cross-stitch, hook chain stitch
23-3/4 x 21-1/2 in.; 3 in. fringe with tassels
(60.3 x 54.6 cm; 7.6 cm fringe with tassels)
Braided-net fringe, embroidered band
Lined
2004.259.76

Uuk kap ilgich
Lakai, late 19th–early 20th century
Silk, wool, cotton, metal; chain stitch, cross-stitch, fishbone stitch, slanted buttonhole stitch
20 x 12-1/4 in.; 12 in. tassels
(50.8 x 31.1 cm; 30.5 cm tassels)
Embroidered band at top
Striped lining
2004.259.77

At torba ilgich
Lakai, late 19th–early 20th century
Silk, wool, cotton; chain stitch
24-1/2 x 24 in.; 3-3/4 in. fringe with tassels
(62.2 x 61 cm; 9.5 cm fringe with tassels)
Braided-net fringe
Pieced ikat lining
2004.259.78

Uuk kap ilgich
Lakai, 19th century
Silk, wool, cotton; chain stitch, cross-stitch
24-1/2 x 15-7/8 in. (62.2 x 40.3 cm)
Embroidered band
Pieced, printed lining
2004.259.79

Tabaklau ilgich
Semiz, late 19th century
Silk, wool, cotton; needle chain stitch, slanted buttonhole stitch, double chain stitch
29-1/4 x 28 in.; 2 in. fringe
(74.3 x 71.1 cm; 5.1 cm fringe)
Fringe with warp-twined heading, warp-twined band
Printed cloth bands on reverse edge
No backing cloth
2004.259.80

Uuk kap ilgich
Lakai, early 20th century
Silk, cotton, metal; cross-stitch, chain stitch
24-1/4 x 15-1/2 in.; 8 in. tassels
(61.6 x 39.4 cm; 20.3 cm tassels)
Pieced, embroidered bands
Pieced lining
2004.259.81

Ilgich
Lakai, 19th century
Silk, cotton, linen; cross-stitch, double chain stitch
21-1/2 x 21-3/4 in. (54.6 x 55.2 cm)
Cloth band
Newly lined
2004.259.82

At torba ilgich
Lakai, late 19th–early 20th century
Silk, cotton; cross-stitch
20 x 20-3/8 in.; 3 in. fringe
(50.8 x 51.7 cm; 7.6 cm fringe)
Braided-net fringe, cloth band
Pieced, printed lining
2004.259.83

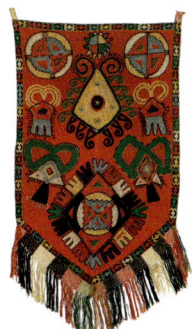

At torba ilgich
Lakai, 19th century
Silk, wool, cotton; needle chain stitch
22 x 20-1/4 in.; 2-1/2 in. fringe
(55.9 x 51.4 cm; 6.3 cm fringe)
Fringe with warp-twined heading, cloth band
2004.259.84

Uuk kap ilgich
Lakai, late 19th–early 20th century
Silk, wool, cotton; chain stitch, cross-stitch
24-1/4 x 16-1/4 in.; 5 in. fringe
(61.6 x 41.3 cm; 12.7 cm fringe)
Braided-net fringe, embroidered band
Pieced lining
2004.259.85

Uuk kap ilgich
Lakai, late 19th–early 20th century
Silk, wool, cotton; chain stitch
23 x 5-1/4 in.; 4-1/2 in. fringe
(58.4 x 13.3 cm; 11.4 cm fringe)
Braided-net fringe, embroidered band
Lined
2004.259.86

Uuk kap ilgich
Lakai, late 19th century
Silk, wool, cotton; chain stitch, slanted buttonhole stitch, cross-stitch
23 x 14 in. (58.4 x 35.6 cm)
Embroidered bands
Pieced, printed lining
2004.259.87

At torba ilgich
Lakai, 19th century
Silk, wool; needle chain stitch
21-1/2 x 23-3/4 in. (54.6 x 60.3 cm)
2004.259.88

Segusha
Lakai, 20th century
Silk, wool, cotton, metal; slanted buttonhole stitch, chain stitch, double chain stitch
19-1/2 x 36 in.; 8-1/2 in. fringe with tassels (49.5 x 91.4 cm; 21.6 cm fringe with tassels)
Braided-net fringe, cloth band
Pieced plaid lining
2004.259.89

Tent decoration
20th century
Silk, cotton, glass, metal; cross-stitch, chain stitch
9-1/2 x 3 in.; 10 in. tassels (24.1 x 7.6 cm; 25.4 cm tassels)
No backing cloth, striped lining
2004.259.90

Uuk kap ilgich
Lakai, 20th century
Silk, wool, cotton; needle chain stitch, cretan stitch
22-3/4 x 12-1/4 in. (57.8 x 31.1 cm)
Bag back: ikat print with printed lining
Pieced, printed linings
2004.259.91

Tent hanging
Dasht-i-Kipchak Uzbek, 20th century
Silk, cotton; chain stitch, detached chain stitch, cretan stitch, back stitch, open chain stitch
33 x 28-3/4 in.; 3-3/4–4 in. fringe (83.8 x 73 cm; 9.5–10.1 cm fringe)
Fringes with warp-twined (tablet) heading, knotted fringe with tassels and warp-twined (LM) heading, printed cloth band
Pieced, block-printed lining
2004.259.92

Ilgich
Kungrat, 19th century
Wool, silk; spaced buttonhole-filling stitch, checkered chain stitch, needle chain stitch
28 x 26-1/4 in.; 2-3/4 in. fringe (71.1 x 66.7 cm; 7 cm fringe)
Fringe with warp-twined heading (LM), ikat and pieced, printed band
No backing cloth
2004.259.93

Tent hanging
Kyrgyz or Kazakh, 20th century
Silk, wool, cotton; chain stitch, fishbone stitch, checkered chain stitch
35 x 25-1/4 in. (88.9 x 64.1 cm)
Cloth band
No backing cloth; pieced, printed lining
2004.259.94

Tent hanging
Kyrgyz, 19th century
Silk, cotton, metal; needle chain stitch, double chain stitch, detached chain stitch
32 x 29 in.; 3-1/2 in. fringe with tassels (81.3 x 73.7 cm; 8.9 cm fringe with tassels)
Knotted fringes with warp-twined headings, plain and printed cloth bands
Pieced, printed lining
2004.259.95

Tent hanging
Kyrgyz, late 19th–early 20th century
Wool; chain stitch, double chain stitch, detached chain stitch, running stitch
25-1/2 x 23-1/2 in. (64.8 x 59.7 cm)
Wool-felt ground cloth
2004.259.96

Altered pillow cover
Probably Hazara, Afghanistan, 20th century
Silk, cotton; cross-stitch
21-1/2 x 14-3/8 in.; 4 in. fringe (54.6 x 36.5 cm; 10.2 cm fringe)
Fringes with plain-weave and warp-twined headings, cloth band
Block-printed lining
2004.259.97

APPENDIX 1

MATERIALS AND TECHNIQUES USED IN UZBEK EMBROIDERIES

Irina V. Bogoslovskaya

Translated from the Russian by Adam Albion, Liv Bliss, and Alexandra Drobova

We will never know precisely who created the first decorative Central Asian embroidery or when, but since antiquity the people inhabiting this vast region have worn clothes and crafted household goods decorated with intricate needlework. Archaeologists have confirmed that the sources of this distinctive embroidery (including that of the city of Shahrisabs and those of the Uzbek Lakai and Kungrat) are evident in the material culture of the original inhabitants of modern Central Asia. For example, prints of textiles on ceramics from the Burgulyuk site in southern Kazakhstan reveal that inhabitants were weaving there at least as long ago as the mid-second millennium BCE.[1] Among the examples of handmade embroidery in techniques similar to *suzani* are veils that were found in the gravesite of a Hun chieftain in Noin-Ula, in northern Mongolia; they are decorated with plantlike images and depictions of horsemen. Scholars surmise that ancient Bactrians in what is now southern Uzbekistan and Tajikistan may have embroidered these in the second century BCE.[2]

In her 1961 book *Suzani Uzbekistana*, G. L. Chepelevetskaya drew direct parallels between the ornaments of nineteenth-century embroideries and murals from Khorezm and Sogdia dating to the third and fourth centuries CE. Although it is difficult to identify the specific techniques of ornamentation based on the fabric designs or individual items of clothing portrayed in those frescoes, it is possible to imagine what types of embroideries were being made at the time.

When Ruy Gonzales de Clavijo, the Spanish ambassador to the court of Tamerlane, visited Samarkand during the years 1403–6, that city was the capital of the Timurid empire. "Spread through the garden were many tents and awnings made of colored silk fabrics sewn with patchwork pieces," Clavijo observed. "Inside and outside the pavilion, textiles with colored shapes and volutes embroidered on them were cast about." As these examples suggest, the history of Central Asian embroidery is as ancient as the manufacture of silk in China or carpets in Persia.

Until the end of the 1880s, the ground cloth for embroideries was hand-spun cotton. *Buz* (*karbaz* in Tajik) and *mata* with a natural reddish tone were produced in Bukhara, Merv, Samarkand, and other urban centers. Wealthier people used half-silk and silk textiles, or *shohi*, for wall hangings. At the end of the nineteenth century, machine-made textiles were imported from England, Russia, and other countries, but a simple cotton ground cloth was preferred for most urban-made embroideries. In the late nineteenth and early twentieth centuries, the seminomadic Uzbeks of Dasht-i-Kipchak origin—the Lakai, Durmen, Kipchak, Kyrk, and Kungrat, among others—did embroidery on both manufactured and homemade cotton and wool textiles. *Ilgich* and other Lakai decorative embroideries were worked on fine local cotton cloth or imported cotton flannelette that was predominantly red or black; occasionally, they were done on a brown, dark blue, or green background.[3]

On the reverse side, *ilgich* and other hangings often had a printed cotton-fabric backing through which the needle also passed. Many of these plain, striped, and patterned backing

Fig. 1 By the end of the nineteenth century, imported factory prints were often used to line embroideries. Floral imagery was especially popular. (2004.259.79, detail)

Fig. 2 Some traditional Central Asian patterns, such as paired almonds and leaves, continued to be popular on commercially printed cloth. (2004.259.71, detail)

Fig. 3 Embroiderers also used traditional handmade textiles. Highly valued pieces, such as the famous resist-dye warp ikats of Central Asia, were recycled as linings for important embroideries. (2004.259.64, detail)

ground cloths were manufactured in Central Asian cities, such as Ferghana, Samarkand, Shahrisabs, and Tashkent. During the nineteenth century, patterned fabrics were made manually by block printing cotton cloth. Wooden stamps, called *kolyb*, were carved from hard woods, such as cherry and pear, and from soft woods, such as poplar. Some material for woodblock printing was saturated with a solution of tannin. Many fabrics were made by block printing the cloth with an alum mixture and an iron-oxide mixture and then dyeing it in a decoction of madder root (*ruyan*) to obtain both red and black colors. Often, resists were applied after this initial process, and the fabric was dipped in an indigo-dye bath to produce a more elaborate pattern with a blue color. At the end of the nineteenth century, dyers began dyeing the block-printed cloth in a solution of alizarin.

Gradually, factory-made fabrics supplied to Central Asia in large quantities by other countries, especially Russia, replaced those woven by hand. Embroiderers began using these materials, especially those with plant and flower motifs, as lining fabric (fig. 1). A typical pattern of Central Asian printed cloth has plant elements, such as paired almonds, and leaves (fig. 2). Competing manufacturers of factory-made textiles took into consideration the aesthetic preferences of each region in an effort to produce fabrics "of such types and patterns as are required by the customs and tastes of the locals."[4] Among the various ground cloths, backing, and lining fabrics on the Central Asian market at the end of the nineteenth century were plain-woven cotton (*mata*), silk warp-faced, cotton-weft ikat (*adras*) (fig. 3), fine, narrow-striped silk (*bekasab*), silk ikat (*padshoi*), and velvet (*baghmal*). Imported cotton chintz, unbleached calico, red calico, plain calico, and lightweight *mitkal* fabric also were available. According to some sources, Russian manufacturers had been producing designs with ikat-style patterns as early as the seventeenth century.

The most common ornament on chintz and on the printed cloth made in Ivanovo, the largest cotton-textile manufacturing town in Russia in the eighteenth and nineteenth centuries, was an almondlike element referred to as a "bean" or "cucumber." G. Grigor'ev described it in detail in a 1937 article.[5] According to him, this element originated as an image of a rooster or pheasant, two birds that were objects of cults in ancient times; their schematized representations were seen as protective devices (fig. 4).

Fig. 4 Some scholars believe that the ubiquitous almond (*bodom*) motif in Central Asian textiles, also referred to as the "bean" and "cucumber" pattern, originated as an image of a rooster or pheasant—ancient symbols of protection. (2004.259.73, detail)

The Uzbek, Kazakh, Kyrgyz, and Turkmen were well acquainted with the spinning of heavy yarn from sheep's wool, which involved the use of a spinning wheel (*charh*). They also used the *charh* to unwind silkworm cocoons. In the cities and certain silk-weaving centers in Uzbekistan, men generally unwound the cocoons and did the commercial weaving, although some sources mention women's participation as well. First, they steamed the cocoons in a large cauldron. Then they hammered two long pegs into the ground beside the cauldron and stretched between them a long thread with a small ring on the end. They threw the cocoons into boiling water, a handful at a time, and stirred them with a stick. As the ends of the loosened silk threads wound around the stick, a master craftsman estimated how many filaments would produce a thread of even thickness.[6] After twisting them slightly in his hands, he passed the filaments through the ring and then on to the person winding the thread: he fixed the threads and wound them on the *charh*.

Silk and woolen yarns were processed in order to remove fats or coatings and to ensure the absorption of dyes. Silk yarn was boiled in water with potash (*ishkor*), while woolen yarn was washed in warm alkaline water with soap, with lye, or with clay extracted from the mountains. The yarns were rinsed in flowing water, then squeezed and put in a boiling cauldron with dissolved dye. Madder was used to dye a red color, cochineal for crimson, indigo for blue, and delphinium (*isparyak*) flowers for black.[7] The yarn made from natural components had to be boiled and then left for one or two days. Alum was always added to the solution to fix the color after boiling. Then the colored yarn was rinsed and dried. The introduction of aniline dyes in the second half of the nineteenth century reduced the time needed to dye threads to about two hours. Because the colors produced by aniline dyes are less stable, the yarn often was not rinsed. Until the 1880s, Central Asian embroiderers used locally manufactured silk threads colored with natural dyes. In Tajikistan, silk was made in Kulyab and Kabadian. The Lakai often purchased ready-dyed silk, which they considered superior, from sellers in Bukhara. When they bought undyed silk, they colored it themselves with dyes purchased from gypsies or small-scale merchants.

The basic instruments Uzbek embroiderers used were various-sized metal needles (*nina, ninaduz, and suzan*), thimbles (*angish*), embroidery frames (*chambarak*) and hooks, and chain-stitch embroidering machines (*popur* or *popon*). (Embroidery frames and embroidering machines were only used in urban contexts.) Embroiderers used *nina* needles to create the basic embroidery pattern and the larger *ninaduz* to join strips of embroidered material. The *ninaduz* was also used to stretch fabric on the embroidery frame. Embroiderers executed chain stitch either with a needle or with an instrument specifically designed for this purpose, called a *bigiz* or *daraush*. It was shaped like an awl, only with a narrower metallic base hafted onto a wooden handle and with an iron hook on the end. Twentieth-century urban master embroiderers generally utilized the round, wood-framed *chambarak* (from the Uzbek *chambar*, meaning circle or hoop). The gold embroiderers of Bukhara, among others, still use this simple device, attaching stretched fabric to its rim before they begin stitching.

By the end of the nineteenth century, the embroidering machine called the *popur* or *popon* (from the Uzbek for embroidery) gained popularity, initially in the big cities of Uzbekistan and later across Central Asia. The chain stitch it created closely resembled the same stitch made by the *bigiz*. Soon, large quantities of machine-made embroideries were being produced in Bukhara, Tashkent, and other cities. For the most part, embroidered hangings (*suzani*) were made by machine. It was difficult, however, to produce the large ornamental forms characteristic of Samarkand and Jizzak in this way; often, the results were coarse and artistically inferior. Ultimately, Uzbek machine-made embroidery became a style in its own right, and embroiderers started using velvet and silk materials together with cotton as a base fabric.

Although almost all young women practiced the art of hand embroidery for their trousseaus, certain female artists, called *kalamkash* or *chizmakash,* were especially skilled at laying down designs, which depended upon the shape, size, and purpose of

Fig. 5 Motif outlines were frequently marked on cloth as a design aid. Embroiderers usually stitched over these general guides, but occasionally, as here, remnants of colored-thread basting outlines remained visible; note the red thread in the blue chain-stitch area. (2004.259.56, detail)

the finished piece.[8] The *kalamkash* drew the patterns to be embroidered on the fabric, rendering them by hand in ink or colored clay with a reed, steel pen, or chalk or by basting outlines in colored threads (fig. 5). Later, pattern samples were outlined or cut out of paper. The art of composition and a sense of proportion were handed down from mothers to daughters. As a rule, designers began by organizing the central area of the piece, which was separated from the border area with straight lines. The width of the border was measured using the fingers or a stick. The *kalamkash* first marked the centers and edges of the basic design elements (rosettes) with dots, and then she drew various floral shapes (bouquets, pomegranate trees, almond motifs), images of fauna (birds, animals), triangular amulets, or household items such as copper water vessels. The drawing started from the center and finished with contours.

The decorative stitches and other techniques of Lakai embroiderers share similarities with the embroidery art of many Turkic-Mongolian peoples whose origins reach back to antiquity. The consistency of ethno-cultural connections gave rise to common techniques and influenced the general development of embroidery. Nevertheless, the Lakai use certain stitches in distinctive ways, and the overall design and composition of their embroideries characterize them unmistakably as Lakai.

One of the most common stitches in Lakai embroideries, as well as in many urban pieces, is the chain stitch (*iurma* or *yo'rma*). Also one of the oldest of stitches, it appears in a Chinese embroidery found in the Pazyryk burial mound in the Altai Mountains dated to the sixth–fifth centuries BCE.[9] This stitch appears on small square and shield-shaped Lakai and Kungrat decorative embroideries (*ilgich*) (see p. 25), on bags to hold mirrors (*ainak push*), bags for carrying tea leaves (*chai khalta*), and other objects. It is done by hand, using either a needle or a *bigiz*. Chain stitching follows the outline of an embroidered element, then gradually fills the area inside right up to the edges. (An example of this technique is the *bodom*, or almond, design motif in an embroidered Lakai piece in the Robinson Collection, fig. 6). The stitches move in gentle curves from the narrow to the wider end of the almond form, drawing together toward the center until the whole space is filled. The surface thus acquires a special texture in combination with the color modulation of the silk threads. The curving rows of chain stitch create a sense of movement and rhythm. A chain of contrasting colored stitches borders each of the design elements: yellow and blue almond shapes are fringed with red, a white one with dark red, and a dark red one with green. Chain stitch was used not only to embroider over an area completely but also to delineate the delicate lines of plant forms.

Chain stitch is the most basic of the looped embroi-

Fig. 6 A skilled and aesthetically sensitive embroiderer not only creates a distinctive surface texture but also emphasizes the movement and rhythm of the pattern through specific placement of individual stitches. (2004.259.64, detail)

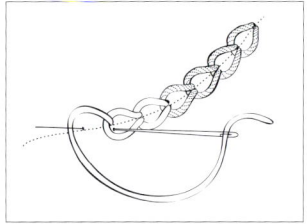

Fig. 7 Chain stitch done with a needle

dery stitches. When this stitch is made with a needle, the working thread remains on the face of the ground cloth and is looped under the tip of the needle, held down with the left thumb (fig. 7). Ideally, the needle is inserted into the same hole from which it has emerged to make the next stitch. However, this occasionally does not happen, offering a clue as to whether the stitch was made with a needle or a *bigiz* (fig. 8).

The loop created by chain stitch worked with a *bigiz* is always formed through a single

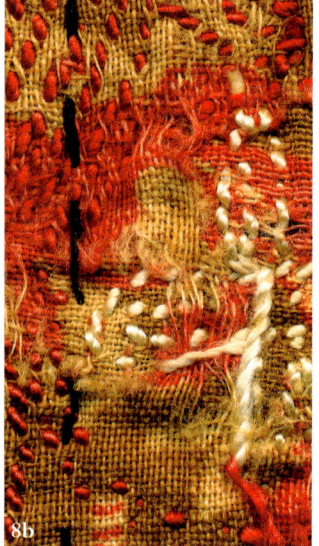

Fig. 8 Examining the face (8a) and reverse (8b) of an embroidered object reveals details about how embroiderers worked and what tools they used. Here, note the spaces between the stitches that have been worked through the ground cloth and its supporting backing cloth of a cotton print — indicating that a needle was used to make this chain stitch. (2004.259.56, details)

piercing of the fabric (fig. 9). Another difference in the stitching process is that, when a *bigiz* is used, the working thread remains on the reverse of the ground cloth. It is generally thought that a *bigiz* allows for greater precision than a needle and therefore creates a more uniform stitch (fig. 10).

A typical example of work done with chain stitch is a Durmen *ilgich* in the Robinson Collection (see p. 31). It displays many similarities with the design of a bag-shaped *ilgich* described by the late scholar Belkis Khalilovna Karmysheva:

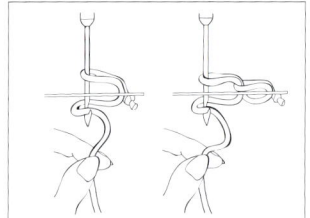

Fig. 9 Chain stitch done with a hook

> The *ilgich* is embroidered on bright red woolen baize. In the center there is a rhombus with hooks on the corners. In the corners, there are circles with a zigzag edge, inscribed with hooks and a rosette in the center of the pattern element. The free spaces between these forms are filled with multi-petaled rosettes. The combination of black and yellow, white and scarlet, green and red colors in the basic patterns makes this embroidery bright.... It is embroidered with chain stitch, and is not starched.[10]

Fig 10 Here is an example of chain stitch executed with a *bigiz*: face (10a) and reverse (10b). Note the even lines of the blue scalped border on the reverse that have been created by the uniform stitches worked through the ground cloth and its supporting backing cloth; this is a distinguishing mark of embroidery done with a *bigiz*. Chain stitch worked with a needle sometimes does not fully penetrate the backing cloth (see fig. 8b). (2004.259.25, details)

Lakai embroiderers are noted for their particularly skillful and aesthetic use of the slanted buttonhole stitch (*ilmoq yaktarafa*). Like the chain stitch it is a looped stitch, but the structure uses an open form and is a variation of the common buttonhole stitch. Instead of the "arm" of the stitch remaining perpendicular, as in the common form of the buttonhole stitch, in the Lakai variation it slants dramatically to the left of the base of the stitch, forming an acute angle (fig. 11). Particularly noteworthy is the consistency of the closely spaced stitches and their extreme slant, both of which reinforce the energy of the pattern (fig. 12).

Many artisans in Uzbekistan created embroideries using a continuous-thread couching stitch called *basma*, which is also known as *suzani* stitch (fig. 13). Base threads (*nakh*) were laid onto the surface of the pattern, horizontally or vertically, and anchored to the ground fabric with one or more securing stitches, depending on the length of the laid thread. These smaller anchoring stitches were placed under one another to form rectilinear horizontal rows. The intervals between the anchoring stitches done in *basma* style differ, ranging from large to barely visible. These variations depended upon the embroiderer's expertise and diligence and especially upon the embroidery traditions of the given region.

Fig. 11 Slanted buttonhole stitch (*ilmoq yaktarafa*)

Several varieties of *basma* stitch are found across Uzbekistan. Although executed identically, their different appearances depend upon their length and direction. The embroidery scholar M. Rassudova described four basic types:

a) *zakhmash daroz*: the laying of the base threads with oblong quilting-type stitches (up to three millimeters);

b) *zakhmash lunda*: the laying of the base threads with very short "round" quilting-type stitches;

c) the laying of the base threads with double quilting-type stitches of typical *basma* length (two stitches made next to each other with little distance between them, the next two at some distance); and

d) *donacha* or *zaraduzi*: the laying of the base threads with "grains." (Each small quilting-type stitch of the successive row is laid between two quilting-type stitches of the preceding base thread.)[11]

Fig. 12 The Lakai are particularly noted for their refined use of the slanted buttonhole stitch. The choice of the stitch is carefully coordinated to enhance the energy and power of the design. (2004.259.77, detail)

Embroiderers in Bukhara, Nurata, and Shahrisabs used more freely placed, loosely twisted base threads that were tightly drawn to the material with anchoring stitches. In Samarkand, where the silk for embroidery was usually tightly twisted, the base thread was stretched tightly and laid flat on the material, and the anchoring stitches created a relief texture.

Another type of continuous-thread couching is *kanda-khayol*, with its characteristic elongated anchoring stitches. In one variation of this stitch, after the embroiderer creates the first row, subsequent rows of anchoring stitches are connected as the work continues (fig. 14). As with all stitches, its appearance varies considerably depending upon the structure of the thread, that is,

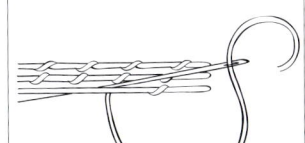

Fig. 13 Continuous-thread couching stitch (*basma*)

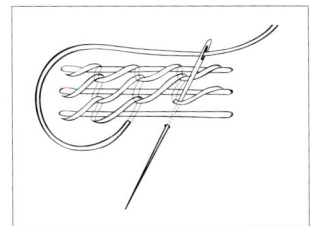

Fig. 14 Continuous-thread couching stitch variation (*kanda-khayol*)

Fig. 15 Both nomadic people and urban dwellers appreciated decorative cross-stitch embroidery. (2004.259.11, detail)

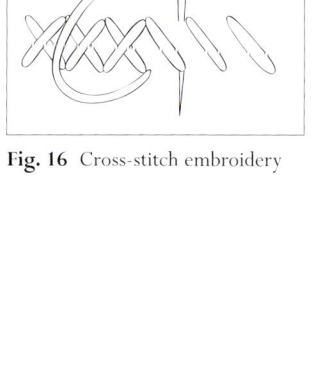

Fig. 16 Cross-stitch embroidery

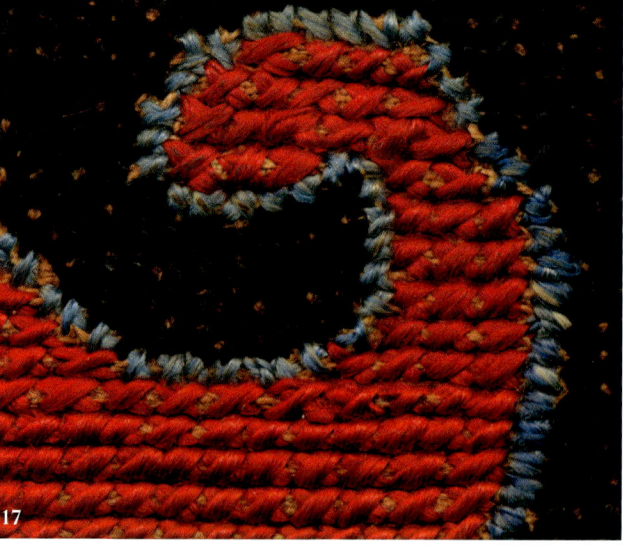

Fig. 17 Close examination of examples of Central Asian cross-stitch reveals a working method that involves working entire rows as a unit, rather than one stitch at a time, to complete the full cross of the stitch (see fig. 16). (2004.259.81, detail)

whether it is floss, tightly twisted single, or plied.

Yet another stitch, the *chinda-khayol* (also known as the *duruiya*, or double-darning stitch), appears most commonly on small items, such as kerchiefs or towels; it is executed so that both sides look the same. Stitches of equal size are laid as close to one another as possible, in neat rows. To make this stitch, the embroiderer directs the needle either toward or away from herself along the fabric in a straight line. When she reaches the edge of a pattern element, she turns the cloth 180 degrees and continues filling the surface of the pattern element in another direction. To increase the density of the surface covering, the embroiderer inserts the needle in the same perforations.

The *khomduzi* or *khomirak* is a simple, double-sided satin stitch. The embroiderer places the base threads either straight or at an angle (with the right end pointing upward). This stitch was typically used to embroider small items that would be seen on both sides.

Iroki cross-stitch, which distinguishes some of the most exquisite Lakai embroideries as well as being widely used in Shahrisabs embroidery, is both difficult to execute and greatly admired (fig. 15; see also pp. 91, 126).

When executing this stitch, Uzbek embroiderers most often lay threads first in one direction and then in the other, thus creating cruciform stitches (figs. 16, 17).

In another visual variation that Uzbek embroiderers consider a half cross-stitch (*kuklyama*), which technically is a type of continuous-thread couching, the embroiderer first lays long base threads vertically, from the bottom edge of a pattern element to the upper edge, and then places small regular stitches at an angle across each base thread from top to bottom to create the appearance of a cross-stitch. The next base thread is laid on the left side of the preceding base thread.

Lakai embroiders frequently do cross-stitch embroidery without using any previously prepared pattern. They either memorize the patterns or improvise them on a *buranboi*, a lightly starched, handmade gauze. Once the main motifs are embroidered in cross-stitch, the background also is embroidered (see p. 101).

In all urban areas, a *kalamkash* typically drew the contours of the pattern on the cloth in pencil or ink. In Shahrisabs, densely patterned cross-stitch embroidery decorated money pouches (*pul khalta*), mirror bags (*aina khalta*), salt pouches (*tuz khalta*), special cloths on which food was served (*dastarkhan*), horsecloths, *suzani*, robes (*khalat*), and even shoes. These cross-stitched items were made for ceremonial gift-giving, as presents for the representatives of the court of the emir, the nobility, and ambassadors. Embroiderers executed the most intricate and difficult stitches on textiles of the highest quality.

Other stitches used by Uzbek embroiderers include several chain-stitch variations: half cross-stitch (fig. 18), open chain stitch (*ilmoq*) (fig. 19), double chain stitch (fig. 20), and checkered chain stitch (which carries two threads in one needle) (fig. 21). Double chain is used as both an outline and as a filling stitch (figs. 22, 23), whereas open chain (fig. 24) and checkered

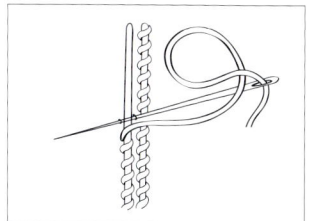

Fig. 18 Half cross-stitch embroidery

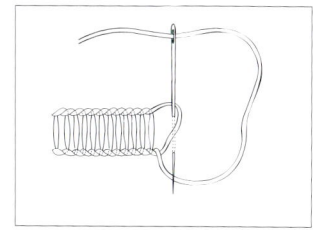

Fig. 19 Open chain stitch embroidery (*ilmoq*)

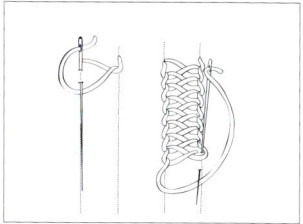

Fig. 20 Double chain stitch embroidery

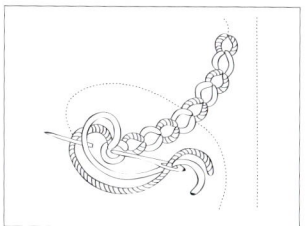

Fig. 21 Checkered chain stitch embroidery

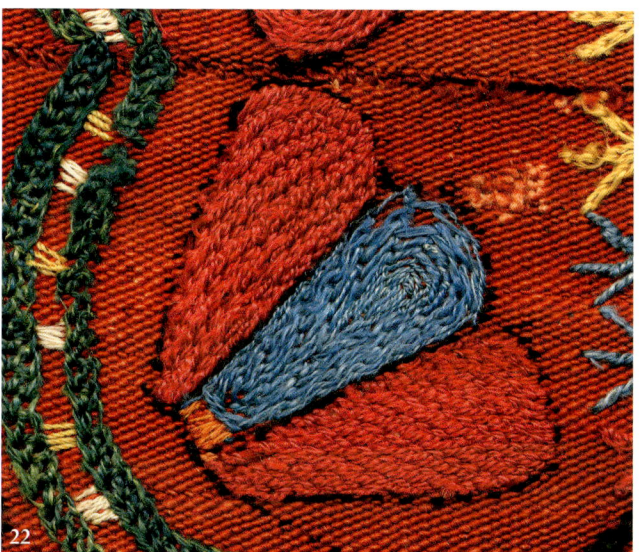

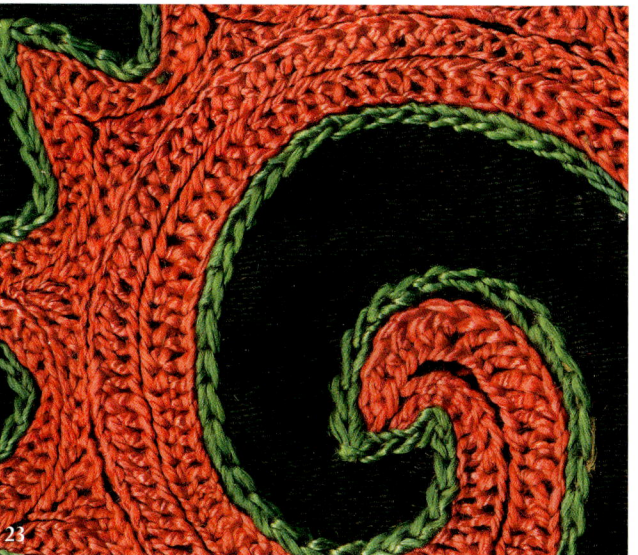

Fig. 22 A number of stitches can be used as an outer line of a motif or as a filling stitch. (2004.259.51, detail)

Fig. 23 Double chain stitch is sometimes mistaken for a cretan stitch, particularly when used as a filling. The ridge on its outer edges helps distinguish it from other stitches. (2004.259.69, detail)

Fig. 24 Sometimes various stitches are employed on a single embroidery. Seen here is a red open chain stitch and multicolored continuous-thread couching with a sienna chain-stitch outline. (2004.259.10, detail)

Fig. 25 Checkered chain stitch is most often seen on urban embroideries. However, some Kungrat women used it occasionally on their wool-ground *ilgich*. (2004.259.48, detail)

chain (fig. 25) are primarily outlining stitches. Another variation of alternating colors that uses the traditional chain stitch, and is frequently employed for guard borders on *ilgich*, reminded the embroiderers of running water and so is called the *su* (water) pattern (see fig. 10a). Cretan stitch (*chamak*) and fishbone stitch are also occasionally used.

The Lakai sometimes supplement their embroideries by adding tassels with golden threads in order to emphasize both the value of the object and the socioeconomic status of its owner. As Karmysheva noted, "Lakai embroideries were valued [for their artistic merits] and quite often were bought by members of other Uzbek tribes and also by Tajiks."[12]

There is no doubt that the Lakai, Kungrat, and Shahrisabs embroideries represented in the Jack A. and Aviva Robinson Collection comprise an important resource for scholars seeking information about the technical and artistic methods used by these exceptional craftspeople, adding substantially to our understanding of the broad range of styles and techniques found in Central Asian embroidery.

NOTES

1. A. I. Terenozhkin, "Monuments of Material Culture on the Tashkent Canal," *Transactions of the Uzbek Branch of the Academy of Sciences of the USSR*, no. 9 (1940): 32–33.

2. K. V. Trever, *Pamyatniki Greko-Baktriiskogo iskusstva* [Monuments of Greco-Bactrian Art], Izdatel'stvo Akademii Nauk SSSR [Academy of Science of the USSR], (Moscow and Leningrad: n.p., 1940): 141–48, tables 39, 40, 42; *Vseobshchaya istoriya iskusstva* [A General History of Art], vol. 1 (Moscow: n.p., 1956), 412; *Istoriya Uzbekskoi SSR* [The History of the Uzbek SSR], vol. 1, no. 1 (Tashkent: n.p., 1955), 92.

3. Many inhabitants of Central Asia, the Caucasus, and Siberia prefer a saturated dark red color. Generally, Turkic people considered scarlet (*al*) the color of the guardian angel. The semantic root of the word for red used by the Kyrgyz is connected with fire; ancient Chinese associated it with the south, Turkmen with the color of pomegranates. For Karakalpaks, there is a similarity between the words *kyz* (girl) and *kyzyl* (red). The red background of Lakai embroidery was dominant because of what was believed to be the color's protective significance.

4. *Tsentral'nii Gosudarstvennii Istoricheskii Arkhiv SSSR* [Central State Historical Archive of the USSR] (n.d., n.p), fol. 22, op. 3, 43.

5. G. Grigor'ev, "Tus-Tupi," *Art* 1 (1937): 124–33.

6. S. P. Rusyaikina, *Narodnaya odezhda Tadjikov Garmskoi oblasti Tadjikskoi SSR* [Folk Costume of the Tajiks of Garm District of the Tajik SSR], Central Asia Ethnographical Collection, vol. 2 (Moscow: n.p., 1959), 145–46.

7. Ivan Krauze, "Zametki o krasil'nom iskusstve tuzemtsev" [Notes on the Painters' and Dyers' Art among the Indigenous Inhabitants], *Russkii Turkestan: Sbornik izdannyi po povodu politekhnicheskoi vystavki. vypusk vtoroi. Stat'i po etnografii, tekhnike, sel'skomu khozyaistvu i estestvennoi istorii* [Russian Turkestan: An Anthology Published for the Polytechnic Exhibition. No. 2: Essays on Ethnography, Manufacture, Agriculture, and Natural History], (Moscow: n.p., 1872), 209–12.

8. The term derives from the Uzbek *chizma* (sketch) and the Tajik *kashidan* (draw); cf. the Kazakh word *syzgysh* or *syzgych* (draftsman).

9. S. I. Rudenko, *Gorno-Altaiskie nakhodki i skify* [Discoveries in the High Altai and the Scyths] (Moscow and Leningrad: n.p., 1952), 82–84.

10. Belkis Khalilovna Karmysheva, "Lokaiski mapramatchi i ilgichi" [Lakai *Mapramach and Ilgich*], in *Soobshchenii Respublikanskogo istoriko-kraevedsheskogo musea Tadjikskoi SSR* [Report of the Republican Historical-Folk Arts Museum of the Tadjik SSR] (Stalinabad: n.p., 1955): 149–50.

11. M. Rassudova, *Uzbekskii khudozhestvennii shov* [Uzbek Artistic Stitches], (Tashkent: n.p., 1961), 12.

12. Karmysheva, "Lokaiski mapramatchi i ilgichi": 149.

APPENDIX II

EDGE TREATMENTS ON UZBEK EMBROIDERIES IN THE ROBINSON COLLECTION

Frieda Sorber

in collaboration with Lotus Stack

The edge treatments, or trimmings, found on many textiles serve to frame these objects and draw attention to their shape and design. Across Central Asia, as throughout the Islamic world, embroiderers in urban and rural areas alike create elaborate trimmings that both adorn and strengthen the textiles they make for daily and ceremonial use. Among some groups, these trimmings even carry spiritual connotations and are believed to shield their owners from harmful supernatural forces. However, many researchers view textile edge treatments as marginal, almost extrinsic to the central designs. At the Minneapolis Institute of Arts, on the other hand, the edge treatments of Uzbek embroideries in the Jack A. and Aviva Robinson Collection are seen as integral to the designs and have been analyzed in detail.

Fig. 1 From bottom to top: V-shaped structures, designs, and textures are prominent on many edge treatments. Fringe with tablet-woven, warp-twined heading structure (structure); integral, loop-manipulated warp-twined structure (structure and design); and three rows of chain-stitch embroidery (texture). (2004.259.37)

Visual Techniques

Almost all the embroideries in the Robinson Collection have multiple borders consisting of edges integral to the object and one or more bands and fringes that have been applied to the object. A characteristic of the multiple borders is the prevalence of V-shaped designs and textures created by warp-twined structures that echo the chain stitch and chain-stitch variations used in many of the pieces in the collection (fig. 1).

This V-shaped feature is not limited to Uzbekistan but can also be found in edge treatments ranging from China to North Africa and from India to Northern Europe. Doubtless this is because they are both

Fig. 2 *2a.* The ends of each braid are tied in a knot to form a simple tassel. *2b.* Pictured is an example of alternating simple and ornate tassels at the end of a braided fringe. *2c.* The ends of several braids are combined to form a single tassel. (a. 2004.259.35; b. 2004.259.44; c. 2004.259.53)

visually pleasing and relatively easy to accomplish, especially when done with a continuous thread and a hooked iron *bigiz*. (See "Materials and Techniques Used in Uzbek Embroideries," pp. 185–86.) Executed in techniques such as loop manipulation and tablet weaving, they provide sturdy, warp-twined structures that strengthen and help preserve the edges.[1]

Openwork, netlike structures are frequently — and incorrectly — termed *crochet* in the literature on Central Asian textiles.[2] Almost all such structures on items in the Robinson Collection are braided with free-hanging ends that are incorporated into a variety of tassels, executed in styles ranging from simple to ornate (fig. 2). Some textiles have larger tassels at the corners; these consist of bundles of threads wrapped into multicolored cords, knots, and multiple small heads with fringed skirts (fig. 3).

Fig. 3 *3a.* Large tassels are sometimes used to add further embellishment to pentagonal *uuk kap ilgich*. *3b.* The top (or head) of an elaborate tassel often has several components. Shown here are four "Turk's head" knots and a centered wrapped element. The fringed skirt is composed of plied threads. (2004.259.24)

Techniques

Frequently, a variety of techniques are used to embellish the edges of a single piece — chain stitch, cross-stitch, loop manipulation, and tablet weaving being among the ones most favored. Except for tablet weaving, all these methods can produce edging that is integral to the object and that also can be made separately and applied later. But no matter what technique is employed, edge treatments are always vital to the design concept.

Embroidered bands are typically made from narrow strips of embroidered fabric and are mitered as they are applied to the corners. Occasionally, however, the fabric strip is cut to shape, and no mitering is required (fig. 4). Warp-twined structures comprised both of twined warps and added wefts are frequently used to make edge embellishments. Depending on the technique used (i.e., loop manipulation or tablet weaving), warp-twined structures can also be integral to the object or can be made separately and attached later.[3]

Loop manipulation requires two people working together. One of them holds a number of loops over his or her fingers and stretches them between himself or herself and the coworker. The person holding the loops creates warp sheds by switching the looped threads between the fingers of one hand and those of the other hand (fig. 5).

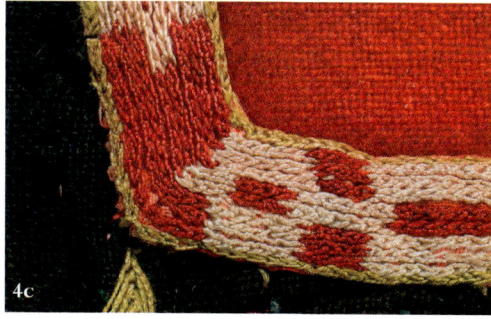

Fig. 4 *4a.* Narrow strips of fabric are embroidered to form decorative bands. Note the printed design of the ground fabric where the embroidery stops. *4b.* This detail shows a mitered corner of an embroidered band. *4c.* This detail shows a shaped embroidered band. (a. 2004.259.40; b. 2004.259.81; c. 2004.259.40)

Fig. 5 The loop manipulator moves thread loops from one hand to the other.

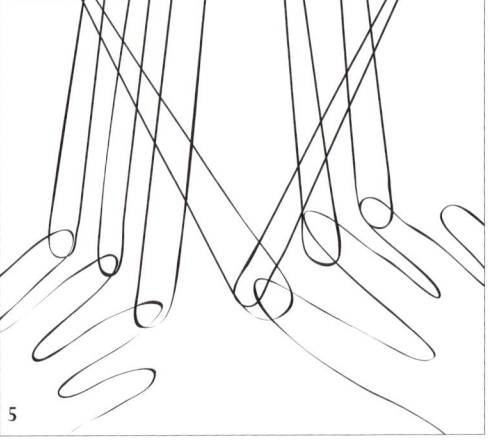

Fig. 6 The weft thread is sewn into the fabric after each shed change. (2004.259.37, detail of reverse)

Fig. 7 7a. *(face)* When the white threads are not active elements of the design, they float on the reverse *(see below)* In addition to the loop-manipulated lower border, a separate cross-stitched band has been added to this embroidery. 7b. *(reverse)* When a warp thread is passive, that is, not integral to the warp-twined structure, it floats on the reverse (or back) of the band. (2004.259.31)

To make a band or a fringe, the coworker inserts a weft into each shed. Two threads make a twined cord.[4] Adjacent pairs of threads make alternating, slanted S-shaped and Z-shaped cords that also create the V forms seen in Figure 1. For both decorative embroideries and clothing, an integral, loop-manipulated edge treatment is sometimes desired; in those cases, each weft thread is sewn into the fabric after it has passed through the shed. This produces a distinctive stitching pattern on the reverse of the fabric (fig. 6). Since this kind of trimming is integral to the object, cutting or removing it would destroy the warp-twined structure.

The warp-pattern designs are often made by using loops in contrasting colors and structurally integrated in either an active or a passive manner, depending on the requirements of the specific pattern. When a thread is passive, that is, not integral to the structure of the embroidery, it floats on the back of the band (fig. 7). The warp threads should be kept under tension throughout the process (fig. 8). However, the quality of both the design and structure can be compromised when the distance between the two workers is too great, and the person manipulating the loops cannot see the design as the "weaver" inserting the weft strives to secure it. This doubtless explains many of the variations and "errors" in some of the Robinson Collection pieces (fig. 9).[5]

Tablet weaving, a technique used extensively in the Islamic world, is done on narrow looms (fig. 10). The warps are inserted into four holes near the corners of square tablets made of bone, wood, or cardboard (fig. 11). Sets of tablets — the exact number determined by the complexity of the design and the desired width of the band — are placed next to one another. The warps form cords, each made up of four threads. This structure is thicker and sturdier than a loop-manipulated band, whose cords consist of two threads.[6] The cords with tablet-woven borders in most of the Robinson Collection pieces alternate in S and Z forms, creating a V texture. One characteristic of tablet weaving is that warps fixed in a loom twine both where the weaver inserts the weft and behind the tablets. The result is that, at some point during the weaving process, the threads behind the tablets become tangled, and the direction of the twine has to be reversed into the unwanted twine. This reversal also affects the band's pattern, creating alternating

V and diamond forms (fig. 12). On most bands in the collection, between twenty and thirty inches were woven before the twine had to be reversed. The tablet-woven borders on all the Robinson embroideries were made separately from the central piece. The wefts never penetrate the fabric, but they often form a fringe. Thus these bands and fringes can be detached and reused on other textiles.[7]

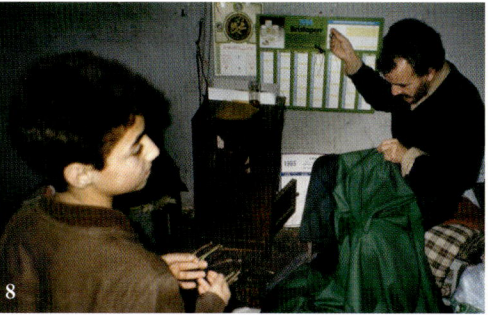

Fig. 8 To keep the warp threads under tension, the loop manipulator (*left*) and the "weaver"/stitcher often must work some feet apart, as in this workshop in Fez, Morocco. That factor can affect the quality of the work.

Wider fringes with short tassels and an interlaced net band are quite common in Uzbek textiles. These braided-net fringes are almost always made specifically for the embroidered work at hand.[8] The net consists of flat, four-strand braids that change from a one-over-one to a paired, two-over-two thread sequence when the braids interlace. Although the braided-net fringes in the Robinson Collection appear to be similar overall, a detailed analysis, particularly of the starting area, reveals certain differences (fig. 13). Presumably, one or two heading cords were stretched horizontally to give the worker a base from which to proceed. The decision about whether to start with a knot, a four-strand braid, or an eight-strand paired braid probably reflects the workers' individual preferences.[9]

Fig. 9 When making this white and black loop-manipulated border, the "weaver" had difficulty creating a corner while at the same time coordinating the warp-twined structure and design. Notice the blue weft elements that are visible in places; these should be entirely hidden by the warp-faced design. Erratic quality in some pieces can be traced to a too-great distance between loop manipulator and weaver. (2004.259.37)

A few bands in the collection were probably woven on a loom in a warp-faced plain weave, their designs created by exchanging different-colored warps.[10]

Particularly ornate tassels are made separately and used to adorn *uuk kap ilgich* and other pentagonal embroidered panels.[11] All the tassels on these pieces are structurally related. They have long heads, consisting of wrapped cords and knots that often branch out to form multiple smaller heads. A simple twined fringe makes a skirt (see fig. 3). When small glass beads are available, the Lakai, in particular, are quite fond of incorporating them into the ends of skirt fringes. To make them, over-twisted threads are twined into a fringe, and a single thread is woven in to anchor the base of each twisted loop. The loops, which stand out over a hidden base consisting of a wrapped piece of fabric, are fastened to the base with a few stitches (fig. 14). Heads consist of bundles of string that are wrapped with silk and gold thread. Short lengths of gold thread and silk are wrapped around a core, which in turn is wrapped around the bundle of strings. In some cases, the bundle is divided into four separate bundles and wrapped to make knots.[12]

Fig. 10 Throughout the Islamic world, tablet weaving is done on narrow looms. The several tablets that this Syrian weaver needed to make this simple band can be seen on the warp threads to his right.

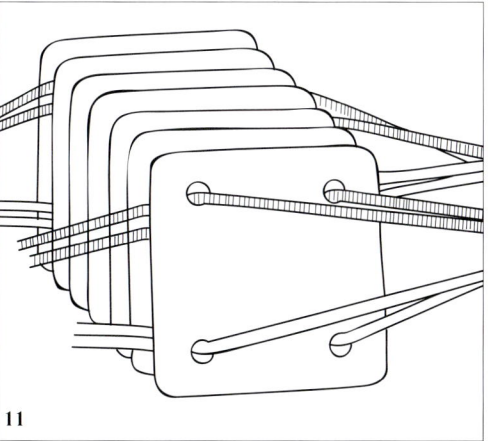

Fig. 11 Warp threads are inserted into all four holes of each tablet. The rotation of the tablets creates specific sheds and controls the design and twined structure of the band-weaving process.

Fig. 12 In many types of tablet weaving, the direction of the twist of the threads must be reversed. This structural change, often an indicator of the technique being used to make the band, also affects the design. (2004.259.33)

Fig. 13 Most braided net fringes have a similar basic structure, but the relationship to the heading cord to the initial braids can be quite varied. *13a.* Shown here is the use of four-strand braids on a heading cord of two elements. *13b.* The twist of the braided threads affects the direction of the braids. *13c.* Seen here is the use of eight strand braids on a heading cord. *13d.* Eight strands are knotted onto the heading cord before braiding begins. (a. 2004.259.65; b. 2004.259.65; c. 2004.259.65; 2004.259.86)

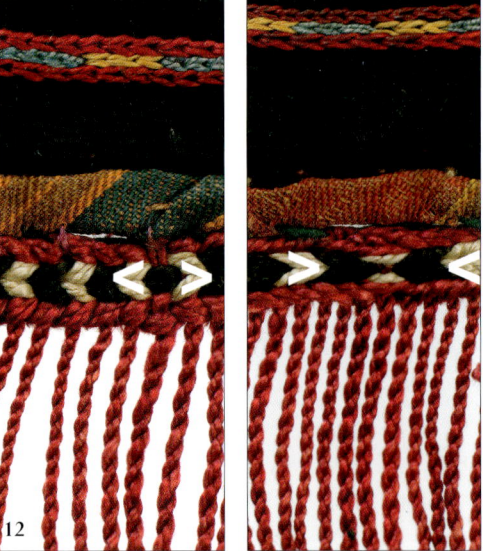

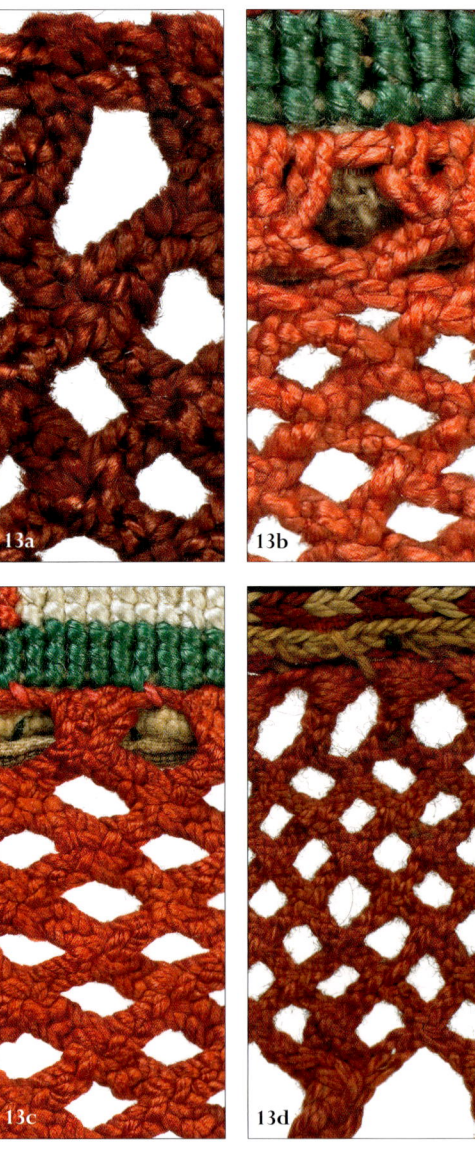

Workmanship

The quality of workmanship on the edge treatments of the Uzbek embroideries in the Robinson Collection ranges from painstaking care that matches and enhances the visual impact of an individual piece to haphazard patchworks of odds and ends of fringe. For example, a few items have up to five pieces of fringe that are roughly the same color and width. In a few cases, worn-out fringes may have been replaced by whatever bits and pieces were at hand. To facilitate the recycling procedure, these fringes have been dyed, usually dark green or black, hiding the original colors.[13] By contrast, other edge treatments have been carefully planned to match the color distribution and thread sheen and proportion of the embroidery. In these, it is clear that the size and shape of the embroidery have been taken into careful consideration. For some embroidered edges, the fabric has been cut to match the shape and size of the object, avoiding the need to make the mitered corners that accompany trimmings from the straight pieces of fabric (see fig. 4c). Depending on the method used, corners are more or less made to shape on some of these objects (see fig. 9). For instance, in bag faces and other objects where the fringe hangs on a diagonal, the first two or three braids were made slightly longer before the actual network was begun. Although this is not readily apparent in the finished piece, it allows the fringe to drape better.[14]

The thrifty use of valuable silk, cotton, and wool threads and fabrics seems to have been of paramount importance for the makers of all these trims. For example, even the smallest scraps of worn-out cotton could be put to use in the invisible cores of tassel heads (see fig. 14). Any sturdy thread could be used to wrap with more valuable silk and metallic thread for the stems and knots of tassels. Gold thread was often used in lengths only a few inches long.[15] Also, remnants of silk were sometimes knotted to make a weft for fringes.[16]

Social and Cultural Context

Analysis of the edge treatments on the Uzbek embroideries in the Robinson Collection raises various questions regarding their cultural context and significance. Even though many Asian and Western collections contain a wealth of embroidered objects that would seem to testify to the importance Central Asian cultures attach to proper finishes and embellishments, there is almost no Western literature available about them.[17]

Due to the paucity of fieldwork data from either Tajikistan or Uzbekistan, it is hard to determine who made the various elements that embellish the edges of the embroideries in the Robinson Collection. What was the role of women in the production of these pieces relative to that of men? Was there an interaction between rural and urban communities that would allow for the general purchase or special commission of edge treatments?

No firm conclusions about gender-specific roles related to embroidery production can be drawn from a purely visual analysis of these edge treatments. Since women make the central objects, it seems logical to assume that they embroider the separate edges as well.[18] Loop manipulation in the Far East, Europe, and North Africa is often done by women, but in Islamic North Africa the warp-twined edges utilizing a weft are mostly done by men; therefore, assumptions about gender specialization can be tenuous. We know that a century ago the Hunza women of what is now northwestern Pakistan wore hats with warp-twined edges embroidered and assembled by women.[19] However, given the absence of documentation, it is hazardous to assume these working patterns are the same for Uzbek women.

Few tools are needed for either embroidery or warp-twined loop manipulation, and both activities can be done in one's home or while visiting relatives or neighbors. Working on a piece of embroidery affords a woman productive moments when there are no pressing domestic demands, such as caring for children or doing household chores. But it is less easy, and more time consuming, to become involved in manipulating a set of long loops.[20]

In much of the Islamic world, tablet weaving is typically a male activity, practiced chiefly in urban settings. If that is also the case in Tajikistan and Uzbekistan, men could have made the tablet-woven fringes in the Robinson Collection after the central embroidery was finished. However, we know that females once did the tablet weaving in the towns and cities of Georgia.[21] Weaving is also a female activity in rural Turkey.[22] But again, because there is scant hard information available, it is not even possible to speculate on patterns of production for edge treatments such as those in this collection. Were several people involved in making a given piece? Did rural and urban, or male and female, worlds interact to produce a particular object? Did rural women commission and buy tablet-woven bands from urban specialists to apply to the edges of their embroidery? Was the embroidery taken to specialists to have edge finishes applied? Did the women who made the embroidery also make the separate tassels, or did male or female specialists produce them? (The fact that threads used in the embroidery and in the tassel usually do not match may indicate that specialist tassel makers were involved.) We simply do not know the answers to these various questions.

However, from the visual evidence alone, one fact seems abundantly clear: edge treatments were vital elements of almost every Uzbek textile. The care taken to plan and implement trimmings that would match the colors and shape of the central embroidery demonstrates that, for both makers and users, these items added substantially to the status and significance of the object.

Fig. 14 Note the economical use of materials: Small sections of silk and metal thread are wrapped around a core of cotton thread and tied into "Turk's-head" knots. Scrap fabric is used as the core of the tassel skirt to create a fuller, more opulent look; the plied threads would normally cover this element. (2004.259.77; detail)

NOTES

1. Westerners often mistake these structures for knitting, based on surface appearance. However, knitted structures consist of interlinked loops formed by a continuous thread.

2. Openwork crochet as a technique for edge treatments on Central Asian embroideries seems to have emerged only in the twentieth century. Just one piece in the Robinson Collection (2004.259.46) has a crocheted edge.

3. For a general description of the differences between tablet weaving and loop manipulation, see Noémi Speiser, *A Manual of Braiding* (Basel: the author, 1983), 118–22. On some objects in the Robinson Collection, the loops remain intact at the end of a band, proving that loop manipulation was used. Examples include: 2004.259.38 (top-right corner), 2004.259.41, and 2004.259.43.

4. Moroccan tailors often use eight loops manipulated by eight fingers to create edge treatments and to connect two pieces of fabric. Due to a lack of documentation, it is not possible to determine just how the loops of Central Asian textiles have been manipulated. Often, nine or more loops are used. Experiments in Stockholm during the 1920s showed that several people working together could manipulate fifteen loops at a time. While doing field research in Morocco during the 1980s, the author saw cases in which one person handled thirteen loops simultaneously.

5. Although they once were prevalent from Central Asia to North Africa and Europe, loop-manipulated edges have rarely caught the attention of researchers. In Europe the technique vanished, almost without a trace, during the seventeenth century. Loop manipulation was often practiced by tailors and is still used in Morocco to connect and trim fabrics. The technique has been employed extensively in Central Asia, but it has rarely been documented there. For wider bands, more than one person may have manipulated the loops. This practice was known in Europe but was not documented in North Africa or Asia.

6. Tablet weaving can also be done with two warps per tablet, but such was not the case with any of the objects under discussion.

7. Good examples in the Robinson Collection are 2004.259.37 and 2004.259.97, in which both tablet-woven bands and loop-manipulated fringes were employed.

8. In the literature on textiles, braided-net fringes are often described as crochet. However, they consist of multiple interlaced threads, unlike true crochet, in which a hook is used to make a structure that consists of the interlinking loops of one continuous thread.

9. See, for example, Robinson Collection objects 2004.259.31, 2004.259.65, 2004.259.76, 2004.259.85, and 2004.259.89.

10. See Robinson Collection object 2004.259.75. The warps float at the back of the fabric on items where they are not needed for the design.

11. See Robinson Collection objects 2004.259.24, 2004.259.59, 2004.259.62, 2004.259.77, 2004.259.81, and 2004.259.90.

12. The tassels in the collection all appear to have been planned carefully so as to avoid loose ends wherever possible. This suggests that their makers produced them one at a time, instead of preparing loose elements for several tassels before assembling them, as workers in Western workshops would normally do.

13. See Robinson Collection objects 2004.259.37 and 2004.259.51.

14. This effect can be seen in Robinson Collection object 2004.259.89.

15. Gold thread was constructed of a gilded metal strip wound around a core thread of linen, cotton, or silk.

16. In Robinson Collection objects 2004.259.25 and 2004.259.97, threads of different colors were knotted together without trying to hide the knots in the heading of the fringe, so as to utilize the available silk to the fullest.

17. Here, my research on textile trimmings in Morocco during the 1980s and 1990s seems relevant. In Morocco, edge treatments are often at least as valuable, in terms of purchase price and/or production time, as the main embroidery itself. See Frieda Sorber, "Trimmings in Fez, Morocco," paper presented at *Textiles in Daily Life*, third biennial symposium, Textile Society of America, Seattle Art Museum, September 24–26, 1992 (see www.textilesociety.org/symposia _1992.htm).

18. This assumption was corroborated in conversations between Lotus Stack and the Lakai embroiderer Aimkhal Ernazarova in Hissar, Tajikistan, May 2005.

19. Jürgen Frembgen, *Stickereien aus dem Karakoram* [Embroideries from the Karakoram] (Munich: Staatliches Museum für Völkerkunde 1998), 55.

20. Outsiders would not often see women embroidering. The arrival of guests, and the accompanying demands of hospitality, would bring an interruption to textile-related tasks. And because few tools are needed for embroidery, there would be little immediately visible evidence of the labor involved. Thus ethnologists or anthropologists would not necessarily notice them.

21. M. Bartels, *Proceedings of the Berlin Association for Anthropology, Ethnology, and Prehistory* (Berlin: Von A. Asher and Company, 1898), 329–32.

22. Peter Collingwood, *The Techniques of Tablet Weaving* (New York: Watson-Guptill, 1982), 49, ills. 25, 26.

GLOSSARY

Included here are significant Uzbek and Persian terms used in this book. Definitions have been limited to the simplest meaning of each term, and transliterated spellings are those most often used in recent literature on Central Asian textiles.

A

adras: silk warp-faced, cotton-weft ikat

ainak push: term widely used in Uzbekistan and Tajikistan for small, rectangular and square embroideries on cloth; also called mirror bags

alacha: handwoven, striped cotton fabric

angish: thimble

apran: felt floor covering

at torba ilgich: square *ilgich* without a triangular flap

atlas: silk satin ikat fabric

B

baghmal: velvet

basma: style of continuous-thread couching embroidery stitch; also called *suzani* stitch

basmachi: derogatory name applied to anti-Soviet resistance movement of the early Soviet period

beg: chief or ruler; an honorifc

bekasab: narrow-striped silk

beshik: cradle

bigiz: hooked iron embroidery tool with a wooden handle; used for making chain stitch; also called *daraush*

bogich: wide woolen tent band

boibosh: headress of kerchiefs wrapped around a *kiigich*; worn by Kungrat women

bokche: Turkoman bread bag

bosaga: hinged wooden door of the yurt; also called *erganak*

bosh: turbanlike head covering consisting of a small cap surrounded by many tightly wrapped scarves; sometimes also called *sallabosh*

bugzhoma: large, envelope-shaped bag, made of embroidered cloth or plain-woven wool fabric, used to store clothing; also, triangular or V-shaped embroidered cloth decorations for the *chuk* (called *segusha* in Afghanistan)

buranboi: lightly starched, handmade gauze used by embroiderers as backing cloth

buz: handwoven, tabby unbleached cotton cloth; also called *karbaz*

C

caroq: technique of piecing fabric or felt to make patchwork; Uzbek patchwork cloth

chachak: silk fringe

chai khalta: bag for carrying tea and other small personal items

chaishab: medium-to-large-sized hanging

chamak: cretan stitch

chambarak: embroidery frame

changarok: large, spoked wheel atop the yurt that holds the wooden poles forming the dome

char-chiroq: four-wicked lamp

charh: spinning wheel

charigich: yurt door made of a piece of felt tied to the frame with a woolen rope

chekmen: robe made of wool or coarse, home-made cloth

chii: reed mats used on the side of a yurt

chillia: first forty days following the birth of a child

chimildik: wedding curtain

chinda-khayol: double-darning stitch

chiraz: trim

chizmakash: woman skilled at drawing embroidery designs; also called *kalamkash*

chuk: elaborately constructed stack of bedding, hangings, quilts, and blankets

cinchi: horse expert

D

da-our: embroidered saddle cover

daraush: hooked iron embroidery tool with a wooden handle, used for making chain stitch; also called *bigiz*

dastarkhan: special cloth on which food is served

djigit: warrior or soldier

doga: triangular cloth amulet; also called *tumar*

dorpech: narrow embroidered strip, sometimes long enough to circumscribe a room at ceiling height; also called *zardevor*

Durmen: Uzbek tribal name; part of Dasht-i-Kipchak group

G

gajari gilam: flat-woven rug with supplementary warp-float patterning

gardich: embroidery hoop

gazhery: technique of supplementary warp-float patterning

gulibadam: almond flower

H

halamat: beadwork necklace; also called *hafamat*

I

ilgich: small square and shield-shaped decorative embroideries

igna nina: embroidery needle; also *nina*

ilmoq yaktarafa: slanted buttonhole stitch

iroki: full cross-stitch

ishkor: potash

isparyak: delphinium

iurma: chain stitch

J

jainamaz: name for the design of arch-shaped *suzani*; literally, prayer place

jelak: long-sleeved, unlined over-robe; also called *kurta*

jinn: evil spirit

K

kaichidon: long, narrow, pentagonal containers used as scissor bags

kalamkash: woman skilled at drawing embroidery designs; also called *chizmakash*

kalib: wooden stamp for block printing; also called *kolyb*

kanaous: all-silk, plain-woven ikat fabric

kanda-khayol: a type of continuous-tread couching embroidery stitch popular in the Shahrisabs region

kara oy: black yurt

karbaz: handwoven, tabby undyed cotton fabric; also called *buz*

Karluk: Uzbek tribal name; part of Dasht-i-Kipchak group

Kauchin: Uzbek tribal name; part of Dasht-i-Kipchak group

keraga: latticework sections making up the lower part of the yurt; each section called a *kanot*, or wing

Kesamir: Uzbek tribal name; part of Dasht-i-Kipchak group

khalat: robe

khalta: bag

khomduzi: simple, double-sided straight embroidery stitch; also called *khomirak*

kiigich: small cloth cap worn by Kungrat women beneath a headdress of wrapped scarves

kishlaq: village

koilak: dress

kolyb: wooden stamp for block printing; also called *kalib*

kozik: stakes driven into the ground to secure the yurt

kuklyama: half cross-stitch

kukrak burma kollak: yoked dress

Kungrat: Uzbek tribal name; part of Dasht-i-Kipchak group

kurta: long-sleeved, unlined over-robe; also called *jelak*

L

Lakai: Uzbek tribal name; part of Dasht-i-Kipchak group

Loqai: alternate spelling of Lakai

M

mahalla: neighborhood

mapramach: pile-woven or embroidered bag backed with plain or striped fabric and shaped to form a rectangular container

Marka: Uzbek tribal name; part of Dasht-i-Kipchak group

mehmankhana: guest room

mogul: napped wool flannel

N

Naiman: Uzbek tribal name; part of Dasht-i-Kipchak group *nakh*: base threads

nina: embroidery needle; also *igna nina*

ninaduz: large embroidery needle

nugai burush koilak: dress with a stand-up collar; sometimes called *eka koilak*

O

okenli-gilam: carpet made of strips of alternating embroidered plain- and pattern-woven wool or embroidered with large-scale designs similar to those encountered in *ilgich* wall hangings

oy: yurt

P

padshoi: silk ikat

paktagul: cotton flower

popuk mashina: sewing machine for chain stitch

popur: embroidery machine; also called *popon*

pul khalta: embroidered money pouch

pustak: felt blanket

pyopyok: tassels

Q

Qataghan: both an Uzbek tribal name and a larger grouping of Uzbek clans

qaum: affinity group; its ties can be based on kinship, clan links, and economic, religious, or political interests

Qunghrat: alternate spelling of Kungrat

R

ruijo: name for both large *suzani* and arched *suzani*

ruyan: madder root

S

sabov: twig tool used for teasing wool

sanama iroki: counted-thread cross-stitch; sometimes called *sanoma terma iroki*

segusha: V-shaped or triangular embroidered cloth decorations for the *chuk*

Semiz: Uzbek tribal name; part of Dasht-i-Kipchak group

shohi: plain-woven silk ikat cloth

sizgich: woman skilled at drawing embroidery designs

sokirchek: base on which the *mapramach* rests

suzani: embroidered hanging

T

tabaklau ilgich: envelope-shaped square *ilgich*, constructed with a flap or false flap

takyamat: felt floor covering

takyr: weft-faced rug with repeating patterns across the entire width

tizma: narrow-woven band

tor: place of honor in the yurt

tumar: triangular cloth amulet; also called *doga*

tumorcha tikish: flat-woven rug made from supplementary warp-patterned wool bands

turlik: outer covering of the yurt, consisting of four or five large felt sections

tuz khalta: embroidered salt pouch

U

uima ekali koilak: everyday woman's attire, consisting of two wide, long-sleeved cloth dresses

ulus: larger tribal grouping or confederation

utov: yurt

uuk: sheaf of curved wooden poles forming the roof of the yurt; also called *uvuk*

uuk kap ilgich: pentagonal or shield-shaped *ilgich*

uzuk: semicircular yurt-dome mat, made of felt

Y

yo'rma: chain stitch; alternate spelling of *iurma*

yurt: round, latticework tent with roof poles and a roof wheel

Z

zandanaji: fabric patterned with large roundels in rows, typically alternating with smaller interstitial designs and surrounded by decorative borders

zardevor: narrow embroidered strip, sometimes long enough to circumscribe a room at ceiling height; also called *dorpech*

SELECTED BIBLIOGRAPHY

Allworth, Edward, ed. *Central Asia: 130 Years of Russian Dominance; A Historical Overview.* Durham, N.C.: Duke University Press, 1994.

Arseneva, Elizaveta Vasilevna. *Ivanovo Sitsi, XVIII–Nachala XX Beka* [Ivanovo Printed Textiles, Eighteenth–Early Twentieth Centuries]. Leningrad: Khudozhnik RSFSR, 1983.

The Baburnama: Memoirs of Babur, Prince and Emperor. Trans. Wheeler M. Thackston. New York: Oxford University Press, 1996.

Baer, Eva. *Islamic Ornament.* New York: New York University Press, 1998.

Bogoslovskaya, Irina, and Larisa Levteeva. "Embroidered Skullcaps of Uzbekistan." *Ornament* 23, no. 3 (2000): 32–35.

Borozna, N. G. "Material'naia kul'tura uzbekov Babataga" [Material Culture of the Uzbeks of Babtag]. In *Materialnaya kultura narodov srednei azii i Kazakhstana* [Material Culture of the Peoples of Central Asia and Kazakhstan]. Moscow: Academia Nauk SSSR, 1966.

Bregel, Yuri, ed. and trans. Munis Khorezmii (1778–1829). *Firdaws al-iqbal: History of Khorezm / Shir Muhammad Mirab Munis and Muhammad Riza Mirab Agahi* (New York: E. J. Brill, 1999).

Burton, Audrey. *The Bukharans.* New York: St. Martin's Press, 1997.

Centlivres, Pierre. "Les Uzbeks du Qattaghan." *Afghanistan Journal* (Graz, Austria: Akademische Druck u. Verlagsanstalt) 2, no. 1 (1975): 2–36.

Chepelevetskaya, G. L. *Suzani Uzbekistana* [*Suzani* of Uzbekistan], Institut Iskusstvoznaia AN UZSSR [Institute of the Arts of Uzbekistan], Gosudarstvennii muzei vostochnih kultur [State Museum of Eastern Culture]. Tashkent: Gosudarstvennoe izdatelstvo khudozhestvennoi literatury [State Publisher of Artistic Literature], UZSSR, 1961.

Cootner, C. M. "Gardens of Paradise." *Hali: The International Journal of Carpets and Textiles,* no. 30 (1986): 46–51.

Cousin, Françoise, and Bernard Dupaigne. *Afghan Embroidery.* Lahore, Pakistan: Ferozsons, 1993.

Curtis, William Eleroy. *Turkestan: The Heart of Asia.* New York: Hodder and Strouton, 1911.

Foltz, Richard C. *Mughal India and Central Asia.* New York and Karachi: Oxford University Press, 1998.

Grube, Ernst. *Keshte, Central Asian Embroideries: The Marshall and Marilyn R. Wolf Collection.* London: Marcuson Publishing Services, 2003.

Haidar, Mansura. *Central Asia in the Sixteenth Century.* New Delhi: Manohar Publishers and Distributors, 2002.

Hiebert, Fredrik T. "Pazyryk Chronology and Early Horse Nomads Reconsidered." *Bulletin of the Asia Institute,* no. 6 (1992): 117–29.

Jarring, Gunnar. *On the Distribution of Turk Tribes in Afghanistan.* Lund, Sweden: Hakan Ohlsson, 1939.

Kalter, Johannes, and Margareta Pavaloi. *Uzbekistan: Heirs to the Silk Road.* London: Thames and Hudson, 1997.

Kandiyoti, Deniz, and Nadira Azimova. "The Communal and the Sacred: Women's Worlds of Ritual in Uzbekistan." *Journal of the Royal Anthropological Institute* 10, no. 2 (June 2004): 327ff.

Karmysheva, Belkis Khalilovna. "Etnograficheskii ocherk zhivotnovodstva u lokaitsev" [Ethnographical Essay on Animal Husbandry among the Lakai]. Leningrad: Academia Nauk SSSR, 1951.

_____. *Uzbeki-Lokaitsi luzhnovo Tadjikistana* [Uzbek-Lakai of Southern Tajikistan]. Stalinabad: Akademii Nauk Tadjikskoi SSR, Institut istorii, arkheologii, i etnografii [Academy of Science of the Tajik SSR, Institute of History, Archaeology, and Ethnography], 1954.

_____. "Lokaiski mapramatchi i ilgichi" [Lakai *Mapramach* and *Ilgich*]. In *Soobshchenii Respublikanskogo istoriko-kraevedsheskogo musea Tadjikskoi SSR* [Report of the Republican Historical-Folk Arts Museum of the Tajik SSR]. (Stalinabad: n.p., 1955): 121–34.

_____. "On the History of Population Formation in the Southern Areas of Uzbekistan and Tajikistan." Paper presented at Seventh International Congress of Anthropological and Ethnological Sciences, August 1964. Moscow: Nauka, 1964.

Katalog Turkestanskovo Otdela [Catalogue of Turkestan Manufacturers]. Exh. cat. Moscow: Polytechnic Institute, 1871.

Knorr, Thomas, and David Lindahl. *Uzbek: The Textiles and Life of the Nomadic and Sedentary Uzbek Tribes of Central Asia.* Exh. cat. Basel: Zbinden Druck, 1975.

Lee, Jonathan. *The Ancient Supremacy: Bukhara, Afghanistan, and the Battle for Balkh, 1731–1901.* New York: E. J. Brill, 1996.

Mardonova, A. "Customs and Rituals of the Childhood Cycle among the Tadjiks of the Upper Zeravshan Valley in the Past and Today." *Soviet Anthropology and Archeology* 24, no. 2 (1985): 35–53.

Mirsky, Jeannette, ed. *The Great Chinese Travelers.* Chicago: University of Chicago Press, 1964.

Morozova, A. S. *Uzbekistanda iurmaduzlik* [Embroidery of Uzbekistan]. Tashkent: Uzbek Academy of Arts, 1960.

Narshakhi, Abu Bakr Muhammad ibn Jafar (899–959). *The History of Bukhara.* Richard N. Frye, ed. and trans. Cambridge, Mass.: Mediaeval Academy of America, 1954.

O'Bannon, George W. *From Desert and Oasis: Arts of the People of Central Asia.* Athens, Ga.: Georgia Museum of Art, University of Georgia, 1998.

Olufsen, Ole. *The Amir of Bokhara and His Country: Journeys and Studies in Bokhara.* Copenhagen: Gyldendal, Nordisk Forlag, 1911.

Paksoy, Hasan B. "Z. V. Togan: The Origins of the Kazaks and the Uzbeks." *Central Asian Survey* 11, no. 3 (September 1992), n. pg.

Petrovich Nalivkin, Vladimir, and Nalivkina [his daughter]. *Essay on the Everyday Life of Women of the Settled Indigenous Population of Ferghana* Kazan: n.p., 1886.

Rasuly-Paleczek, Gabriele. "Kinship and Politics among the Uzbeks of Northeastern Afghanistan." In Ingeborg Baldauf and Michael Friederich, eds. Bamberger Zentralasienstudien: Konferenzakten ESCAS IV [Bamberg Central Asia Studies: Conference Documents IV] (Bamberg, October 8–12, 1991). Series: Islamkundliche Untersuchungen [Investigations in Islamic Art]. Berlin: Klaus Schwarz, 1994.

_____. "Ethnic Identity versus Nationalism: The Uzbeks of North-Eastern Afghanistan and the Afghan State." In Touraj Atabaki and John O'Kane, eds. *Post–Soviet Central Asia.* London and New York: Tauris Academic Studies, 1998.

Richards, D. S., ed. *Islam and the Trade of Asia: A Colloquium.* Published under the auspices of the Near Eastern History Group Oxford and the Near East Center University of Pennsylvania. Oxford, England: Bruno Cassirer; Philadelphia: University of Pennsylvania Press, 1970.

Roy, Olivier. *The New Central Asia: The Creation of Nations.* New York: New York University Press, 2000.

Rudenko, Sergei I. *Frozen Tombs of Siberia: The Pazyryk Burials of Iron Age Horsemen.* Berkeley and Los Angeles: University of California Press, 1970.

Schuyler, Eugene. *Turkestan.* 2 vols. New York: Scribner, Armstrong, 1877.

Shalinsky, Audrey C. "Özbegs." In P. J. Bearman et al., eds. *The Encyclopaedia of Islam.* Leiden: Brill, 2005, 233–34.

Sitnyakovskii, K. "Rodoslovnaia tablitsa sem'i kungradov" [Genealogical Table of the Kungrad Family]. *Bulletin of the Imperial Geographic Society* (Tashkent) 7 (1907): 26.

Snesarev, G. P. *Remnants of Pre–Islamic Beliefs and Rituals among the Khorezm Uzbeks.* Pt. 4, chap. 2: "The Magic of Family and Household Ritual." *Soviet Anthropology and Archeology* (Winter 1971–72).

_____. "Remnants of Pre–Islamic Beliefs and Rituals among the Khorezm Uzbeks." *Soviet Anthropology and Archeology* (Spring 1974).

Sokolovskaia, Ludmila, and Axelle Rougeulle. "Stratified Finds of Chinese Porcelains from Pre–Mongol Samarkand (Afrasiab)." *Bulletin of the Asia Institute,* no. 6 (1992): 87–98.

Soucek, Priscilla P., ed. *Content and Context of Visual Arts in the Islamic World: Papers from a Colloquium in Memory of Richard Ettinghausen* (Institute of Fine Arts, New York University, April 2–4, 1980). University Park, Pa.: Pennsylvania State University Press for the College Art Association, 1988.

Sukhareva, Olga Aleksandrovna. *K istorii gorodov Bukharskogo khanstva* [History of the Bukharan Khanate]. Istoriko-etnograficheskie ocherki [Historical-Ethnographic Studies]. Tashkent: Izd-vo Akademii nauk Uzbekskoi SSR, 1958.

_____. "The Design of Decorative Embroidery of Samarkand and Its Connection with Ethnic Ideas and Beliefs." *Soviet Anthropology and Archeology* (Winter 1983–84).

Sumner, Christina. *Beyond the Silk Road: Arts of Central Asia from the Powerhouse Museum Collection.* Sydney, Australia: Powerhouse Museum of Applied Arts and Sciences, 1999.

Sumner, Christina, and Guy Petherbridge. *Bright Flowers: Textiles and Ceramics of Central Asia.* Sydney, Australia: Powerhouse Museum of Applied Arts and Sciences, 2004.

Thomas, Mary. *Dictionary of Embroidery Stitches.* 1934. Reprint, London: Hodder and Stoughton, 1977.

Vok, Ignazio. *Suzani: The Textile Art of Central Asia; Vok Collection.* Introduction and catalogue text by Jakob Taube. Munich: Edition Vok, 1994.

Wilkinson, Charles K. *Nishapur: Pottery of the Early Islamic Period.* New York: Metropolitan Museum of Art and Greenwich, Conn.: New York Graphic Society, 1973.

INDEX

Illustrations are indicated in **boldface** type.

A

Abdul Rashid Dostum, 37
Abul Ghazi, 27
Adras, 183
Afghanistan, 15, 16, 20, 28, 33, 37, 43, 50, 57, 62, 64, 69, 70, 72, 79, 86, 96, 100, 116, 163n11, 165n5, 165n26, 169n22, 169n23, 170n28, 170n31, 170n33
Agriculture, 28, **32**, 33, 37, 123
Aibak, 28, 163n11
Ainak push, 69, 90, 137–38, **139–40**, 141, 173–74
Amir Abdur Rahman, 33, 37, 164n24
Amu Darya (river), 20, 27–28, 33, 44–45, 47, 50, 82, 165n5
Amulets, 70, 72, 79, 166n27, 185
Andreev, M. S., expedition, 16, 117
Aq oy, 50, 164n1
Aral Sea, 28
Atlas, 137

B

Babur (1483–1530), 27, 130, 147
Badra-Oglu Lakai tribe, 33, 45, 59
Bags, *bugzhoma*, 62, 65, **76**, 96, 106, 169n24
Bags, *khalta*, 96, 167n5, 169n24, 185, 189
Baljuan, 28, 33, 45, 86
Balkh, 16, 27, 28, 36, 44, 163n1, 165n5
Basmachi, basmachestvo, 33, 37, 163n16
Batik, 156
Bazaars, 86, 135, 137
Beads, beadwork, 72, 82, 96, 106, 167n14, 195
Begs, 28, 33, 37, 132, 164n24
Belts, 85–86, 100, 135, 137, 141–42, 158, 169n24
Bolshevik policies, 33, 117, 161
Bolshevik Revolution, 33, 62
Boteh, 100, 106
Bronze Age design, 123
Bukhara, 28, 33, 64, 85, 132, 135, 147, 152, 169n15, 169n26, 170n28, 171n45, 171n47, 181, 184, 187
Bukhara, emir of, 28, 33, 132, 137, 163n13
Buzkashi, **84**, 85–86

C

Calico, 62, 69, 135, 183
Caroq, 62, 64, 72, 74, **77**, 79, 100, 165n15, 165n18

Carpets, 37, 39, 62, 64, 69, 74, 90, 123, 137, 142, 165n19, 167n23, 169n22, 181
Ceramics, 96, 117, 156, 170n43, 181
Chachak, 105
Chagatai, 20, 46, 163n1, 163n3, 168n6
Chambarak, 141, 184
Char-chiroq, 147, 150, 156
Chechka Uzbek, 70
Chengiz (Genghis) Khan (c. 1162–1227), 27, 44–46
Childbirth, 36, 43, 70, 72, 74, 79, 87, 164n4, 166n27
Chillia, 74
Chimildik, 72, **145**, **151**
Chintz, 96, 183
Chit, 156, 171n47
Chuk, 58, **59**, 61–62, **63**, 64–65, 69, 72, **73**, 90, 96, **97**, 100, 165n23, 174
Cinchi, 44, 85, 166n45
Clan relations, 15, 27–28, 33, 36–37, 43, 50, 72, 74, 82, 85, 90, 117, 162, 165n27
Collective farms, 20, 33, 36, 163n17
Costume, 36–37, 50, 70, 72, 79, 82–83, 85, 130, 135, 164n22
Cotton cultivation, 33, 36, 62, 165n10
Curtis, William Eleroy, 161

D

Dagdan, 72
Da-our, **81**, 86, **104**, 105, **107**, 167n10
Dasht-i-Kipchak, 15–16, 27–28, 36, 50, 64, 70, 90, 96, 100, 105, 107, 123, 132, 138, 150, 181, 164n2, 165n11, 167n2, 167n14
Delhi sultanate (1206–1526), 156
Demographic data, 28, 168n7
Diet, 58
Djigit, 79, 85
Doga, 72, 96, 169n27
Dorpech, 141
Dowry, 72, 74, 90, 138, 141, 161
Dress, 70, 72, 79, 82–83, 86, 158
Dudin, Samuel Martinovich, **4**, 16, **26**, **45**, 65, 111, 124, **157**, 168n25
Durmen, 28, 36, 44, 50, 64, 69, 90, 100, 111, 117, 163n6, 164n1, 165n11, 166n41, 168n26, 182, 186, 196
Dyes, 62, 64, 117, 123, 141, 165n18, 182–84

E

Edge trimmings, 57, 106, 193–98
Enver Pasha, 33

Ethnicity, ethnic identity, 27, 36, 43, 132, 164n22, 168n6, 168n7
Evil eye, 70, 79, 111, 165n26, 166n29

F
Factories, 161, 183
Felts, 26, 57–58, 65, 74, 90, 117, 123, 143, 169
Flannel, 100, 105, 117, 181
Funerals, 43, 50, 86

G
Gardens, 127, 130, 142, 147, 150, 181
Gladyshev (Russian envoy), 28
Gold embroidery, **134**, 163, 169n13
Golden Horde, 27, 163n3
Grube, Ernst, 156
Gulibadam, 162, 171n55

H
Hats, 96, **133**, 135, 137–38, **158**, 167n1, 171n55, 197
Headdresses, 82–83, 127, 166n41
Herders, 28, 50, 85
Hissar, 28, 33, 44–46, 69, 132
Hordet, 160
Horse culture, 50, 69, 85–86
Horses, Khotal, 85
Household goods, 33, 37, 57–58, 64, 69, 90, 100, 117, 138, 141, 165n21, 165n23, 185
Hujum, 161

I
Ibrahim Beg, mullah, 33
Iroki, 140, 188
Ishan Isa Khodja, 135
Ishan Khoja Lakai, 33
Islam, Islamic practices, 16–17, 43, 70, 150, 156, 166n28, 169n23, 169n37

J
Janid dynasty (1598–1740), 28
Jinns, 70, 79
Jochi, 27
Jurabaev, 16, **22**, **32**, 33, **47**, **59**, **60**, **76**, **84**

K
Kaichidon, **54**, **98–99**, 100
Kalamkash, 138, 142, 161, 184–85, 189
Kanaous, 137
Kara oy, 57
Karakalpak culture, 36, 191n3
Karbaz, buz, 135, 141–42, 147, 150, 156, 169n25, 181

Karmysheva, Belkis Khalilovna, 16, 28, 62, **66–67**, 85–86, **89**, 100, **105–6**, 111, **117**, **127**, 186, 190
Katalog Turkestanskovo Otdela, 135, 137
Kauchin tribe, 28, 163n1
Kazakhstan, 27, 181; see also *Borat*
Keneges tribe, 132, 168n6
Kesamir tribe, 28, 50
Kherga, 28
Khojent, 33, 132, 135
Kiigich, 82
Kipchak ethnic origin, 27–28, 36, 50, 70, 90, 123, 132, 150, 165n5, 165n11, 168n6
Kishkes, removal, see Appendices I, II
Kishlaq, 51
Kitab, 130, 132, 137, 147, 150, 156, 168n4, 168n6
Koilak, 82
Kuklyama, 141, 188–89
Kulabi, 20
Kunduz, Beg of, 28
Kungrat ethnic origin, 27–28, 37, 43–44, 46

L
Lakai ethnic origin, 27–28, 36–37, 43, 46
Lansdell, Henry, 137
Linings, 105, 156, 183
Lochik, 50, 165n8
Loop manipulation, 192–97

M
Mapramach, 58, 62, 64, 74, 100, 105–6, 168n28
Marka tribe, 28, 50, 90, 165n11
Marriage, 36, 43, 50, 69, 72, 74, 82, 87, 138, 140, **145**, 151
Mirror bags, 69, 90, 137, 169n24, 185, 189
Mohammed Alim Khan (1880–1944), 137
Mongols, 27, 85, 137, 156, 181, 185
Movements, political and religious, 33, 36–37, 43, 117, 132
Mughal empire (1526–1858), 27, 156, 171n45
Muhammad Shaibani (1451–1510), 27
Muravin (Russian envoy), 28

N
Naiman tribe, 50
Nikoh, 72, 74
Nina, 141, 184
Nodir, Binafsha (photographs), **49**, **55**, **56**, **59**, **76**, **78**, **83**, **101**
Nurata, 142, **146**, 147, 170n34, 187

O

Oglak-chakmog, 85

Okenli-gilam, 64

P

Panj river, 50

Pashtu, Pashtun, 35, 164n24

Pazyryk, 123, 185

Patchwork, 62, 64, 72, 90, 100, 123, 166n37–38, 169n18, 181, 196

Penson, Max (photographs), **19**, **42**, **77**

Persian language and ethnicity, 36, 50, 90, 132, 137, 147, 164n22, 168n3

Q

Qataghan, 28, 37, 45–46, 50, 70, 163n11, 165n5

Qaum, 43, 74, 164n27, 168n6

Quilts, quilting, 58, 62, 69, 74, 85, 96, 137, 141, 169n21, 187

R

Religion, pre-Islamic, 70, 150, 166n35, 166n39, 170n37, 170n39, 170n41

Ritual, 36, 50, 70, 72, 74, 85–86, 100, 105, 130, 138, 165n26, 166n31, 170n41

Robe trim, **158**

Rugs, 37–38, 62, 64, 117, 138

Ruijo, 141

Russian conquest, 33, 117, 132

Rusyaikina, S. T. 16, 117

S

Saddle trappings, 100, 105–6, 130, **134**, 137, 165n21, 167n10, 166n45, 166n48, 189

Safavid empire, 27

Samangan province, 28, 37, 79

SAMIIR expedition, 16, 96, 100, 117, 123

Schuyler, Eugene, 132, 135

Scorpion motif, 90, 100, 105–6, 111, 123, 162, 171n55

Semiz tribe, 28, 50, 64, 90, 111, 168n26, 179

Shahrisabs, 130–62

Shaibanid confederation, 27–28, 163n1

Sizgich, 90, 111

Sogd, Sogdian, 137, 140, 169n15, 181

Sokirchek, 58

Sukhareva, Olga Aleksandrovna, 132, 138, 150, 168n4, 168n6–7, 169n19, 170n41

Sukkot sukkah, **144**

Surkhandarya province, 20, 28, 36–37, 70, 82, 132

T

Tabaklau, 105–6, 111

Tablet weaving, 192–97

Tajik ethnicity, 16, 20, 27, 36, 163n1

Talismans, 72, 106, 127, 138, 162, 164n4, 166n40, 166n45, 169n18, 171n55

Tashkent, **148–49**

Tassels, 62, 72, 96, 100, 105–6, 111, 165n21, 167n14, 190, 192–98

Tent bands, 57–58, 62, 96

Tents, 28, 150, 181; see also yurts

Termez, 20

Timur Leng (Tamerlane) (c. 1336–1404/5), 130, 147, 181

Timurid empire, 27, 130

Tor, 58, 91

Torba, 105–6, 111

Tumar, 72, 165n26, 169n18

Turbans, 82, 85–86, 135

Turk tribe, 27–28, 36, 46, 163n19, 164n24

Turkestan, 28, 33, 132, 135, 161, 163n11, 163n20, 168n7, 169n13, 169n25

Turkestanskii Al'bom, **132**, **133**, **134**, **144–45**, **151**

Turkic languages, 36, 163n19

Turkic tribes, 27–28

U

Umbilical cord, 74, 79

Uuk kap, 105–6, 111

Uzbek ethnicity, 27–28, 33, 36–37, 43–46, 50, 57, 70, 82, 111, 117, 130, 132, 163n1, 163n3, 163n11, 164n22, 164n26, 165n10

Uzbek Khan (1282–1341), 27

V

Veiling, 72, 74, 150, 181

W

Warp twining, 192–97

von Kaufman, Konstantin Petrovich, 132, 169n13

Weddings, see dowry, marriage

Wolves, 74, 79, 166n31

Y

Yurts, **26**, 28, 37, 51, **56**, 57–58, 62, 64, 69, 72, 74, 86, 90, 96, 100, 106, 150, 164n1–2

Z

Zandanaji, 142, 147, 165n7, 165n8, 165n11, 165n23, 165n27

Zardevor, 141, 169n24

Zoroastrianism, 150, 167n52

REPRODUCTION CREDITS

Photographic reproductions in this book were provided by the individuals and institutions listed below. Names of photographers are in parentheses following the pages on which their photographs appear.

Anahita Gallery, Inc., Santa Fe, New Mexico: 8–9 (M. P. Petrovsky); 4, 26, 45, and 157 (S. M. Dudin); 22, 32 (top and bottom), 47, 59, 60, 76 (top), and 84 (bottom) (Jurabaev); 66–67, 89, and 127 (Belkis Khalilovna Karmysheva); 84 (top), 129, 136, 143, and 160 (unknown photographers). Photographs © Anahita Gallery, Inc., Santa Fe.

Dirk Bakker: 13 (Dirk Bakker). Photograph © Dirk Bakker.

Library of Congress, Washington, D.C.: From the *Turkestanskii Al'bom*: 132 (LC digital file from Part 3, pl. 6, no. 33), 133 (LC digital file from Part 2, vol. 2, pl. 138, no. 419), 134 (LC digital file from Part 2, vol. 1, pl. 56, no. 143), 144 (LC digital file from Part 2, vol. 1, p. 8l. 138, no. 259), 145 (LC digital file from Part 2, vol. 1, pl. 73, no. 227), 151 (LC digital file from Part 2, vol. 1, pl. 72, no. 223). Photographs courtesy The Library of Congress, Prints and Photographs Division.

Minneapolis Institute of Arts: All photographs of the Jack A. and Aviva Robinson Collection (Dan Dennehy); detail images in Appendix I and Appendix II (Charles Walbridge). Photographs © Minneapolis Institute of Arts.

Binafsha Nodir: 49, 55–56, 76 (bottom), 78, 83 (left and right), and 101 (Binafsha Nodir). Photographs © Binafsha Nodir.

Dina Penson: 19, 42, and 77 (Max Penson). Photographs © Dina Penson Khojaeva, courtesy Anahita Gallery, Inc., Santa Fe, New Mexico.

Edward Stack: 195 (Fig. 8) and 196 (Fig. 10) (Edward Stack). Photographs © Edward Stack.

Lotus Stack: 73, 97, and 101 (Lotus Stack). Photographs © Lotus Stack.

State Historical Museum, Tashkent, Uzbekistan: 14, 17, and 43. Photographs © State Historical Museum, Tashkent.

Map (23) and line drawings by Kristine Mudd: 118, 186 (Figs. 7 and 9), 187 (figs. 11, 13, and 14), 188 (Fig. 16), 189 (Figs. 18–21), 194 (Fig. 5), and 195 (Fig. 11).